ENDORSEMENTS

I so enjoy Alan DiDio's topical versatility and inquisitive approach. *They Lied to You About the Rapture* is sure to be a thought-provoking addition to the riveting discussion on the Rapture. Be sure to add this to your eschatological reading.

David Diga Hernandez
Author, *Holy Spirit: God Within You*

Alan DiDio's book, *They Lied to You About the Rapture,* will unlock mysteries, answer your end-time questions, lay the future out for you in a way you will easily understand, and provide you with an end-time glossary like I've never seen in any other work. I enjoyed reading this riveting book so much that I devoured it in a single sitting. It's difficult to cover a subject like this in one volume, but Alan has done it masterfully. Congratulations on this new book, my dear friend. *BRAVO* you've done it again!

T0370202

Rick Renner, ThD
Minister, Author, and Broadcaster
Moscow, Russia

Alan DiDio's latest book is a full-blown wake-up call for believers everywhere. *They Lied to You About the Rapture* isn't just another book on end-times prophecy—it's a deep dive into the heartbeat of God's Word about the Rapture and the urgency of the hour. Alan has a gift for pulling back the curtain on what is really happening, making complex truths not only understandable but absolutely life-changing. This isn't just theology, it's a call to live with purpose, urgency, and a fiery passion for Jesus.

What I love most about Alan's approach is his authenticity and his love for the body of Christ. He doesn't just lay down truth bombs; he invites you into a deeper walk to understand the times and fall even more in love with the appearing of our Savior. Every chapter draws you closer to King Jesus and reawakens the anticipation of His return.

As a friend and a fellow warrior in the faith, I can tell you Alan lives out these words. He has been a constant source of encouragement and wisdom to me and so many others. His fire for Jesus and his mission to prepare believers for what's ahead is all over this book. I wholeheartedly endorse

They Lied to You About the Rapture and believe it's a must-read for anyone hungry to understand the hour in which we're living.

Troy Brewer
Senior Pastor, Open Door Church, Burleson, Texas
Founder, Troy Brewer Ministries

The topic of the Rapture, accompanied by all things eschatology, appears to be at an all-time moment of polarization, in some cases, even displaying an ungodly hostility toward opposing points of view. Much of the discussion is charged from a drive-by argue-tainment culture. Misfired statements win the day rather than solid truth backed by factual understanding. Social media has fostered low attention and high-emotion responses against substantive clarity, underscored by the many loud voices claiming credibility with little to no trustworthiness. Most collisions over the Rapture, or end-time topics, are often devoid of any real substance, which can only be revealed through venturing under the hood for verification after an honest examination of these critical issues.

As I read my friend Alan DiDio's book, what I came across was honesty with facts, not only historically and biblically, but the presentation is done in such a manner that I found myself falling into much of the well-articulated structure, giving solid answers and even lessons to the issues. Alan's work answered questions I had not even thought to ask—that is called good writing!

You must know that as you read *They Lied to You About the Rapture*, it is written in good faith; but make no mistake, Alan pulls no punches. Prepare for sound exegesis and surgical provision of apologetic insights relating directly to these hotly debated issues. Along the informative, even revelatory ride, you will undoubtedly discover difficult-to-dispute aha moments and musings you may not have considered.

It was refreshing to discover this is NOT A BOOK FOR ESCAPISTS! Instead, it is just the opposite. Alan takes the gloves off and makes the readers own what they believe. Whatever point of view you are coming from, there will certainly be thought-provoking moments that will not easily be dismissed.

Among the many strong points of clarity was the call to responsibility—this is not a message about checking out. It is about checking in! Belief should never be defined by abuse; in other words, the extremes of any message can distort the foundational truth, no matter what the message is.

A point of fascination and interest for me was Alan defining which part of the armor of God, as listed in Ephesians 6, he believes describes the

Rapture of the Church. I also found the stark parallels between Jesus and the antichrist gripping when considering the judgment seat of Christ compared to the times of the great tribulation judgment. A big question was confronted with multiple exact historical references relating to the Rapture being invented in the 1800s that will give any skeptic a lot to consider.

In his new book, my friend does what he does best: dive deep into the issue and provide clarity for those who have ears to hear. This is a work for every believer who loves His appearing and desires to add clarity and depth to what the Bible and history state on the matters at hand.

Not only is Alan DiDio my friend, he is also a respected voice and articulate communicator of truth. *They Lied to You About the Rapture* is an excellent work, and I want to thank Alan for writing it. May this book bless you, dear reader, as much as it did me!

Joseph Z
Author, Broadcaster, and Prophetic Voice
JosephZ.Com

I love Alan DiDio's book! Just reading through the table of contents makes me want to stand at my desk raise my hands in the air and shout MARANA-THA! DiDio makes it very clear that we are not appointed to wrath, as the purpose of the Tribulation is The Time of Jacob's Trouble! The seven years deals with ISRAEL! As he points out, the Church is not here as we are not appointed to wrath.

The Rapture is nothing new and was not "invented" by Darby. Remember, the Bible was kept from the common man for over 1,000 years. All Darby and others of his ilk did was have access to the Scriptures and from there they would read this:

> *For the Lord himself shall descend from heaven with a shout, with the voice of the archangel, and with the trump of God: and the dead in Christ shall rise: first then we which are alive and remain shall be caught up together with them in the clouds, to meet the Lord in the air: and so shall we ever be with the Lord* (1 Thessalonians 4:16-17 KJV).

Reading DiDio's book will bolster your faith and strengthen your relationship with Jesus! This IS our blessed hope!

Dr. L.A. Marzulli
Author, *Rungs of Disclosure*
Host/Director of 30 films

Bishop DiDio delivers a unique and thrilling way of presenting the facts about the last days, and he makes the hope we have as believers clear and concise for all. This is so important at a time when controversy, misunderstandings, and even lethargy on the topic are rampant. Bishop Alan's new release, *They Lied to You About the Rapture*, will stir you to action and make you ever more aware that Jesus is coming soon, and He's excited to see you face to face.

Joseph Morris
Author of *End Times Made Easy and Countdown*

I highly recommend Alan's book, *They Lied To You About the Rapture*, as a great introduction to eschatology in general and the rapture question in particular. This volume is also suitable for more advanced students who want to grapple with the full range of questions that revolve around the rapture, but not at an academic level. It was a refreshing, challenging, encouraging, and hope-inspiring presentation. I especially appreciated the emphasis on heart readiness to meet the Lord and on occupying until he comes. The rapture question is far more than merely getting the timeline correct.

Lee Brainard
Soothkeep Ministries

In *They Lied to You About the Rapture*, Bishop Alan DiDio delivers a bold and timely message that challenges the Church to wake up and reclaim the truth about Christ's return. With profound biblical insight, compelling storytelling, and a fearless approach to tackling the myths and distortions surrounding end-time teachings, this book cuts through the noise and points readers back to the heart of the gospel. Bishop DiDio reminds us that preparing for what's coming isn't about fear or sensationalism—it's about falling in love with His appearing and living with holy urgency.

This is more than a theological exploration; it's a call to action for every believer to align their heart with God's Word and to be ready for the moment when the sky splits, and everything changes. In a world desperate for truth, this book is a beacon of hope and clarity. It will convict, inspire, and challenge you to live with boldness and anticipation in these prophetic times. I highly recommend this powerful work to anyone longing to walk in truth and prepare for His glorious return.

Pastor Todd Coconato
President of Todd Coconato Ministries, National Speaker,
and Author of *Come Out from Among Them*

With global interest in the Rapture of the Church at an all-time high, Alan DiDio's *They Lied to You About the Rapture* arrives as a thorough and thought-provoking exploration of this prophetic event. DiDio's careful examination of Scripture, combined with historical research and practical insights, makes this book an important resource for anyone engaging in a serious study of end-time prophecy and the blessed hope of Christ's return.

Mike Signorelli
Lead Pastor, V1 Church

THEY LIED

TO YOU ABOUT THE

RAPTURE

DESTINY IMAGE BOOKS BY ALAN DIDIO

*Armed for Victory: Prayer Strategies That Unlock
the End-Time Armory of God*

Summoning the Demon: AI, Aliens, and the Antichrist

They Lied to You About the Rapture: How to Prepare for What's Coming

THEY LIED

TO YOU ABOUT THE

RAPTURE

HOW TO *PREPARE*
FOR WHAT'S COMING

ALAN DIDIO

DESTINY IMAGE® PUBLISHERS, INC.
P.O. Box 310, Shippensburg, PA 17257-0310
"Publishing cutting-edge prophetic resources to supernaturally empower the body of Christ"

This book and all other Destiny Image and Destiny Image Fiction books are available at Christian bookstores and distributors worldwide.

For more information on foreign distributors, call 717-532-3040.
Reach us on the Internet: www.destinyimage.com.

ISBN 13 TP: 979-8-8815-0187-7
ISBN 13 eBook: 979-8-8815-0188-4

For Worldwide Distribution, Printed in the U.S.A.
1 2 3 4 5 6 7 8 / 29 28 27 26 25

CONTENTS

FOREWORD BY JIMMY EVANS

When Alan DiDio visited with me on my *Tipping Point Show*, I was immediately struck by his unique ability to address complex prophetic themes with both scholarly precision and pastoral warmth. Like me, Alan recognizes that we're living in a unique moment in history—a time when the prophecies of Scripture are clearly unfolding right before our eyes.

The topic of the Rapture has never been more relevant than it is today. With global uncertainty, increasing persecution of Christians, and the rapid alignment of nations against Israel, many believers are asking serious questions about what the future holds. Sadly, there's also a lot of confusion and misinformation circulating about the Rapture, even within the Church. That's why this book is so timely and necessary.

I've spent decades teaching about end-times prophecy, and I can tell you that one of the biggest challenges we face is addressing the misconceptions that have crept into our understanding of the Rapture. Some view it as an escape hatch from responsibility, while others dismiss it entirely as a modern invention. Both extremes miss the profound truth and power of this "blessed hope" that the apostle Paul wrote about.

As the founder of Encounter Church in Charlotte and host of the popular *Encounter Today* YouTube channel, Alan brings a unique perspective to this subject. His ministry combines careful biblical exposition with an understanding of current events that helps believers grasp the relevance of prophecy for today. What impressed me most during our interactions was his ability to cut through misconceptions with clear-eyed biblical precision. He doesn't just defend the doctrine of the Rapture, he helps readers understand *why it matters* for their daily walk with Christ.

What sets this book apart is its balanced approach. Alan doesn't shy away from addressing difficult questions and challenges to the pre-tribulation position, but he does so with grace and scholarly attention to detail. His extensive research into church history and careful examination of Scripture provide a solid foundation for understanding why the Rapture isn't just a modern invention but a truth that has been present in the Church from the very beginning.

I particularly appreciate how Alan addresses the claim that belief in the Rapture leads to passive Christianity. Like me, he has found the opposite to be true. When properly understood, the imminent return of Christ motivates believers to greater engagement in the Great Commission, deeper commitment to holiness, and more passionate worship. This book helps readers grasp how the "blessed hope" of Christ's return should inspire us to occupy until He comes.

I recognize in Alan a kindred spirit—someone who shares my burden to prepare the Church for the days ahead. When he visited my program, our conversation revealed a shared conviction that end-times teaching shouldn't produce fear but faith, not anxiety but anticipation. This book reflects that same heart.

What I find most compelling about *They Lied to You About the Rapture* is its pastoral approach to an often-controversial subject. Alan doesn't just present arguments, he provides comfort and encouragement while maintaining doctrinal integrity. His careful handling of Scripture, combined with practical application, makes complex theological concepts accessible without compromising their depth.

In these increasingly challenging times, the Church needs clear, biblical teaching about the end times more than ever. This book provides exactly that. It offers hope without hype, encouragement without compromise, and truth without sensationalism. I believe Alan's work represents the kind of balanced, biblical teaching about the end times that the Church desperately needs today.

Whether you're new to the study of prophecy or have been studying it for years, you will find fresh insights and practical applications that will strengthen your faith and deepen your walk with Christ. At a time when our culture is increasingly dominated by fear and uncertainty, Alan's message reminds us that the blessed hope of Christ's return remains our greatest source of comfort and motivation.

As someone who has devoted much of my ministry to teaching about biblical prophecy, I'm encouraged to see voices like Alan's adding to this important conversation. This book isn't just another end-times study, it's a call to live with purpose and hope in light of Christ's imminent return. I wholeheartedly recommend it to anyone seeking to better understand the blessed hope of the Rapture and its practical implications for their life today.

Jimmy Evans
Founder & CEO, Tipping Point Ministries
www.EndTimes.com

FOREWORD BY PERRY STONE

Alan has done an outstanding job outlining the biblical proof of the Catching Away of the Bride of Christ, an event that Christians refer to as the Rapture. I, too, hold the belief that the Rapture will be a pre-tribulation event, and I also have spent years researching this doctrine throughout the Bible and early church historical writings. This is why I can agree with Alan and say with conviction that the Rapture is an actual event that will occur before the Seven-Year Tribulation.

Holding a pre-tribulation stance often brings hateful rhetoric and name-calling from people with opposing beliefs, the most common accusation being that we are heretics. It's comical to imagine standing before God at the Bema judgment and being chastised because we taught people that His Son was going to return for His Bride. It is also astonishing the lengths to which people will go to try to convince us that we are wrong. My experience has been that people who criticize us the loudest have done the least amount of research, and they often base their opinions on two or three verses in the Bible. Or worse, they simply think that God wants to pour out His wrath on His Bride to purify us. They have not done due diligence by studying Scripture, line upon line, and precept upon precept. The truth is that there are shadows of the Rapture throughout the Bible, including throughout the Old Testament. But it requires a desire to dig into Scripture to find the treasure nuggets that God placed there for us to discover.

As Alan says succinctly in this book, the differing eschatological views and disputes have often overshadowed the core message and added to the confusion. Much of the Church today has lost its ability to sit down together and have a civil discussion about topics such as this because too many people would rather resort to emotionalism, divisiveness, and name-calling. Engaging in this behavior overshadows the real message of the Rapture: that we are to look for and love Christ's appearing, just as believers did in the days of the early Church. We can look for and love His appearing while still occupying until He comes. In fact, this is exactly what we are called to do.

One thing we are not called to do is devour each other with hostility. God isn't sitting in Heaven listening to us argue and then drawing conclusions or changing His mind based on our debates. His mind was made up long ago. The timing of the Rapture is what it is, and no amount of fighting amongst ourselves is going to change God's mind. Believers should be able to discuss and learn from each other. When our opinions differ on this topic, we should civilly disagree, still love each other, and not turn off non-believers because of our words and attitudes.

Even if you disagree with this specific timing of the Rapture, I recommend that you read this book anyway so you will understand some of the biblical reasons for why we hold this viewpoint. Regardless of your belief, Alan encourages us to remain vigilant, keep oil burning in our lamps, and ,just like the picture provided by the ancient Jewish wedding, anticipate the day that the bridegroom arrives to take us to His home.

Let us all be like the early Church as they spread the message of the Gospel and lived with anticipation of the Lord's coming. There will be a generation that will experience this great event, and nobody will want to miss it. Maranatha! Our Lord, come!

Perry Stone
Voice of Evangelism Ministries / Manna-Fest Television

INTRODUCTION

THE CLOCK STRIKES MIDNIGHT

Not long after I was born again, I found myself standing in the open field next to my childhood home. The familiarity of the place was comforting but there was also a sense of anticipation that set my heart pounding.

People were scattered throughout the field, their voices a low hum as they chatted among themselves. Friends and neighbors, faces I recognized and some I didn't, all lost in their own conversations.

Suddenly, a sound broke through the mundane chatter, a noise unlike any I had ever heard. It was as if the sky itself was singing. Instinctively, I looked up and there, breaking through the clouds, I saw it, a massive clock with Roman numerals, its hands almost straight up. The second hand rounded the 9, crept past the 10, and moved steadily toward the 11. Midnight was near.

I turned to see if anyone else had noticed, but only a few seemed to see what I saw. The rest continued their conversations, oblivious to the celestial event unfolding above them. My heart raced as I realized what was happening. This was *the* moment, the one for which we had been waiting. Jesus was coming.

As the second hand approached the 12, a strange sensation gripped me. Like metal drawn to a magnet, I began to rise, my feet leaving the ground. Everything seemed to move in slow motion. I glanced around and saw that only a few others were rising with me. The excitement was mixed with sorrow as I saw the faces of those I was leaving behind me.

One of my friends, eyes wide with the realization of what was happening, reached out, trying to join us. But it was too late. Midnight had come, and he wasn't ready. His fingers grasped at the air, but he remained earthbound, a look of desperation etched on his face.

The sky seemed to pull me upward, closer to the clock, now glowing with a brilliant light. My heart swelled with a mix of joy as I ascended and the field, the people, my childhood home all faded away as I was drawn toward the my Savior.

Then suddenly I awoke. It was just a dream, but it lingered, vividly and powerfully in my mind. The words, "Jesus is coming" were on my lips as a divine reminder of the urgency of the hour.

WAS IT "JUST" A DREAM?

The dream followed me long after I awoke, its stark images and profound message forever etched into my heart and mind. I immediately knew it was more than just a dream; it was a divine encounter that set me on a new path, a journey to prepare not only my heart but also the hearts of others for Jesus's imminent return.

As I reflected on the dream, I felt an overwhelming urgency to understand the times in which we live. This desire led me to the study of eschatology, a branch of theology concerned with what the Bible says about the final events of history and the Second Coming of Christ.

> **eschatology** | es-kə-ˈtä-lə-jē
> **noun**
> 1: a branch of theology concerned with the final events in the history of the world or of humankind[1]

2: a study of the ultimate destiny of mankind, dealing with topics such as the Second Coming, the Rapture, the Millennium, and the eternal state of man

3: the part of theology that examines the prophetic scriptures to understand God's divine plan for the end of days

Origin: from the Greek eschatos (last) + -logia (study of)

The Bible's message on this subject seemed clear to me, but the many and varied views I ran into in different Christian camps were surprising. I never would have imagined the Church would be so divided on these issues.

My passion for eschatology grew with each passing day. I devoured books, attended seminars, and spent countless hours in prayer and study. The more I learned, the more I realized the importance of being prepared and vigilant. The dream had ignited a fire within me, a fire that burned with a desire to see others come to the same understanding and readiness for the return of our Lord.

Let me be clear, as much as the dream had impacted me, I know that we are not be led by dreams alone. The Word of God is our principal source of instruction, the infallible guide for our lives. The Bible warns us about false prophets and deceptive dreams, reminding us to test every spirit and hold fast to what is true. Dreams, while potentially powerful, must always be measured against the truth of Scripture, and their only value is in their ability to arrest our attention and bring our focus back to the Word of God.

Incorporating dreams into the believer's life is a delicate balance. Dreams that point us to the Bible, that confirm God's teachings, and align with Scripture can be significant and should not be ignored. They can serve as reminders, warnings, or encouragements, prompting us to dig deeper into Scripture and drawing us closer to Him. But they can never be allowed to replace the Bible as our primary source of truth. Dreams, visions, and prophecies must always direct us to the Bible.

The dream I experienced did just that. It was a catalyst, a divine nudge that propelled me into a deeper understanding of eschatology and a more fervent commitment to live out and share the Gospel.

MY FIRST SERMON

It was my first semester at the University of North Carolina at Charlotte (UNCC), and I found myself enrolled in a speech class in which I would experience a defining moment in my end-time journey. The assignment was straightforward: prepare a speech and include an illustration to help convey the message. Little did I know this would be the first time I would preach about the incredible signs pointing to Jesus's return.

As I considered the topic for my speech, I felt a strong prompting to speak about something close to my heart: the miraculous rebirth of the nation of Israel. I remembered the dream, the urgency, and the calling to prepare myself and others for the return of Jesus. With this in mind, I knew that highlighting the fulfillment of biblical prophecy through Israel's restoration would be a powerful message.

On the day of the speech, I rolled in a large world map, eager to share what I had learned. I remember being so nervous!

I began by explaining the significance of Israel in Bible prophecy. "The rebirth of the nation of Israel in 1948 was not merely a political event," I said, pointing to the map. "It was a miraculous fulfillment of ancient prophecies that predicted its return." I referenced several key Scriptures to underline my point:

> Isaiah 66:8 (KJV): *"Who hath heard such a thing? Who hath seen such things? Shall the earth be made to bring forth in one day? or shall a nation be born at once? for as soon as Zion travailed, she brought forth her children."*

I explained how this prophecy was astonishingly fulfilled when Israel was declared a nation on May 14, 1948, and was recognized internationally as a nation overnight.

> Ezekiel 37:21-22 (KJV): *"And say unto them, Thus saith the Lord God; Behold, I will take the children of Israel from among the heathen, whither they be gone, and will gather them on every side, and bring them into their own land: And I will make them one nation in the land upon the mountains of Israel; and one king shall be king to them all: and they shall be no more two nations, neither shall they be divided into two kingdoms any more at all."*

I highlighted how God promised to regather His people from all the nations and bring them back to their land, a prophecy that has been unfolding since 1948 and 1967 and continues today.

> Amos 9:14-15 (KJV): *"And I will bring again the captivity of my people of Israel, and they shall build the waste cities, and inhabit them; and they shall plant vineyards, and drink the wine thereof; they shall also make gardens, and eat the fruit of them. And I will plant them upon their land, and they shall no more be pulled up out of their land which I have given them, saith the Lord thy God."*

I spoke about the incredible agricultural and technological advancements in Israel, transforming it from a desolate land into a thriving nation, fulfilling the prophecy that they would rebuild and inhabit the land permanently.

Emphasizing how these fulfilled prophecies were clear signs pointing to the imminent return of Jesus, I stated, "The rebirth of Israel is not just a historical fact; it's a divine signal that we are living in the last days. Jesus Himself spoke of the fig tree budding as a sign that His return was near" (Matthew 24:32-34) and we are that generation.

There was more to the speech, but you understand the premise. Israel's very existence is a sign that points to the return of our Lord Jesus Christ.

I concluded my speech with a passionate call to action, urging my classmates to recognize the times in which we are living and to prepare their hearts for Jesus's return: "The rebirth of Israel is a clarion call to all of us.... It's time to wake up and to get ready for His coming."

The response from my classmates was mixed; some were intrigued, others indifferent, but a few followed up with questions. This first sermon, born out of a simple class assignment, marked the beginning of my journey to share the urgent message of Jesus's return, a journey fueled by the prophetic truths found in God's Word and the ever-present reminder that we are in the last days. I encourage you to seize every opportunity you have to share this truth that Jesus is coming.

ARE YOU READY TO SEE JESUS?

"Are you ready to see Jesus?" is a question that cuts through the noise of life's distractions and goes straight to the heart. Whether you're a lifelong believer or someone who's just now beginning to consider eternity, the reality is the same: at any moment, the sky could split, the trumpet could sound, and everything will change in the blink of an eye. This isn't meant to instill fear, it is a call to live with a sense of purpose that only comes when eagerly anticipating meeting Jesus face-to-face.

So how do you get ready? It starts with the simple yet sincere decision to surrender. Surrender your plans, your ambitions, and your heart to Jesus. If you've never made Him Lord of your life, now is the time. The Bible says, *If thou shalt confess with thy mouth the Lord Jesus, and shalt believe in thine heart that God hath raised him from the dead, thou shalt be saved"* (Romans 10:9 KJV). It's not about striving to be perfect; it's about accepting His perfect sacrifice on the Cross and allowing His love to transform you from the inside out.

For those who already know Him, the question still stands: Are you living like you're ready to see Him? Being ready means more than just having your theological "ducks" in a row; it means actively pursuing His will, staying vigilant, and refusing to be lulled to sleep by the comforts and cares of this world. Now is the time to recommit, to realign your focus, and to ignite that first love again. Because when that moment comes, when we finally stand before the King of kings, we'll want to hear just one thing:

"Well done, thou good and faithful servant"
                                        (Matthew 25:21 KJV).

1

A STRANGE THING HAPPENED ON THE WAY TO THE RAPTURE

In essentials unity, in non-essentials liberty, in all things charity.
—Rupertus Meldenius, German Lutheran Theologian[1]

As I delved deeper into the study of eschatology, I was taken back by the level of divisiveness surrounding this topic within the Christian community. The prophetic Scriptures that had filled me with such excitement and urgency also seemed to spark intense debates and disagreements among believers. This realization not only surprised me, but it also left me feeling disappointed and discouraged.

Eschatology, as already defined as being the study of the end times, covers a wide range of interpretations and beliefs. From the timing of the Rapture to the specifics of the Tribulation and the millennium, there are various perspectives, each with its passionate adherents. As I shared my newfound insights and convictions about the Pre-Tribulation Rapture, I found myself facing criticism and opposition from those who held different views. Let's look at some of those views.

THE MAIN VIEWS OF THE RAPTURE EXPLAINED

When it comes to the Rapture, the moment when believers will be "caught up" to meet Jesus in the air, Christians have been arguing over the timing for decades, if not centuries. Many view Bible prophecy like a jigsaw puzzle and, depending on where you think the pieces fit, you'll land in one of four main camps: Pre-Tribulation, Pre-Wrath, Mid-Tribulation, and Post-Tribulation.

First let's define the word *Rapture.*

> **rapture | ˈrap-chər**
> **noun**
> the event in which believers are caught up to meet Jesus Christ in the air, resulting in the glorification of their bodies and being transformed into a state of eternal perfection.
> **Origin**: from the Latin word *raptura*, which means "to seize" or "to snatch away in the nick of time." The term is derived from *rapere*, to seize, carry off, or transport. It comes from the Latin translation of the Greek word *harpazō* found in 1 Thessalonians 4:17, which describes believers being "caught up" to meet the Lord in the air.[2]

Theologically, the Rapture refers to the moment when believers, both living and dead, will be transformed and receive glorified bodies, completing Christ's redemptive work in their lives. It's not just about an escape from the earth, it's the *crown jewel* of Christ's salvific work in our lives, the final act in God's redemptive drama for believers. This glorification is the culmination of what Christ secured through His death, burial, and resurrection.

ARE YOU READY FOR AN UPGRADE!?

Imagine for a moment stepping into a version of yourself who knows no pain, no fatigue, and no limitations. No more aches, no more sickness, no more "What was I supposed to do again?" moments. It's a body that will never grow old, never wear out, and never know sin. When we talk about receiving a *glorified body*, we're talking about experiencing life as God originally intended, full of energy, vitality, and boundless strength. The best part? Jesus gave us a sneak peek.

After His resurrection, Jesus didn't just come back to life in the same form. He rose with a *glorified body*, a body that still bore the marks of His crucifixion, yet was infused with the glory of God. This same Jesus, who once grew tired, hungered, and suffered in agony, emerged from the grave in a form that defied natural laws as we know them. He could appear and disappear at will (Luke 24:31), pass through locked doors (John 20:19), and yet still eat and fellowship with His disciples (Luke 24:42-43). His glorified body retained a physical nature. He wasn't a ghost, but His natural body operated on a whole new level.

Now consider that *our glorified bodies will be like His.* The apostle Paul tells us that Christ *"shall change our vile body, that it may be fashioned like unto his glorious body"* (Philippians 3:21 KJV). In other words, the same power that transformed Jesus's beaten, bruised body into a glorified state will transform us as well. What does that mean practically? Think of the possibilities:

1. **No Limitations**: Right now, our bodies are bound by gravity, time, and space. Jesus, in His glorified state, could transcend those boundaries. Imagine a life where you can move effortlessly, where distance is irrelevant, and time no longer dictates your experience. Some suggest that we'll travel at the speed of thought. No more jet lag, no more traffic jams!

11

2. **Perfect Communion**: Jesus's glorified body wasn't hindered by fear, doubt, or weakness. He could converse deeply and freely with His disciples. With glorified bodies, we'll experience perfect fellowship with God and one another, with no miscommunication, no selfish impulses, and no relational breakdowns.

3. **Resurrected Power**: Jesus's glorified body was infused with resurrection power. He existed in a state of absolute mastery over death. He has promised to share that very same power with us.

> *For this corruptible must put on incorruption, and this mortal must put on immortality*
>
> (1 Corinthians 15:53 KJV).

Our bodies will be bursting with supernatural energy, able to accomplish anything God desires, forever.

BREAKING FREE FROM THE CURSE

Right now, we live in a world where everything is tainted by the curse of sin. From the weariness in our bones to the diseases that plague us, our bodies are in a constant state of decay. But in a glorified state, we'll be free from all of it. No more creaky knees, no more failing eyesight, no more doctor's appointments! Imagine each and every day in *eternity* feeling better than you've ever felt…no caffeine required.

Even our emotions and thoughts will be transformed. We'll also be free from mental and spiritual torment. No more guilt. No more shame. No more struggles with anxiety or fear. Our minds will be crystal clear, our emotions perfectly balanced, and our spirits completely aligned with God's. We will reflect Him in ways we can't even imagine. These are all things that we can strive for "in Him" right now as children of God; but at the Rapture, it will all be made complete. Nothing missing and nothing broken.

In His glory, Jesus shone like the sun at the Mount of Transfiguration (Matthew 17:2), and John describes Him in Revelation as having a face *"as the sun shineth in his strength"* (Revelation 1:16 KJV). When we're glorified, we'll shine like that, too. Daniel 12:3 (KJV) tells us, *"And they that be wise shall shine as the brightness of the firmament; and they that turn many to righteousness as the stars for ever and ever."*

In our glorified state, we will *radiate* the brilliance of our King. What a blessed hope! It's hard to even wrap our minds around what it will be like to live in a glorified body, especially when we're so used to dealing with fatigue, sickness, and constant limitations. But the promise stands: we will be like Jesus, enjoying eternal life not just in spirit, but in a body that's finally, fully alive.

So whether you're facing illness, discouragement, or just the daily grind, remember this: one day, in the twinkling of an eye, all of that will be gone. It's the moment we've all been waiting for, the final act of Christ's redemptive work in our bodies. When it happens, every pain, every limitation, and every struggle will fade away in the light of His glory and grace.

Are you ready for that upgrade? Because it's coming, and it's going to be out of this world.

ALL CHRISTIANS BELIEVE IN THE RAPTURE

No wonder the enemy tries to muddy these waters with division and rob us of our hope. This is a core doctrine and all Christians believe in the Rapture in one form or another because it's tied to the promise of the resurrection and the transformation of our bodies (1 Corinthians 15:51–52).

Where most Christians differ is on the *timing*. Whether you're Pre-Tribulation, Mid-Tribulation, or Post-Tribulation, we all agree that Jesus will one day glorify His Church, completing the work He began when He rose from the dead.

So when we talk about the Rapture, we're talking about more than just being "caught up" in the sky. We're talking about our ultimate transformation, the moment when everything broken and corrupted in us is made perfect forever. In other words, the Rapture is not an exit strategy, it's our eternal upgrade.

The significance of this event cannot be overstated, especially as you dive deeper into Bible prophecy and notice that sometimes it seems conspicuously absent from key passages. So, could it be that these "missing" mentions are deliberate because the Holy Spirit wants us to differentiate between the Rapture (when Jesus comes for His saints) and the Second Coming (when He returns with His saints)? Possibly. We'll unpack this distinction more in the coming chapters. But for now, keep this in mind: the Rapture is a separate and central piece of God's end-time plan.

Now that we've established that every camp agrees on the reality of the Rapture, let's delve into the debate over when it will actually happen.

The following is a brief breakdown of what each camp believes:

1. Pre-Tribulation Rapture

This is the view I hold. "Pre-Tribbers" believe that Jesus is coming back to snatch His bride (that's us) out of here *before* the chaos of the seven-year Tribulation kicks off. We see the Rapture happening as an imminent event, meaning it could happen *at any moment*, and the Church won't have to go through any of the coming wrath of God described in the book of Revelation. It's a message of hope and urgency, not escapism.

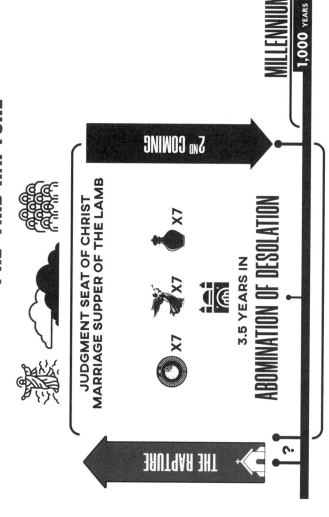

PRE-TRIB RAPTURE

THE RAPTURE

2ND COMING

JUDGMENT SEAT OF CHRIST
MARRIAGE SUPPER OF THE LAMB

X7   X7   X7

3.5 YEARS IN
ABOMINATION OF DESOLATION

7 YEAR TRIBULATION
70TH WEEK

?

WHITE THRONE
JUDGMENT

NEW HEAVENS
& NEW EARTH

MILLENNIUM
1,000 YEARS

2. Pre-Wrath Rapture

Pre-Wrath folks have a different take on the timeline. They believe that the Church will be here for the *beginning* of the Tribulation, but will be rescued before God's full wrath is unleashed, specifically, before the *"wrath of the Lamb"* mentioned in Revelation 6:16-17. They see the first few seals being opened as something the Church might have to face, but they draw the line when it comes to the more intense judgments.

3. Mid-Tribulation Rapture

This group believes that the Church will experience the first half of the Tribulation but will be taken up at the midpoint right before things really get ugly. They often key in on the timing of the *"abomination of desolation"* spoken of by Jesus in Matthew 24:15 and the two witnesses in Revelation. To them, the Rapture is a halftime exit right before the antichrist goes full beast mode. So for the Mid-Tribulation camp, the Church will see some tough times, but won't be here for the worst of it.

4. Post-Tribulation Rapture

"Post-Tribbers" are the spiritual equivalent of the "no pain, no gain" crew. They believe the Church will go through the entire seven-year Tribulation, enduring every seal, trumpet, and bowl of judgment until Jesus returns. For them, the Rapture and the Second Coming are essentially the same event, believers get caught up to meet Jesus in the air and then immediately come back down with Him as He sets up His Millennial Kingdom. Some Post-Tribbers say that we'll be raptured before the final battle of Armageddon at the tail end of The Great Tribulation.

While these are the main views on the Rapture's timing, there are a few more eschatological perspectives that color the end-time debate:

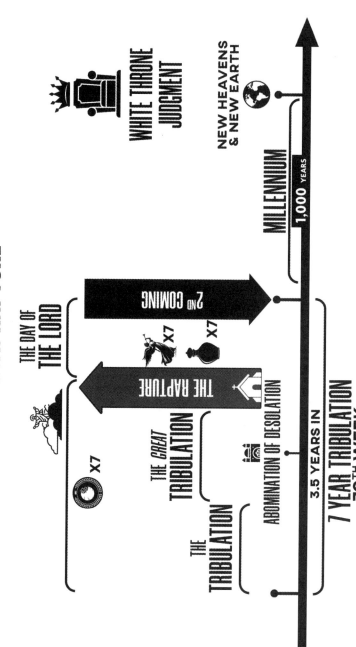

MID-TRIB RAPTURE

WHITE THRONE JUDGMENT

NEW HEAVENS & NEW EARTH

MILLENNIUM

1,000 YEARS

2ND COMING

THE RAPTURE

ABOMINATION OF DESOLATION

x7

x7

x7

3.5 YEARS IN

7 YEAR TRIBULATION
70TH WEEK

POST-TRIB RAPTURE

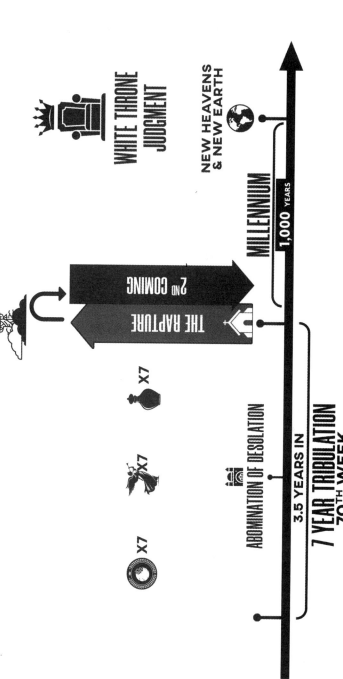

WHITE THRONE JUDGMENT

NEW HEAVENS & NEW EARTH

MILLENNIUM

1,000 YEARS

2ND COMING

THE RAPTURE

x7

x7

x7

ABOMINATION OF DESOLATION

3.5 YEARS IN

7 YEAR TRIBULATION
70TH WEEK

AMILLENNIALISM

Amillennialists are in a completely different camp altogether. They believe that the "millennium" isn't a literal thousand-year reign of Christ on earth, but rather a symbolic period that we're living in right now. For them, the Rapture is more of a metaphor, and the Second Coming will happen at the end of this symbolic "millennium," with no separate Rapture event beforehand. In other words, they take much of Bible prophecy as a spiritual allegory, not future prophecy.

POSTMILLENNIALISM

Postmillennialists are the eternal optimists of the eschatological world. They believe that the world will gradually get better through the influence of the Church until we enter a golden age of Christian rule, *then* Jesus will return. For them, the Tribulation is either historical or symbolic, and the Rapture isn't really a focus. In their view, it's not about Jesus rescuing us *from* chaos, but about us establishing His Kingdom on earth *before* He comes back.

As you can imagine, there seem to be as many differing views about the Rapture as there are churches; however, this summarizes the majority of them.

SO WHICH ONE IS RIGHT?

"Which one is right?" Good question. While each view has its arguments, one thing is clear: getting the timing right is less important than being *ready*. Jesus warned us to watch, pray, and stay alert (Mark 13:33). Whether He comes before, during, or after the Tribulation, the most crucial question is: *Are you prepared to meet Him?*

At the end of this chapter, I include a more comprehensive biblical timeline to give you a clearer understanding of how these events unfold according to Scripture. However, the most important question is this: *When He comes, will you be caught up or caught off guard?*

This is where things get tricky because the Church seems to be split between two extremes: those who are always ready to go to war over the issue, and those who avoid confrontation like it's the plague. The reasonable voices often stay quiet while the loudmouths dominate the discussion, leaving everyone else frustrated and turned off from engaging in the topic altogether.

In an effort to keep the peace, some prefer to sidestep this debate entirely. But that's a mistake, too. There's nothing unchristian about having passionate disagreements, as long as we can still walk away loving each other at the end of the day. Healthy debate sharpens us while avoiding the hard conversations weakens us.

SARCASM AND THE END TIMES

When I first stepped into this debate, I was stunned at the hostility of some people. It was like I'd unknowingly wandered into a battlefield, and suddenly everyone had a theological axe to grind. Feeling attacked, my natural reaction was to defend my beliefs vigorously. Since my personal "love language" is sarcasm, I often used it as a tool in these theological "discussions."

Unfortunately, my sarcasm was not always appreciated, and instead of fostering healthy discussions, I often contributed to the problem. My attempts to engage others in dialogue sometimes came off as condescending or dismissive, further cementing the divisions.

It took time and introspection to recognize that my approach was not helping. The very thing I loved, eschatology, was becoming a source of contention rather than illumination. I realized that if I truly valued these prophetic truths, I needed to find a way to share them with love and respect, even when faced with differing opinions.

My study of eschatology taught me to appreciate the depth and complexity of the subject. I learned to respect others' deeply held beliefs, understanding that sincere Christians can hold various opinions on the end times and that they often have good reason for their views. In fact, regardless of which view you hold, you're in good company. Many great men and women of God feel as you do. This is not an issue that should be dividing the Church. Instead, it should be an area where we can engage in fruitful, biblical discussions that strengthen our faith.

Though I may have fun throughout this book and you might sense a hint of sarcasm here and there, know that if you differ in your eschatological views, I love and respect you. My hope is to win you over with biblical evidence and thoughtful discussion, but regardless of whether you come to share my perspective, the goal is to foster unity and growth within the body of Christ.

You will also find that I "attack" those on my own side, for misrepresenting the Pre-Tribulation view as much as I do those with differing views. In fact, that's how this book began. I truly believe that rapture teaching is not the problem with today's Church, as some detractors believe; rather, it's weak and ineffective rapture teaching that is the culprit.

In this book we answer questions including:

- Why does the timing of the Rapture matter?
- Is the Rapture an escapist mentality?
- Shouldn't Christians be prepared for the Tribulation?
- What problems do Post-Tribulationists have with their view?
- Are there two second comings?
- Is the Rapture a new idea?
- What about the Last Trump?

- Is the Rapture in the armor of God?
- And many more…

In the end, engaging in meaningful conversations about the end times can bring us all closer to Jesus, the Author and Finisher of our faith. We can sharpen and challenge one another, ultimately growing in our understanding of God's Word. Make no mistake about it, I aim to challenge you. In this book, I call out the lies, mischaracterizations, and misinformation surrounding the Rapture of the Church. But my goal is to do this in love, and hopefully, we'll have a little fun along the way.

> In the future there is reserved for me the [victor's] crown of righteousness [for being right with God and doing right], which the Lord, the righteous Judge, will award to me on that [great] day—and not to me only, but also to all those who have loved and longed for and welcomed His appearing
>
> (2 Timothy 4:8 AMP).

My goal is to see a generation fall in love with the return of Jesus Christ.

This passion for the rapture began with a dream and has led to a life dedicated to learning what the Bible truly says about the last days. Eschatology became my passion, and the Word of God has remained my anchor. For it is in God's Word that we find the ultimate preparation for Jesus's imminent return, the blessed hope that sustains and motivates us to live for His glory and to occupy till He comes.

PROPHETIC TIMELINE: PRE-TRIBULATIONAL/PRE-MILLENNIAL

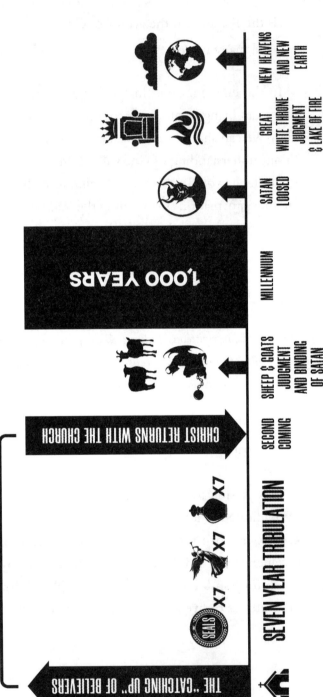

THEOLOGICALLY, THE RAPTURE REFERS TO THE MOMENT WHEN BELIEVERS, BOTH LIVING AND DEAD, WILL BE TRANSFORMED AND RECEIVE GLORIFIED BODIES, COMPLETING CHRIST'S REDEMPTIVE WORK.

JUDGMENT SEAT OF CHRIST
MARRIAGE SUPPER OF THE LAMB

THE "CATCHING UP" OF BELIEVERS

SEVEN YEAR TRIBULATION

SEALS x7

x7 x7

CHRIST RETURNS WITH THE CHURCH

SECOND COMING

SHEEP & GOATS JUDGMENT AND BINDING OF SATAN

1,000 YEARS

MILLENNIUM

SATAN LOOSED

GREAT WHITE THRONE JUDGMENT & LAKE OF FIRE

NEW HEAVENS AND NEW EARTH

2

FALLING IN LOVE WITH HIS APPEARING

The question of whether we are living in the last days has captivated a substantial segment of the US population, reflecting a deep-seated curiosity both about the future and the end times. Consider these striking statistics:

- 4 in 10 adults believe humanity is living in the end times.
- 55% are convinced that Jesus will return someday.
- 29% of individuals from non-Christian religions share the belief that we are in the end times.
- 23% of non-religious adults think we are experiencing end-time conditions.
- 9% of atheists and 14% of agnostics also entertain the idea that we are living in the end times.[1]

This topic is becoming a cultural phenomenon. The Pew Research Center highlights this widespread interest, underscoring a collective sense that something significant is unfolding in the world around us.

Yet amid this surge of interest, the subject has become a double-edged sword. The media and some so-called ministries often exploit these fears, turning profound questions into profit-making ventures and clouding the discourse with sensationalism. This commercialization of the end times can leave the public feeling more confused and disillusioned, struggling to discern truth from hype.

The Church, too, has not been immune to this uncertainty. In a landscape polarized by differing eschatological views, doctrinal disputes have often overshadowed the core message. Pre-Tribulation proponents face accusations of heresy, while Post-Tribulation adherents are labeled as deceitful. Such divisions have only added to the confusion, leaving many believers feeling isolated or misrepresented.

Despite the muddied waters, the call remains clear. We must return to the steadfast truth of God's Word. In the middle of all of the controversy, falling in love with His appearing means embracing the truth of what the Bible says, rather than succumbing to sensationalism, fearmongering, or divisiveness. It also means surrendering to the Word of God rather than yielding to our emotional preferences.

LET NO ONE STEAL YOUR CROWN

The Bible speaks of several crowns that await those who are in Christ Jesus. First is the **Crown of Righteousness**. Second Timothy 4:8 (KJV) states, *"Henceforth there is laid up for me a crown of righteousness, which the Lord, the righteous judge, shall give me at that day: and not to me only, but unto all them also that love his appearing."*

This verse highlights the crown reserved for those who live righteously and in eager anticipation of the return of Jesus. The Crown of Righteousness symbolizes the reward for a life lived in faithful expectation of Christ's coming.

Second is the **Crown of Life.** James 1:12 (NIV) declares, *"Blessed is the one who perseveres under trial because, having stood the test, that person will receive the crown of life that the Lord has promised to those who love him."* This crown is promised to those who remain steadfast under trial and temptation, showing a deep, enduring love for God despite life's challenges.

Next is the **Imperishable Crown.** First Corinthians 9:25 (NKJV) reveals, *"And everyone who competes for the prize is temperate in all things.*

Now they do it to obtain a perishable crown, but we for an imperishable crown." This incorruptible crown is awarded to those who exercise self-discipline and perseverance, likened to an athlete training for a race. It symbolizes the reward for a disciplined, dedicated life in Christ.

The next crown is the **Crown of Glory.** First Peter 5:4 (NKJV) says, *"And when the Chief Shepherd appears, you will receive the crown of glory that does not fade away."* This crown is given to faithful shepherds and leaders who have guided others in the faith with diligence and care. It signifies the reward for those who shepherd the flock with humility and love. It's also important to note when this takes place—at the moment of His appearing.

Last is the **Crown of Rejoicing.** First Thessalonians 2:19 (NKJV) states, *"For what is our hope, or joy, or crown of rejoicing? Is it not even you in the presence of our Lord Jesus Christ at His coming?"* This crown is associated with those who have led others to Christ, reflecting the joy and reward of seeing new believers in the presence of the Lord.

I don't think we can be dogmatic about the exact number or meaning of these crowns, but they do show that there will be specific rewards for different forms of faithfulness.

Given the importance of these crowns, it is clear why the enemy works tirelessly to create division and confusion around the doctrine of Christ's return. By causing discord and misinformation, he aims to divert believers' focus from the hope and preparation of Christ's appearing. As Revelation 3:11 (NKJV) warns, *"Behold, I am coming quickly! Hold fast what you have, that no one may take your crown."* This verse indicates that it's possible for these crowns to be taken from us.

STILL HIS CHILD WHILE HOLDING DIFFERING RAPTURE VIEWS?

Can we still be a child of God while holding different views on the Rapture? Absolutely. Our salvation isn't tied to getting the eschatology chart just right. But here's the thing, our relationship with God is about so much more than just making it to Heaven by the skin of our teeth. We're not in this just to secure some sort of "fire insurance." The Bible speaks of heavenly rewards and crowns that symbolize faithfulness, endurance, and a love for His appearing. These aren't heavenly participation trophies handed out to everyone. They're opportunities for each of us to bring glory to Jesus in a very real and tangible way.

On that day when we finally stand before Him, what will we have to offer? All our earthly achievements, titles, and possessions will be meaningless in the light of His glory. The only thing that will matter is what we've done out of love and obedience to Him. By contending for these rewards, especially the precious Crown of Righteousness, you're ensuring that you have something of eternal value to lay at His feet. Isn't that what every true believer longs to be able to offer our King? Don't we all want to stand before our Savior and give Him something that reflects our devotion? That's what makes this issue so critical.

The quest for these crowns represents a life of true and selfless worship. Every Sunday, in churches around the world, millions lift their hands and sing songs of worship, but their hearts are far from Him. However, *every move you make in response to your love for His appearing is an act of true worship.*

I want this generation to fall in love with His appearing!

Earlier, I shared how my profound love for Christ's return dramatically reshaped my life and, in turn, led to some unexpected friction within the Christian community. The very hope that fueled my passion became a battleground, where I found myself under attack from fellow believers. My instinctive response was to defend my beliefs with fervor, and given my aforementioned propensity for sarcasm, I often wielded it like a double-edged sword in these theological debates.

Regrettably, my sarcasm rarely fostered productive conversation. Instead of bridging gaps, it often widened them. I can assure you that it has never been my intention to do so, but when conversations generate more heat than light, my natural reaction is to try to lighten the mood with a little humor. I realize it's seldom appreciated, but what can I say? I'm still a work in progress.

The level of animosity exchanged in debates about the Rapture continues to astonish me. Few topics seem to provoke such an intense reception among believers. While vitriol can be found on all sides, my experience suggests that the Pre-Tribulation Rapture position often bears the brunt of the most vehement hostility and misrepresentations. It's as if a switch is flipped in some people's minds, transforming reasoned discussion into aggressive confrontation. This reaction feels almost supernatural in its intensity, underscoring the deep divisions and passionate emotions surrounding this subject. The individuals who exhibit the most intense and emotional reactions are often the ones who lack a fundamental understanding of the Pre-Tribulation Rapture position. They can rarely, accurately communicate what I believe, but they're sure it's wrong.

This is the most discouraging aspect about this subject matter. I eventually came to understand that if I truly wanted to honor these prophetic truths, I needed to approach discussions with a spirit of love and respect, rather than defensiveness.

Our arguments and carnal quarrels will not inspire others to fall in love with His appearing. All of us should have the same mission to ignite a passion for the return of Jesus within this generation. I believe that we can do this, even when we disagree on the timetable, if we'll acknowledge our love for one another.

By this all will know that you are My disciples, if you have love for one another

(John 13:35 NKJV)

We can also achieve this mission by coming to a unified understanding of what it means to "love His appearing."

So what does it truly mean to *love* His appearing? Let's explore this concept through the lens of 2 Timothy in the Amplified Version of the Bible:

> *In the future there is reserved for me the [victor's] crown of righteousness [for being right with God and doing right], which the Lord, the righteous Judge, will award to me on that [great] day— and not to me only, but also to all those who have loved and longed for and welcomed His appearing*
>
> (2 Timothy 4:8 AMP).

This verse reveals a powerful truth: our relationship with Christ isn't merely focused on being saved from hell, it involves loving Him, longing for Him, and eagerly welcoming His return.

Loving His appearing is not about sitting around, hoping that someday, maybe, Jesus will return to clean up the mess we've created here on earth. It's more than a passive, wishful hope; it's a deep, active, passionate longing to finally see our Savior face-to-face. It's the kind of anticipation that stirs you up, changes how you live, and keeps your heart full of expectation, waiting for that moment when the sky will split and He'll call your name.

A beautiful picture of this longing is painted in the Song of Solomon. It's often overlooked, but its poetic portrayal of the relationship between a bride and her bridegroom serves as a powerful metaphor for Christ and His Church. In chapter 2, we see a bride breathlessly watching for her beloved:

> *The voice of my beloved! behold, he cometh leaping upon the mountains, skipping upon the hills. My beloved is like a roe or a young hart: behold, he standeth behind our wall, he looketh forth at*

the windows, shewing himself through the lattice. My beloved spake, and said unto me, Rise up, my love, my fair one, and come away (Song of Solomon 2:8-10 KJV).

Her heart leaps when she hears his voice. It's a joyful anticipation that makes everything else fade into the background. That's what it means to "love His appearing." Living with the constant expectation that any day now we'll hear the shout, the trumpet will sound, and we'll be swept up into His everlasting arms.

This is not some casual, "Oh, I hope He comes back eventually" kind of attitude. The bride in the Song of Solomon is yearning for her beloved. Every day she's listening, looking, and longing for his appearing. She's not getting distracted by the daily grind or lulled into complacency. This kind of urgency makes you live differently. This is one reason why this teaching matters so much.

When Paul talks about the "crown of righteousness" laid up for all those who "love His appearing," it is not a crown handed out universally to everyone who intellectually agrees that Jesus is coming back someday. No, this is a reward reserved for those who ache to see Him, who live like they could be swept off their feet at any second. Just as the bride in the Song of Solomon exclaims with joy when she sees her beloved coming, we too should be living with that same sense of joyful anticipation for the Rapture. We're not watching for signs like a detective piecing together clues; we are actively listening for His voice, leaning forward in expectation, and keeping our hearts ready.

Why shouldn't we? This isn't a day to dread or fear. For the Church, the Rapture isn't the beginning of some grim escape plan, it's the start of a glorious reunion when suddenly the One who shed His blood for us, who calls us by name, who has been preparing a place for us in glory, finally comes to take us home. It's the ultimate culmination of everything we've been living for, praying for, and hoping for.

THE BRIDE AND THE BRIDEGROOM

The anticipation of the Rapture isn't simply a doctrine; it's a love story. Christ isn't returning to rescue us out of obligation. He's coming for His bride, the one He loves, the one He has been waiting to embrace. The bride's cry of "Come quickly!" in Revelation 22:17 isn't wishful thinking. It's a yearning from deep within, a longing that mirrors His own desire to be united with His Church. Even as we talk about it, doesn't your heart just burn within you?

So when we talk about loving His appearing, it's not just about prophecy charts and theological arguments. It's about a relationship. It's about leaning out the window, like the bride in the Song of Solomon, watching and waiting for that first glimpse of the One we love. On that day when He calls, we won't hesitate. We'll rise up, run to meet Him, and finally, finally be with Him forever.

That's what it means to love His appearing. It is a craving. To *crave* means to have an intense, almost insatiable longing for something. It's an active, consuming hunger that shapes your actions and thoughts. To crave His appearing means every decision, every prayer, every act of kindness, every effort to share the Gospel is motivated by the desire to be ready and to make others ready.

THE DANGER OF HESITATION

The Song of Solomon not only captures the joy of anticipation but also warns us about the dangers of hesitation. In chapter 5, we see a striking example of what happens when the bride delays in responding to her beloved's call:

> *I sleep, but my heart waketh: it is the voice of my beloved that knocketh, saying, Open to me, my sister, my love, my dove, my undefiled: for my head is filled with dew, and my locks with the*

drops of the night. I have put off my coat; how shall I put it on? I have washed my feet; how shall I defile them?

(Song of Solomon 5:2-3 KJV)

You can almost hear her inner debate: "I'm already comfortable, I've settled in for the night… do I really want to get up now?" But by the time she finally decides to act, it's too late. When she opens the door, her beloved is gone. The opportunity has passed, and she's left to wander the streets, desperately searching for him in the darkness. It's a haunting picture of what can happen when we hesitate to respond to the Lord's call in our personal lives.

How many of us have been in her shoes? We hear the Spirit's gentle prompting, but we delay. We think, "I'll obey tomorrow," or "I'll get serious about my faith next week." But tomorrow turns into next week, and next week turns into never. Before we know it, we've missed our moment of visitation.

DON'T MISS YOUR MOMENT

Jesus echoed this same warning in Revelation 3:20 (KJV): *"Behold, I stand at the door, and knock: if any man hear my voice, and open the door, I will come in to him, and will sup with him, and he with me."*

Here, Jesus is not talking to unbelievers but to the Church and to those who already claim to follow Him. He's knocking, calling, and waiting for a response. But if we delay, if we hesitate to answer His voice, we risk missing out on the intimate fellowship He desires to have with us.

Hesitation can lead to a missed visitation.

It's more than a missed opportunity. It is the loss of a divine moment when God wanted to meet with you, speak to you, or use you in a way that would change your life forever. It's the reason Jesus wept over Jerusalem, saying, *"If thou hadst known, even thou, at least in this thy day, the things which belong unto thy peace! but now they are hid from thine eyes"* (Luke 19:42 KJV). They missed their hour of visitation because they weren't prepared to receive Him.

THE PARABLE OF THE VIRGINS

Jesus drives this point home again in Matthew 25 with the Parable of the Wise and Foolish Virgins. Ten virgins wait for the bridegroom, but only five are wise enough to bring extra oil for their lamps. When the bridegroom finally arrives, the foolish ones, who were unprepared, find themselves locked out in the dark. Jesus's warning is clear: be vigilant, be ready, and don't delay.

That darkness outside the door isn't just symbolic of missing a wedding celebration. For some, it's a picture of The Great Tribulation, a time of unprecedented suffering and judgment that the foolish virgins could have avoided if only they had been prepared. It's not enough to believe that Jesus is coming, we have to live like it.

To truly love His appearing means to be *vigilant*, actively waiting, always ready, and never growing weary. The word *vigilant* literally means being "alertly watchful, especially to avoid danger or seize opportunities."[2] You're not just staying awake, you're living in a constant state of readiness, always anticipating the moment when our Bridegroom will arrive.

Think of it like being on call for the most important event of your life. If you knew a king was coming to your house, would you be lounging around in your pajamas, half-heartedly glancing at the driveway every now and then? Of course not! You'd be watching out the window, ready to fling the door open the moment his car pulls up. That's the kind of urgency and excitement we should have when it comes to the return of Jesus. When that moment comes, hesitation isn't an option.

WE WOULD SEE JESUS

This longing and vigilance can be seen in a seemingly small but profound moment recorded in John 12:21 (NKJV). Some Greeks, outsiders to the Jewish faith, approached Philip with a simple request: *"Sir, we wish to see Jesus."* These Gentiles, restricted to the outer court of the temple and separated from Jesus by physical and cultural barriers, expressed a desire that resonates through the ages. They just wanted to see Him.

Their plea is the heart's cry of today's generation: "We wish to see Jesus." But the question remains: When He comes, will we be ready to see Him? Will we respond the moment He knocks, or will we hesitate, weighed down by distractions, doubts, and excuses?

When Jesus comes for His bride, there will be no time for last-minute scrambling, no time to run out and buy oil, and no time to shake off the spiritual slumber. Loving His appearing means being so prepared that when He knocks, we can say, "Yes, Lord! I've been waiting for You!"

The truth is, we don't know when that moment will be. One thing is certain, when He comes, it will be sudden, it will be swift, and it will be glorious.

THE QUESTION IS: WILL YOU BE READY?

Like those Greeks in John 12, we also find ourselves in a world that often feels like it has erected walls between us and our Savior. Jesus has gone beyond the veil, into the heavenly courts, and while we live in this present world, our hearts yearn to see Him. We don't long for mere cultural renewal or social transformation, our deepest desire is to see Him face-to-face.

In John 14:3 (KJV), Jesus promised, *"And if I go and prepare a place for you, I will come again, and receive you unto myself; that where I am, there ye may be also."* This is not a vague metaphor, it is a literal and personal assurance from Jesus that He will return. I believe that every Christian has a deep desire for this blessed hope regardless of what they say their eschatology is. Even so, there are those who attempt to rationalize or spiritualize His coming, claiming that the prophecies were fulfilled in the past, and that His return is merely symbolic. But the Bible answers them sharply:

> *When everything is ready, I will come and get you, so that you will always be with me where I am*
> (John 14:3 NLT).

> *Ye men of Galilee, why stand ye gazing up into heaven? this same Jesus, which is taken up from you into heaven, shall so come in like manner as ye have seen him go into heaven*
> (Acts 1:11 KJV).

> *And then shall appear the sign of the Son of man in heaven: and then shall all the tribes of the earth mourn, and they shall see the Son of man coming in the clouds of heaven with power and great glory*
> (Matthew 24:30 KJV).

> *...Hereafter shall ye see the Son of man sitting on the right hand of power, and coming in the clouds of heaven*
> (Matthew 26:64 KJV).

> *Behold, he cometh with clouds; and every eye shall see him, and they also which pierced him: and all kindreds of the earth shall wail because of him. Even so, Amen*
> (Revelation 1:7 KJV).

And, behold, I come quickly; and my reward is with me, to give every man according as his work shall be

(Revelation 22:12 KJV).

He who testifies to these things says, "Surely I am coming quickly." Amen. Even so, come, Lord Jesus!

(Revelation 22:20 NKJV)

The fulfillment of these promises is not in some kind of societal reformation or even death; it is in His triumphant return. This is why, as the world grows darker, our excitement grows brighter. We are not called to hasten that day or to create the conditions for His return, but we do have a promise, and we see a pattern in Scripture. God is coming to receive His people unto Himself.

The signs of the times are all around us, and the promise of His coming stands as a beacon of hope. Don't be found unprepared. The day is coming when the wall that separates us from our Savior will be torn down, and we will see Him as He is.

Those who truly love His appearing aren't sitting idly by, as some detractors might suggest. It's easy for critics to caricature believers in the Rapture as passive, twiddling their thumbs, not doing a single thing…just waiting. But nothing could be further from the truth. Those who have a proper understanding of the Rapture know that there's a world of difference between "just waiting" and actively watching for Jesus's return. They're not simply marking time, they're living with purpose, eyes wide open, fully engaged, and eagerly antic-ipating the moment they will meet their Savior.

There's a profound difference between waiting and watching; it's a distinction that speaks directly to the heart of every Christian's life. To "wait" is to singularly mark time, to pass the days in expectation. But to "watch" is something entirely different; watching is an active, eager anticipation, a vigilant readiness that can shape every moment of our lives.

THE SOLDIER RETURNS HOME

Imagine a soldier returning home after a long and grueling deployment. As his ship docks, he scans the crowd for the face of his beloved. There, among the throng, he sees families straining to catch the first glimpse of their loved ones, eyes bright with expectation, hearts pounding with the thrill of reunion. These are not merely people who have been waiting; rather, they've been watching, every day longing for this moment, preparing for it, their hearts and minds fixed on the day of their loved one's return.

In contrast, consider now the story of a sailor who disembarked from his ship, only to find that his wife was not among the eager faces on the dock. Disappointed, he made his way home, his heart heavy with unspoken questions. When he arrived, he found her sitting in their living room, calmly knitting. She looked up and greeted him with a simple, "Welcome home, I've been *waiting* for you."

"Yes," he replied with a quiet sadness, "but the other wives were *watching* for their husbands."

This story speaks volumes. Waiting can be passive, almost indifferent. It's what we do when we know something will eventually happen, but we're not engaged in the process. Watching, however, is active. It's how we respond when we're fully invested, when our hearts are so entwined with the one we're expecting that every part of our day and every action is affected by the anticipation.

In our personal walk, Jesus calls us not just to wait for His return, but to watch for it. In Matthew 24:42 (KJV), He says, *"Watch therefore: for ye know not what hour your Lord doth come."* It's the difference between living each day with a deep, abiding hope, and merely existing with a vague expectation of what the future might hold.

The story of the sailor's wife serves as a cautionary tale. How often are we like her, simply waiting, going about our lives, passively assuming that we'll be ready when the time comes? Christ calls us to something greater, to a life lived in the active anticipation of His return, to be like the wise virgins in Matthew 25, whose lamps were filled and ready.

To *watch* is to live with our hearts and minds fixed on Jesus, actively engaging in His work, preparing ourselves and others for the day when He will appear. It's to live with a sense of urgency, not out of fear, but out of love knowing that the One we long to see could arrive at any moment. It's the difference between merely passing time and making the most of every opportunity, so that when He does come, we're found faithful, ready, and rejoicing.

> Blessed Hope is a powerful enticement for believers to seek to become holy, to be perfect even as He is perfect and to be watchful, waiting for Jesus' return. When He returns is not as important as the fact that we are ready for Him when He does return. The crucial question is, When He returns, will He find us waiting?
>
> —A. W. Tozer[3]

When that day comes, it will be the watching hearts that are filled with the greatest joy, ready to welcome Him with open arms and hear those precious words, "Well done, thou good and faithful servant."

Are you just waiting, or are you watching?

3

OCCUPY TILL HE COMES

Where will all of our worldly enjoyments be, when we are laid in the silent grave?
Resolved, to live as I shall wish I had done, when I come to die.
Resolved, to live as I shall wish I had done, ten thousand ages hence.
Lord, stamp eternity on my eyeballs!

—*Jonathan Edwards*[1]

The essence of Christianity is wrapped up in the expectation of Jesus' imminent return....

—*A.W. Tozer*[2]

If you are looking for a book that will liberate you from the responsibility to plan for tomorrow or console you while you cower in a corner hoping to escape tough times, this is not the book for you. These are the last days! There's no time for defeatism, and we must give no place to any kind of "Fearful Eschatology." We've been called to *occupy till He comes* (Luke 19:13).

For years now, we've heard the same tired narrative: "Rapture believers are just escapists!" They say we're so obsessed with the return of Jesus that we've become useless in the here and now, disengaged from society, and indifferent to the needs of our generation. But is that really the case?

Let's break it down. Critics argue that believing in the Rapture leads to irresponsibility, claiming that we're the type who won't save for retirement or plan for the future because, "Hey, Jesus could come back at any moment!" However, it's difficult to find a prominent Rapture teacher who actually espouses such views. This stereotype is just a straw man and isn't rooted in biblical teachings or in practical reality. It usually comes from misunderstandings or misrepresentations.

Yes, there have been some well-meaning believers who've taken the idea of the Rapture to unhealthy extremes, cashing out their savings, quitting their jobs, or disengaging from society. I don't personally know any, but I've heard stories. However, to say that's the norm for Pre-Tribulation believers simply isn't true. The claim that *"looking for that blessed hope"* (Titus 2:13) somehow causes Christians to surrender is like saying every runner who sees the finish line quits. That's not how this works. On the contrary, seeing the finish line encourages people to work harder.

In fact, those who are most convinced of Christ's imminent return are often the ones who work the hardest.

In 1952, Florence Chadwick jumped into the chilly waters of the Pacific Ocean with a singular goal: to become the first woman to swim the 22-mile stretch from Catalina Island to the California mainland. She wasn't new to challenges like this because she had already conquered the English Channel, twice. But this day would prove to be a different kind of test.

The ocean was relentless, and a thick, soupy fog hung over the water, making it impossible to see beyond her outstretched hand. Florence swam for 15 hours, pushing herself through exhaustion, her muscles aching from the cold. But the fog was unrelenting, blocking her view of everything, including her destination. Finally, overwhelmed with fatigue and unable to see how much farther she had to go, she cried out, "I can't go on! Help me!" Her support team pulled her out of the water and into the boat.

Once aboard, she learned the truth that almost broke her spirit: she had swam 21.5 miles. She was only half a mile away from the California coast. Later, when she spoke to reporters, Florence said, "If only I could have seen the shore, I would have made it."

There's something powerful about catching a glimpse of the finish line and seeing the other side. It reminds us why we endure, why we press on when every muscle in our body screams for us to quit. Florence's story is a reminder that sometimes the only thing between us and our victory is a clear vision of the promise that awaits.

This was certainly true in the early Church whose expectation of Jesus's return didn't make them retreat; rather, it propelled them forward, spreading the Gospel with such urgency that they *"turned the world upside down"* (Acts 17:6 KJV).

Believing in the Rapture isn't about checking out; it's about fully checking in. It's about living with a sense of urgency, knowing that what we do right now matters for eternity. When you really grasp that Jesus could return at any moment, it doesn't make you slack off, it makes you lean in, wanting to make every moment count for His glory.

So, let's set the record straight: true Rapture theology isn't an excuse to sit on the sidelines. It's a call to action. It's about being ready, yes, but also about being busy. As Jesus said, *"Occupy till I come"* (Luke 19:13 KJV). If anything, the belief that we could meet Him at any moment should drive us to engage more deeply, to give more sacrificially, and to serve more passionately.

Because when the King returns, I want to be found faithful. Don't you?

WATCH OUT FOR EXTREMES

If we start using the extremes, or the crazies in any movement, to define a belief, then every doctrine we hold dear will fall apart under that same flawed scrutiny. We'd have to abandon grace because of the "hyper-grace" crowd and throw holiness in the trash because some people took legalism to Pharisaical levels.

Every core doctrine has its fringe elements. But we don't define a belief by its abuse. Just because someone took a biblical truth and twisted it doesn't mean the whole thing is rotten. Misrepresentation is not a reflection of the message, it's a reflection of human error. That's why it's crucial to anchor ourselves in what the Word actually teaches, not in what some have distorted it to be. Otherwise, we'll end up throwing the baby out with the bathwater every single time. If the bad behavior of a few misguided people is enough to discredit a doctrine, then what's left? Absolutely nothing.

I began writing this book to address those misinformed believers who have stirred up this farcical controversy through their own apathy. God's reputation is often more damaged by His advocates than by His detractors. When someone acts foolishly as a Christian, I often tell skeptics, "Listen, that person was crazy before they got saved. Jesus didn't do that to them." Every move of God has had those on the fringes who somehow managed to become the poster child of the movement, a notion reinforced and amplified by its critics.

This same lazy escapism can be attributed to the Post-Tribulation view. If the world and half-hearted Christians know that specific prophecies must be fulfilled before Jesus returns, why wouldn't they just sit back in their doubt and wait to see what happens before getting serious? I've personally encountered this mindset many times. People often say, "I'll get serious when I begin to see these things come to pass." Should I then paint the entire Post-Tribulation movement with a broad brush of fostering apathy because of these encounters? Absolutely not.

There are apathetic Christians who use the idea of the Rapture as an excuse to avoid engaging in culture. But the truth is that they were lazy and complacent before they believed in the Rapture. If it wasn't the Rapture, they'd find some other reason to disengage and avoid fulfilling the call of God on their lives.

Christians do *not* disengage from culture because of Rapture teaching. They disengage because of poor Rapture teaching.

Let's quickly consider a few keys: The Bible reveals that the anticipation of the Rapture is a transformational hope that actively shapes the lives of believers. The following are several powerful ways that the expectation of Christ's return drives spiritual growth and maturity:

1. ENCOURAGES HOLINESS AND PERSONAL RESPONSIBILITY

The apostle John tells us, *"And everyone who has this hope in Him purifies himself, just as He is pure"* (1 John 3:3 NKJV). The hope of the Rapture inspires believers to pursue holiness, to align their lives with Christ, and to take personal responsibility for their walk with God.

2. FOSTERS CHURCH ATTENDANCE AND MUTUAL ENCOURAGEMENT

Hebrews 10:24-25 (KJV) urges us to *"consider one another to provoke unto love and to good works: not forsaking the assembling of ourselves together, as the manner of some is; but exhorting one another: and so much the more, as ye see the day approaching."* The knowledge that Jesus could return at any moment propels believers to be committed to their local church, fostering deeper fellowship and accountability. It instills a "so much the more" mentality. To gather with a heightened intensity and purpose as we see "the day" approaching. Everything we do for the body of Christ should be turned up a notch in the light of the Rapture. Whether it's attending church, encouraging one another, or serving others, the message is clear: do it "so much the more" when the Rapture is in view.

3. DRIVES PASSION FOR EVANGELISM AND DISCIPLESHIP

When you truly grasp that Christ's return is imminent, the urgency of the Great Commission becomes undeniable. The Rapture encourages believers to evangelize and make disciples, knowing that time is short. Jesus said, *"Night is coming, when no one can work"* (John 9:4 NIV), reminding us that the opportunity to reach the lost won't last forever. The anticipation of the Rapture pushes us to share the Gospel, now, and even more so.

4. INSPIRES EARNEST PRAYER

In Luke 18:1 (KJV), Jesus taught that we *"ought always to pray, and not to faint."* We are called to be found in prayer, persistently lifting up the needs of others and seeking God's will, knowing that soon we may be face-to-face with Him.

5. ENCOURAGES LOVING OTHERS AND GUARDING OUR CONDUCT

In Matthew 24:48-49 (KJV), Jesus speaks of a wicked servant who says, *"My lord delayeth his coming,"* and then begins to mistreat others. The expectation of the Rapture keeps us vigilant, reminding us to treat others with love and grace, knowing that Christ could come at any moment. It encourages us to fulfill the commandment to *"love thy neighbour as thyself"* (Matthew 22:39 KJV) and to avoid the pitfalls of complacency or cruelty.

6. PROMOTES GOOD STEWARDSHIP

Jesus taught His followers that they must be as those who *"wait for their lord...that when he cometh and knocketh, they may open unto him immediately"* (Luke 12:36 KJV). Paul also reminds us in 2 Corinthians 5:10 (KJV) that *"we must all appear before the judgment seat of Christ"* to give an account of our lives. This reality drives believers to be good stewards of their time, talents, and resources.

7. ENERGIZES DISCIPLESHIP AND SPIRITUAL GROWTH

The anticipation of the Rapture greases the wheels of discipleship like nothing else. Knowing that Jesus could come at any moment stirs us to make every day count, to grow in Christ-likeness, and to invest in the spiritual growth of those around us. It provides a divine urgency to every act of service, every prayer, and every word of encouragement, propelling us forward in our faith journey.

The Rapture is a catalyst for spiritual growth. It urges us to pursue holiness and deepen our fellowship, all while waiting for our soon-coming King.

> In the days of primitive Christianity, it would have been deemed a kind of apostasy not to sigh for the return of the Lord.
>
> —Jean Baptiste Massillon[3]

The lie that Rapture believers are mere escapists is not only unfounded but also contrary to the transformative power of the Gospel. Our eyes can be set on the heavens, while our hands are diligently at work on earth. These two are not mutually exclusive. So, let's dispel this myth once and for all. Believing in the Rapture doesn't mean we're escaping reality. It means we're more engaged than ever, driven by the hope of Christ's return to be His hands and feet in this world because at any moment we will stand before the Judgment Seat of Christ.

THE JUDGMENT SEAT OF CHRIST

The Rapture is inextricably connected to the Judgment Seat of Christ. As we consider the "lie" that the Rapture of the Church creates apathy or disengagement, we must bring to light this crucial event. The apostle Paul talks about this in 2 Corinthians 5:10 (KJV):

> *For we must all appear before the judgment seat of Christ; that every one may receive the things done in his body, according to that he hath done, whether it be good or bad.*

This judgment is not about salvation, for that is secured through faith in Christ, but it is about reward and accountability.

The Greek word for "judgment seat" is *bema*, which originally referred to a raised platform where officials, particularly judges, would sit to render decisions or hand out rewards. In the context of ancient Greek cities, the bema was the place where the judge of the city sat to hear cases, pass judgments, and reward those who had competed in public games.

In the New Testament, the Bema is used to describe the Judgment Seat of Christ, where believers will appear not for condemnation, but for the purpose of receiving rewards based on their faithfulness, service, and obedience to God's call. Just as athletes in ancient Greece would stand before the bema to receive their crowns of victory, Christians will stand before Christ to be rewarded for what they have done in their lives for His Kingdom. This is where our works will be evaluated for the rewards that will last into eternity.

At the Judgment Seat of Christ there will be many believers who will question within themselves, *Why didn't I do more with what Christ gave me?*

This should wake us up to the eventuality that everything we do, or don't do, matters. Every choice, every act of service, and every

opportunity to share Christ carries eternal weight. When you consider that His return is imminent, it's even more urgent. We only have
a short window left to make every moment count for His Kingdom.
Time is running out!

Leonard Ravenhill, a man known for his passionate preaching and
heart for revival, has this etched on his tombstone: *"Are the things you
are living for worth Christ dying for?"*

Knowing that we will stand before Christ and give an account
of how we lived should ignite a fire within us to serve Him
wholeheartedly.

WATCH OUT FOR LEGALISM

There are many today who have come out of harsh legalism, carrying
the scars of their past, who understandably recoil at the idea of the
Judgment Seat of Christ. They've experienced a life-changing revelation of God's goodness and mercy and can't quite reconcile how
this aligns with the concept of His severity, as seen in Romans 11:22
(KJV) which says, *"Behold therefore the goodness and severity of God."* It
can seem like a contradiction. How can a loving, gracious God also
be a righteous judge?

I understand their hesitancy, and there's no shortage of these kinds
of seeming contradictions as we grow in our knowledge of God. But
just because we can't fully comprehend how these truths fit together
doesn't mean they don't fit together. Nor does it make them any less
biblical. God's goodness and His justice are not opposing forces, but
rather two sides of the same coin. His love doesn't negate His holiness, nor does His grace cancel out His righteous judgment.

The Judgment Seat of Christ is meant to compel us to take the
Luke 19:13 command seriously. It is a call to use our time, talents, and
resources for His glory, knowing that our efforts will be weighed in
the balance when we stand before our Lord.

Others, realizing they can't escape the concept of the Judgment Seat of Christ in Scripture, often attempt to minimize its significance by saying that we'll simply be judged "good." While this is true in part, it overlooks the deeper reality of what this judgment entails. They act as if this judgment will be over in a flash and we'll never even know it happened; but, that gives no glory to God. We're going to feel this moment deeply and the grace shown here will mark us for eternity.

Yes, as believers, we are clothed in Christ's righteousness, and we won't face condemnation. But the Judgment Seat of Christ is about more than just a blanket declaration of "You're good." It's a place where our works, our faithfulness, and the way we've stewarded our lives for God's Kingdom will be examined. It's about assessing the depth of our faithfulness and the fruit of our lives in service to God's Kingdom. Here we'll learn from our mistakes and our successes. We should approach it with reverence, recognizing the seriousness with which the apostle Paul viewed it.

WOOD, HAY, STUBBLE VERSUS GOLD, SILVER, PRECIOUS STONES

In 1 Corinthians 3, Paul contrasts two sets of materials: "wood, hay, stubble" and "gold, silver, precious stones." These materials represent the quality and enduring value of our works as believers, which will be tested by fire at the Judgment Seat of Christ.

Now if anyone builds on this foundation with gold, silver, precious stones, wood, hay, straw, each one's work will become clear; for the Day will declare it, because it will be revealed by fire; and the fire will test each one's work, of what sort it is. If anyone's work which he has built on it endures, he will receive a reward. If anyone's work is burned, he will suffer loss; but he himself will be saved, yet so as through fire
(1 Corinthians 3:12-15 NKJV).

Wood, hay, and stubble are materials that are easily consumed by fire. They symbolize works done with impure motives, selfish ambition, or earthly focus. These are the actions and efforts that, while possibly well-intentioned, are ultimately of little eternal value. Let's look a little closer at each one:

Wood: works done with fleshly strength, relying on human wisdom rather than the Spirit.

Hay: temporary or superficial actions. Hay can look impressive in bulk, but it is lightweight and lacks substance. These are deeds done for appearance or immediate reward, rather than out of a heart for God.

Stubble: the remnants leftover after harvesting, symbolizing things of little worth. Stubble is easily scattered and has no lasting value. It represents trivial or insignificant actions that have no eternal impact.

When tested by the fire of God's judgment, these works will be consumed, showing that they have no lasting worth in the Kingdom of God. In contrast, gold, silver, and precious stones are materials that withstand fire and become purer through the refining process. They represent works done with pure motives, in obedience to the Spirit. These include:

Gold: Could symbolize our service to God and the motives behind that service. Gold is valuable, enduring, and reflects the glory of God. These are deeds rooted in faith, love, and obedience, which will stand the test of time.

Silver: Often associated with redemption in Scripture, silver could also be linked to our words. Proverbs 10:20 says that the tongue of the just is as *"choice silver."* Silver retains its value and is resilient, just like the enduring impact of any word we speak which glorifies Christ. In Matthew 12:36-37, the Bible also says that our words will be judged.

Precious Stones: These could represent the diversity and beauty of the fruit of the Spirit in a believer's life, or they could represent our prayer lives. The High Priest in the Old Testament would wear a breastplate made of twelve precious stones as he prayed for the nation. Our time committed to praying for one another could be a key factor in how we are judged on this day.

THE TERROR OF THE LORD

Paul had a healthy fear of this moment because this is where the believer's work will be tested by fire at the Judgment Seat of Christ. The fire will reveal the true nature of our deeds, whether they were temporary and self-serving (wood, hay, stubble) or enduring and God-glorifying (gold, silver, precious stones). Only the works that pass through the fire will receive a reward.

I want you to see how 1 Corinthians 3:15 is worded in different translations:

> But if the work is burned up, the builder will **suffer** great loss. The builder will be saved, but **like someone barely escaping through a wall of flames**
>
> (New Living Translation).

> If your work passes inspection, fine; if it doesn't, your part of the building will be torn out and started over. But you won't be torn out; **you'll survive—but just barely**
>
> (The Message).

> If it is burned up, the builder will **suffer loss** but yet will be saved— even though only **as one escaping through the flames**
>
> (New International Version).

The Bible paints a vivid, even jarring, picture of our entry into Heaven via the Rapture. We're told we will "suffer loss" and be like someone "barely escaping through a wall of flames." This doesn't produce an "escapist mentality," but it does convey the profound transformation and purification that awaits us as we stand before the holy presence of God.

How do we prepare for such a momentous encounter? While the world below grapples with the Tribulation, believers will face their own trial by fire, a divine refining process described by Paul. Would you rather face the antichrist or the piercing gaze of Christ Himself? The difference is immeasurable, like comparing a local t-ball tryout to the World Series.

UNPREPARED FOR THE ANTICHRIST? REALLY?!

Some argue that those who believe in the Rapture will be unprepared to face the antichrist should they remain on earth. This is simply not true. Preparing to meet Christ is the ultimate training, far surpassing anything needed to withstand the antichrist. Those who fear God, fear no man.

Imagine an athlete training rigorously for the World Series. Would he be intimidated by a minor league game? Hardly. In the same way, those who prepare for the Rapture, for that face-to-face encounter with the Almighty, will be more than equipped to handle any challenge the antichrist presents. The reverse, however, is not true. Those who merely prepare for earthly trials will find themselves woefully unprepared for the divine scrutiny that awaits us all.

The Rapture isn't about escaping hardship or persecution (more on this later); rather, it's about preparing our hearts for the most important encounter of our eternal lives. It's about standing before the Judge of all the earth, not in fear, but in confident expectation, knowing we have been purified and made ready for eternity.

This passage serves as a sobering reminder that not all actions are equal in the eyes of God. It challenges us to build our lives on the foundation of Jesus Christ with materials that will endure, aiming for eternal impact rather than earthly success.

ARE YOU READY TO MEET JESUS?

How, then, could the knowledge of such a significant event, one that could happen at any time, cause believers to disengage or become indifferent? It doesn't! It drives us to engage more passionately with our faith, our communities, and our calling.

The Rapture and the Judgment Seat of Christ are deeply interconnected, offering a profound incentive for believers. Understanding that we will give an account for our service at this Judgment Seat inspires diligence, not withdrawal. This connection dispels the myth that belief in the Rapture encourages spiritual laziness. In reality, if a Christian becomes lethargic, it is more likely due to a lack of accurate teaching about the Rapture rather than the doctrine itself. The anticipation of standing before Christ's judgment will drive us to be faithful in our service, knowing that every action will be weighed and rewarded.

POST-TRIBULATION PROBLEM: THERE'S NO TIME FOR THE JUDGMENT SEAT OF CHRIST

The Post-Tribulation view seems to rob the believer of the significance and imminence of this pivotal moment. According to Paul, this event is a seminal moment when each believer's life and works are judged by the Lord Himself. The reality of this moment should be at the forefront of every believer's mind, not an afterthought rashly wedged into a rigid eschatological timeline.

The Post-Tribulation timeline struggles to adequately account for this event. If believers are to endure the entirety of The Great Tribulation and only then be raptured at Christ's Second Coming, where does this judgment fit? The chronology becomes cramped and convoluted, with little to no room for this important event to take place before the Millennial Kingdom. The Judgment Seat of Christ must occur before believers can receive their rewards and take their place in the Kingdom. According to Revelation 19:14, they are already adorned with white robes and seen coming with Christ to the earth.

Moreover, the Post-Tribulation view, along with other eschatological perspectives that deny the Pre-Tribulation Rapture, diminishes the doctrine of imminence; the idea that Christ could return at any moment. Imminence is a driving force behind the urgency to live faithfully, to engage in good works, and to *occupy till He comes*. If Christ's return is delayed until after the tribulation, believers might be tempted to adopt a wait-and-see approach, undermining the call to constant vigilance and readiness.

The Pre-Tribulation Rapture, on the other hand, fully embraces the imminence of Christ's return. It keeps believers on their toes, knowing that at any moment, we could stand before our Lord to give an account. This perspective fuels a sense of responsibility and purpose. The Post-Tribulation view not only fails to adequately account for the Judgment Seat of Christ but also diminishes the powerful motivator of Christ's imminent return.

Proper Rapture teaching will compel the Christian to know and walk out what it means to *occupy till He comes*, to be found faithful when He returns, and to hear those precious words, *"Well done, thou good and faithful servant"* (Matthew 25:21 KJV).

THE MEANING OF "OCCUPY"

The term *occupy* is both a military and business term. It means "to carry on the business of a banker or trader." The Greek word for *occupy* is *pragmateuomai* (πραγματεύομαι) or *pragma* (πρᾶγμα), which is where we get our word *pragmatism*.

Pragmatism is defined as a practical approach to problems and affairs.[4]

Something that is **practical** is something that can actually be put to use.[5]

If we want to **occupy till He comes**, we cannot get caught up in useless theological debates. We need an eschatology that can be put to good use. We must be about the *"Father's business"* (Luke 2:49).

REJECT FEAR-FILLED ESCHATOLOGY

We are the *"salt of the earth"* (Matthew 5:13) and should deny anything that robs us of our usefulness. A fearful approach to eschatology is dangerous, no matter what label it carries. This is where we should be able to agree with many who have differing views on the Rapture. No one should be looking to escape their responsibilities as Christ's ambassadors on earth.

Escapism: the habitual diversion of the mind to purely imaginative activity or entertainment as an escape from reality or routine.[6]

Based on what we've learned so far, it's clear that labeling the Rapture of the Church as mere escapism is both misleading and erroneous. Such a characterization either intentionally or unintentionally distorts the true biblical understanding of this doctrine.

Some will even go so far as to say that we are afraid of the antichrist. Nothing could be further from the truth. We fear God and, knowing the "terror of the Lord," we *occupy till He comes.* We are not afraid; rather, the enemy is afraid of us. We're not hiding from the antichrist. The antichrist is hiding from us.

ESCAPING WITHOUT ESCAPISM

Now that we've debunked the notion that the Rapture is merely a form of escapism, it's essential to consider whether Christians have a legitimate reason to anticipate a great escape of some kind. The Bible provides a clear and compelling case for the expectation of a divine deliverance. The concept of a great escape is not a baseless fantasy but a promise grounded in Scripture.

First Thessalonians 1:10 (NKJV) states, *"And to wait for His Son from heaven, whom He raised from the dead, even Jesus **who delivers us from the wrath to come**."* This verse underscores that Jesus's return is associated with delivering believers from impending wrath. Chapter 5 adds, *"For God did not appoint us to wrath, but to obtain salvation through our Lord Jesus Christ"* (1 Thessalonians 5:9 NKJV). Here Paul is again talking about the Day of the Lord and reinforces the idea that believers are destined for salvation, not God's judgment.

In Luke 21:36 (NKJV), Jesus puts the icing on the cake saying, *"Watch therefore, and pray always, that you may be counted worthy to **escape** all these things that will come to pass, and to stand before the Son of Man."* Whether you feel the context of this passage aligns with the Rapture or not, you cannot discount the scriptural evidence for a great escape, especially when you consider the pattern of past deliverances. For examples:

Noah and the Flood: Noah was raised above the flood through the ark, which was a type of deliverance before God's judgment engulfed the world (Genesis 6:8-9). Noah was supernaturally sealed up in the ark for seven days before the rains fell.

Enoch: Many overlook the fact that if God hadn't snatched Enoch (Noah's great-grandfather) away, it's possible that he would have been alive during the Flood. His sudden departure could be a powerful picture of the Rapture.

Lot and Sodom: Lot was rescued from Sodom before its destruction, illustrating God's method of delivering the righteous from His wrath (Genesis 19:15-16).

Rahab and Her Family: The safety of Rahab's family was secured before judgment came to Jericho (Joshua 6:22-23).

I address this more in other portions of the book, but you have to admit that a case is building. Revelation 3:10 (KJV) says, *"Because thou hast kept the word of my patience, I also will keep thee from the hour of temptation, which shall come upon all the world, to try them that dwell upon the earth."*

IMMINENCY AND THE EXPECTATION OF ESCAPE

The doctrine of imminency, the belief that Christ's return could happen at any moment, further fuels the expectation of an escape. Philippians 3:20 (NKJV) states, *"For our citizenship is in heaven, from which we also eagerly wait for the Savior, the Lord Jesus Christ."*

While the term "escapism" can imply a desire to evade responsibility or reality, the anticipation of a great escape as described in Scripture is a legitimate expectation. It is rooted in God's promises of deliverance, the biblical pattern of rescuing the righteous remnant before judgment, and the hope that believers will be kept from the wrath of God being poured out in The Great Tribulation.

When you consider the imminent reality of the Judgment Seat of Christ, the notion of escaping earthly trials might seem like merely jumping from the frying pan into the fire. It's akin to attempting to leap out of an airplane to avoid a minor dispute with the stewardess. The Rapture, however, is not about evading responsibility, persecution, or judgment but about being spared from divine wrath and preparing to be held accountable by Jesus Christ. The great escape is not a retreat from accountability but a transition to a higher responsibility, where every action and intention will be laid bare before our righteous Judge. It's not just about avoiding the hardships of the world but ensuring that we meet Christ with something of eternal value to offer.

MORE QUESTIONS

I understand that, depending on your background, there may be many questions still stirring and burning in your mind. Rest assured, I will do my best to address them as we travel through the pages of this book. I ask for your patience as we delve into these profound mysteries. We need to walk together in meekness and humility if we wish to understand them.

Paul said, "*Behold, I tell you a **mystery**...*" (1 Corinthians 15:51 NKJV). The Bible also says, "*It is the glory of God to conceal a matter, but the glory of kings is to search out a matter*" (Proverbs 25:2 NKJV).

Jesus promised that the Holy Spirit, the Spirit of truth, would guide us into all truth: "*...for he shall not speak of himself; but whatsoever he shall hear, that shall he speak: and he will shew you things to come*" (John 16:13 KJV).

The Greek word for *shew* is *anangello* (ἀγγέλλω), meaning "to announce, make known, report, or rehearse." This word shares its root with *angelos* (ἄγγελος), or *angel*, reminding us that the Holy Spirit often uses supernatural messengers to convey His message.

My prayer is that this book will serve as an envoy of hope, guided by the Holy Spirit. I believe it is filled with inspired promises and principles from the Word of God, designed to breathe new life into your walk with Jesus. As we uncover these truths together, may your faith be strengthened and your understanding deepened as you prepare to stand before Jesus at His Bema Seat.

4

ENOCH'S LOST PROPHECY

By faith Enoch was translated that he should not see death; and was not found, because God had translated him: for before his translation he had this testimony, that he pleased God

(Hebrews 11:5 KJV).

The ramifications that come from lies, misconceptions, and errors about the Rapture have far-reaching implications. How a Christian views this subject can have a major effect on their spiritual vitality and resilience. When errors and distortions about this pivotal principle infiltrate our understanding, they can pose a significant threat.

In this chapter I make the case that the *blessed hope* functions not merely as a comforting expectation but as a crucial piece of spiritual armor. This hope fortifies believers against the deceptions of the antichrist and the pervasive uncertainties of the end times. By depriving believers of this crucial protection, we inadvertently leave them exposed to the very deceptions that threaten to undermine their faith. The loss is not just doctrinal but profoundly practical, stripping believers of a defense designed to guard their minds against the unfruitful works of darkness.

Critics of the Pre-Tribulation Rapture often argue that this doctrine might leave believers ill-prepared for the coming tribulation. They worry that prominent teachers of the Rapture are falsely reassuring people with the notion that, *"You'll be raptured out before anything bad happens to you,"* potentially fostering complacency and a lack of readiness for adversity.

Let me unequivocally say that, although I have not encountered anyone teaching this misguided view, I would strongly oppose it if I did. Scripture clearly promises that we will face tribulation and that the world will grow increasingly dark. The intensity of these trials before the Rapture remains uncertain, but it is certain that the challenges will be more severe than anyone has ever experienced. It is essential that we equip believers for the reality of persecution. I delve into the distinctions between persecution, tribulation, and The Great Tribulation later in a subsequent chapter.

WILL RAPTURE BELIEVERS BE DECEIVED INTO TAKING THE MARK OF THE BEAST?

While we're on this subject, others have suggested that a belief in a pretribulation rapture somehow sets Christians up to receive the mark of the beast. The argument runs like this: if we don't expect to be here during the Tribulation, then if we do encounter something like the mark, we'll assume it can't be "the" mark and carelessly accept it. Such accusations not only misunderstand what pretribulation teachers actually say, they also show a lack of awareness about the very nature of the mark itself.

First, consider that the overwhelming majority of teaching and warning about the mark of the beast actually comes from the pretribulation camp. We've been the ones consistently sounding the alarm. In fact, many have taken these warnings so seriously they've gone to extremes, rejecting any new technology out of fear it might be the mark. Far from setting anyone up, we have been the primary voice urging caution and discernment.

Second, the notion that a committed Christian could somehow "accidentally" receive the mark betrays a misunderstanding of its fundamental purpose. The mark of the beast isn't some piece of tech you might mindlessly opt into. It's inseparable from the act of worshipping the antichrist. No true believer will stumble into it. It will require a clear, deliberate decision: to serve God or to serve the antichrist. It won't be a matter of confusion or poor timing; it will be a stark, conscious choice. No matter what one's view on the timing of the Rapture may be, this choice will be anything but subtle.

What is essential to understand right now is that the Pre-Tribulation Rapture doctrine does not undermine our preparedness for difficult times; rather, it provides a unique protection against the antichrist's end-time agenda. The hope of the Rapture is not an escape from suffering but a helmet against the profound spiritual deceptions that will characterize the end times. Not just a helmet but, THE Helmet.

THE HELMET OF THE BLESSED HOPE

I have contended for years that we have misunderstood a vital piece of armor listed in Ephesians chapter 6. The Bible instructs us to put on *"the helmet of salvation"* (Ephesians 6:17). Does being saved mean we already have this helmet on? If that were the case, why would Paul, writing to a church of believers already saved, emphasize the need to put it on?

Paul's exhortation to put on the helmet of salvation holds a deeper and more profound meaning. What exactly is he referring to? To fully appreciate his instructions in Ephesians 6, it's important to understand that this wasn't Paul's first attempt to draw a parallel between Roman armor and the Christian defense system. Ten years earlier, he had addressed a similar theme in his letter to the Thessalonians. Here's what he said then:

> *But let us, who are of the day, be sober, putting on the breastplate*
> *of faith and love; and for an helmet, the hope of salvation. For God*
> *hath not appointed us to wrath, but to obtain salvation by our Lord*
> *Jesus Christ*
>
> (1 Thessalonians 5:8-9 KJV).

This passage explains that the helmet of salvation is closely connected with the *"hope of salvation,"* specifically, the hope of the Rapture.

The term *helmet* in Greek denotes "something that encircles and protects the head." In spiritual terms, this helmet is designed to guard our minds. If we are struck in the head, our thinking and decision-making can be severely impaired. Similarly, *the hope of our salvation,* which is embodied in the expectation of the imminent return of Christ, acts as a crucial defense against false doctrines and the deceptive schemes of the enemy. This blessed hope keeps us steadfast, knowing that Christ's return could happen at any moment.

IMMINENCE AND SPIRITUAL VIGILANCE

Imminence refers to the biblical concept that nothing needs to be fulfilled prophetically before the Rapture can occur. This doctrine emphasizes that the return of Christ is imminent and could happen at any moment.

If Christ were to return to save us midway through the Tribulation, we would not need to remain vigilant because we could simply wait for specific signs that we know must happen first. This would even be more true if His return were scheduled for the end of the Tribulation.

The Pre-Tribulation Rapture provides believers with profound comfort and assurance. We are promised that we will meet the Lord in the air, go before the judgment seat of Christ, and be with Him before later returning with Him.

The helmet of salvation, representing the blessed hope of the Rapture, is not just an unnecessary accessory. It's a vital component of our spiritual armor. It protects our minds, fortifies our faith, and keeps us vigilant in anticipation of Christ's imminent return. These things alone make us the antichrist's worst nightmare. Even if believers were to face the judgment of the Tribulation, they would be the most equipped and prepared for it because of what the anticipation of the Lord's return does in the believer's life.

THE MARANATHA MINDSET

This is what I call, "The Maranatha Mindset." The word *Maranatha* is an Aramaic term found in 1 Corinthians 16:22, which translates to *"Our Lord, come!"* or *"The Lord is coming."* In the Early Church, this phrase was a powerful declaration of hope and expectancy, a reminder that Christ's return was imminent and that believers should live in readiness for that glorious event. Maranatha is how they greeted one another.

The Maranatha Mindset is a way of life that protects the mind of the believer in the last days.

> *Beloved, now we are children of God, and it has not yet been revealed what we shall be, but we know that when He* [Christ] *is revealed, we shall be like Him, for we will see Him as He is. And everyone who has this hope in Him purifies himself, just as He* [Christ] *is pure*
>
> (1 John 3:2-3 NKJV).

The Maranatha Mindset encourages self-purification. As discussed previously, the knowledge that you could see the Lord at any moment is a strong motivator. Only this blessed "hope of salvation" can produce desire to stay in right-standing with God.

The Maranatha Mindset encourages church attendance and discipleship: *"Not forsaking the assembling of ourselves together, as is the manner of some is; but exhorting one another, and so much the more as you see the Day approaching"* (Hebrews 10:25 NKJV).

As we look to that glorious day, we are exhorted not to forsake our connection with the body of Christ. Only the Pre-Tribulation Rapture position allows for this kind of imminence. Every other view requires certain signs and prophecies to be fulfilled first and therefore could cause a Christian to look for those signs instead of looking for Jesus.

I've written about this in my book *Summoning the Demon: AI, Aliens and the Antichrist,* but I want to go deeper here. Good people get confused about Matthew chapters 24 and 25, where Jesus gave very specific information regarding the end of the age. Matthew 24 is often called the mini-apocalypse because in the first few verses, Jesus lays out the precise events of the last days, as they were later disclosed to John in Revelation chapter 6. Matthew began his discourse with a shocking prediction of the overthrow and destruction of the temple: *"Now as He sat on the Mount of Olives, the disciples came to him privately, saying, 'Tell us, when will these things be? And what will be the sign of Your coming, and of the end of the age?'"* (Matthew 24:3 NKJV).

There were three questions:

1. When will this happen?
2. What will be the sign of Your coming?
3. What is the sign of the end of the world?

Jesus did not always answer questions in the order in which they were asked. He would often answer in a way His listeners did not expect. Among the many dramatic evidences Jesus gave of the conditions surrounding His return (His triumphant return to earth, not the blessed hope of the Church), was this, from Matthew 24:37-42 (KJV):

> *But as the days of Noah were, so shall also the coming of the Son of man be. For as in the days that were before the flood they were eating and drinking, marrying and giving in marriage, until the day that Noe entered into the ark, and knew not until the flood came, and took them all away; so shall also the coming of the Son of man be. Then shall two be in the field; the one shall be taken, and the other left. Two women shall be grinding at the mill; the one shall be taken, and the other left. Watch therefore: for ye know not what hour your Lord doth come.*

Jesus did not say it was wrong to eat, drink, get married, have a job, or fulfill other necessary responsibilities. What He was saying in this passage can be summarized by the last statement: *"Watch therefore: for ye know not what hour your Lord doth come."*

He is talking about not being mindful of spiritual things in the midst of natural things. He's talking about not being aware of the potential of imminent judgment. People in Noah's day had no thought that judgment was coming. They were going through their day, working their job, feeding their family and all of the same kinds of things that people do today, without a thought that anything would change. Some even mock the idea of the end of the age or the imminent return of our Savior. The Bible addresses this in 2 Peter 3:3-10 (KJV):

> *Knowing this first, that there shall come in the last days scoffers, walking after their own lusts, And saying, Where is the promise of his coming? for since the fathers fell asleep, all things continue as they were from the beginning of the creation. For this they willingly are ignorant of, that by the word of God the heavens were of old,*

and the earth standing out of the water and in the water: Whereby the world that then was, being overflowed with water, perished: But the heavens and the earth, which are now, by the same word are kept in store, reserved unto fire against the day of judgment and perdition of ungodly men.

But, beloved, be not ignorant of this one thing, that one day is with the Lord as a thousand years, and a thousand years as one day. The Lord is not slack concerning his promise, as some men count slackness; but is longsuffering to us-ward, not willing that any should perish, but that all should come to repentance. But the day of the Lord will come as a thief in the night; in the which the heavens shall pass away with a great noise, and the elements shall melt with fervent heat, the earth also and the works that are therein shall be burned up.

Peter is saying the same thing that Jesus was communicating in Matthew 24 and 25. He forecasts that there will be scoffers who taunt the faithful by asking why they can be so sure Jesus is coming, since He hasn't appeared yet. Peter was accurate in that prediction.

God makes no promises that He does not fulfill.

- God said Jesus would come as a baby in Bethlehem, and He did.
- God said Jesus would be crucified and rise from the dead, and He was, and He did.
- God said Jesus would come again, and He will.
- God will not settle for being right two out of three times. He is faithful to His promises.

Peter also refers to the days of Noah, referring to the flood. The scoffers and mockers of Noah's day said the same things then that they do today. They ridicule the concept of the return of the King of kings and Lord of lords. They maintain that they must attend to much more important affairs than the obscure predictions of an uncertain future event.

Peter reminds us that the world in the time of Noah was destroyed by water. He goes on to say that the current world will not be destroyed by water, rather, it will be burned by fire. He is right. The mockers are wrong. They insist Jesus is not coming, and they live like their assertions are true. Peter says they are *"willfully ignorant."* The reason for what may seem like a delay in Jesus's return is not that God is unaware of the time, but because He is patient and awaiting the repentance of multitudes before the end-time countdown begins.

Look at Paul's resolve when writing to the Thessalonians. Fifty percent of the book of 2 Thessalonians references the end times directly, and even more of that letter makes indirect reference to the Second Coming of Jesus. Think about the urgency behind his words in 2 Thessalonians 3:14-15 (NKJV), where he warned against those who lived as though Jesus was not coming: *"And if anyone does not obey our word in this epistle, note that person and do not keep company with him, that he may be ashamed. Yet do not count him as an enemy, but admonish him as a brother."*

Paul is not talking about someone in the *world* who questions Jesus's return. He is speaking of someone in the *Church* who does so. He goes on to say that other believers should not fellowship with those who live contrary to the expectation of His return. He does not say this because brothers and sisters may disagree on this issue and it therefore may disqualify them from the kingdom of God. The reason is that complacency and carelessness are contagious. If you spend all your time with those who mind only worldly things, chances are good that you will begin to mind only worldly things, giving no thought to Jesus's coming. A serious study of the end times, whether from the teaching of Jesus, Peter, or Paul, can be summed up in one word: **WATCH**.

All scriptural eschatology emphasizes the concept of watchfulness. Every person who teaches Bible prophecy should center their instruction on this concept. Any eschatological teaching that does not emphasize the urgency of watching should be viewed as untrustworthy. This one word can keep you straight about the last days. As the old saying goes, we should live every day like it is our last, because one day we will be right.

WHY WATCH?

Let's take a look at what it means to watch and why. The word *imminent* means "ready to take place or happening at any moment." It means to hang over one's head. It speaks of something ready to befall or overtake us. Ultimately it means that something is close at hand in its incidence. It does not mean "soon," but it does mean that it *could* happen at any moment.

Here is an illustration of imminency and the urgency it conveys. Imagine you are a rebellious teenager. (For some of us, this exercise will be a little easier than for others.) Imagine your parents are going out of town, and you decide to throw a party at your house (which is actually their house). The music is blaring, and a variety of activities are going on that you are certain your parents never would have allowed. The house is a mess. The driveway is full of vehicles. The backyard looks like a homeless encampment. In the midst of all this confusion, the phone rings. It's your dad. He tells you that their plans have changed unexpectedly and they'll be home at *any moment!*

Your rebellious streak suddenly evaporates like a drop of water in the desert. Your expectation of a good time partying with your friends pops like an overinflated balloon, and it is replaced with an entirely different expectation. You begin a frantic flurry of activity that has nothing to do with fun and games. This is serious business. Your life and your future are at stake. You turn off the music, announce that the party is over, try to recruit some disappointed friends to help you clean up the disaster zone that your home has become, and kick everyone else out the same door you welcomed them in just a short time ago. What happened? You have had a revelation of imminence!

Now imagine that same scenario, but the message from your parents is quite different. The music is blaring, and the party is rocking as your parents tell you, "It looks like we are going to be gone longer than we planned." What's your reaction? You'd probably say, "Thanks, Mom and Dad! Call me when you're on your way!" Then you would end the call and tell everyone that it looks like the party just got a little more epic.

This is just an analogy, but I think it's a fitting one. Some might try to poke holes in it, saying, "We're not rebellious or immature teenagers." Fine, let's remove that part. Imagine you're a responsible teenager, one who genuinely honors your parents and wants to please them. They've given you a task, something important that they expect you to finish. Now, if you know they could be home at any moment, what happens? You rush to complete that task, not out of fear of punishment, but out of honor and love for your parents, because you want to be ready for them and fulfill the trust they have placed in you.

Let me give you another real-life example. A few years ago around Christmas, my daughter and I bought my wife a new car. The plan was to get it home, clean up the garage, and place a big red bow on it for when she arrived and opened the garage door. We were thrilled as we pulled the new car into the garage and started straightening up, eagerly anticipating her arrival. Then, we got the call: She'll be home *any minute!*

Suddenly, the excitement kicked into overdrive. It was like someone hit the fast-forward button in our home. We were rushing around, making the final touches, not out of fear or disapproval, but out of love and anticipation. I wasn't scared of my wife, and I certainly wasn't nervous about what she would think of us. There was no concern about judgment or condemnation. Our love for her was what drove us to hustle and get everything ready, because we knew her arrival was imminent.

IMMINENCE EQUALS EXPECTATION

In the same way, the imminent return of Christ isn't something we fear, it's something we eagerly anticipate. We prepare, not because we're afraid, but because our love for Him compels us to be ready.

Imminence is a sound foundational doctrine concerning the return of Jesus, since an *"at any moment"* understanding can radically change our behavior. First John 3:3 (KJV) says, *"And every man that hath this hope in him purifieth himself, even as he is pure."* Jesus spoke to this in Matthew 24:44-51 (KJV):

> *Therefore be ye also ready: for in such an hour as ye think not the Son of man cometh. Who then is a faithful and wise servant, whom his lord hath made ruler over his household, to give them meat in due season? Blessed is that servant, whom his lord when he cometh shall find so doing. Verily I say unto you, that he shall make him ruler over all his goods.*
>
> *But and if that evil servant shall say in his heart, my lord delayeth his coming; and shall begin to smite his fellowservants, and to eat and drink with the drunken; the lord of that servant shall come in a day when he looketh not for him, and in an hour that he is not aware of, and shall cut him asunder, and appoint him his portion with the hypocrites: there shall be weeping and gnashing of teeth.*

When approaching a subject that even the apostle Paul, in 1 Corinthians 15:51, called a *mystery,* there should be a level of humility that accompanies our study. There are things that we may not understand or that seem to be contradictions, but there are also some things that are made indisputably clear. We must anchor ourselves in the certainty of what the Bible teaches before we venture out to discover new revelation or endeavor to give our opinion.

What should we do when confronted with seeming contradictions? We cling to sound doctrine, and humbly ask God for clear understanding. If any new information seeks to take us away from our anchor of the Word of God, we should disregard it no matter how fascinating it may be.

There is one theme about the appearing of the Lord Jesus Christ that should ground us when seeking to understand the events, the signs, and the prophetic forecasts of the last days: imminence. Throughout the New Testament, we read words such as *watch, look, wait,* and *quickly.* All these terms describe the principle of imminence.

21 SCRIPTURAL PROOFS THAT JESUS COULD APPEAR AT ANY MOMENT

1. "Watch therefore, for ye know neither the day nor the hour wherein the Son of man cometh"

(Matthew 25:13 KJV).

2. "But of that day and hour knoweth no man, no, not the angels of heaven, but my Father only"

(Matthew 24:36 KJV).

3. "Watch therefore: for ye know not what hour your Lord doth come. But know this, that if the goodman of the house had known in what watch the thief would come, he would have watched, and would not have suffered his house to be broken up. Therefore be ye also ready: for in such an hour as ye think not the Son of man cometh. Who then is a faithful and wise servant, whom his lord hath made ruler over his household, to give them meat in due season? Blessed is that servant, whom his lord when he cometh shall find so doing"

(Matthew 24:42-46 KJV).

4. *"Take ye heed, watch and pray; for ye know not when the time is. For the Son of Man is as a man taking a far journey, who left his house, and gave authority to his servants, and to every man his work, and commanded the porter to watch. Watch ye therefore: for ye know not when the Master of the house cometh, at even, or at midnight, or at the cockcrowing, or in the morning: Lest coming suddenly He find you sleeping. And what I say unto you I say unto all, Watch"*

(Mark 13:33-37 KJV).

5. *"Knowing the time, that now it is high time to awake out of sleep: for now is our salvation nearer than when we believed. The night is far spent, the day is at hand: let us, therefore, cast off the works of darkness, and let us put on the armour of light"*

(Romans 13:11-12 KJV).

6. *"And the God of peace shall bruise Satan under your feet shortly…"*

(Romans 16:20 KJV).

7. *"So that ye come behind in no gift; waiting for the coming of our Lord Jesus Christ"*

(1 Corinthians 1:7 KJV).

8. *"For our conversation is in heaven; from whence also we look for the Saviour, the Lord Jesus Christ"*

(Philippians 3:20 KJV).

9. *"Let your moderation be known unto all men. The Lord is at hand"*

(Philippians 4:5 KJV).

10. *"And to wait for his Son from heaven, whom he raised from the dead, even Jesus, which delivered us from the wrath to come"*

(1 Thessalonians 1:10 KJV).

11. *"Therefore let us not sleep, as do others; but let us watch and be sober"*

(1 Thessalonians 5:6 KJV).

12. *"That thou keep this commandment without spot, unrebukable, until the appearing of our Lord Jesus Christ"*

(1 Timothy 6:14 KJV).

13. *"Looking for that blessed hope, and the glorious appearing of the great God and our Saviour Jesus Christ"*

(Titus 2:13 KJV).

14. *"So Christ was once offered to bear the sins of many; and unto them that look for him shall he appear the second time without sin unto salvation"*

(Hebrews 9:28 KJV).

15. *"Let us consider one another to provoke unto love and to good works: Not forsaking the assembling of ourselves together, as the manner of some is; but exhorting one another: and so much the more, as ye see the day approaching"*

(Hebrews 10:24-25 KJV).

16. *"Be patient, therefore, brethren, unto the coming of the Lord. Behold, the husbandman waiteth for the precious fruit of the earth,*

and hath long patience for it, until he receive the early and latter rain. Be ye also patient; stablish your hearts: for the coming of the Lord draweth nigh. Grudge not one against another, brethren, lest ye be condemned: behold, the judge standeth before the door"

(James 5:7-9 KJV).

17. *"Wherefore gird up the loins of your mind, be sober, and hope to the end for the grace that is to be brought unto you at the revelation of Jesus Christ"*

(1 Peter 1:13 KJV).

18. *"But the end of all things is at hand: be ye therefore sober, and watch unto prayer"*

(1 Peter 4:7 KJV).

19. *"Behold, I come quickly: hold that fast which thou hast, that no man take thy crown"*

(Revelation 3:11 KJV).

20. *"Behold, I come quickly: blessed is he that keepeth the sayings of the prophecy of this book"*

(Revelation 22:7 KJV).

21. *"He which testifieth these things saith, Surely I come quickly. Amen. Even so, come, Lord Jesus"*

(Revelation 22:20 KJV).

I've just proven to you that there is one word that can sum up all New Testament eschatology: *Watch!* This attitude was central in the teachings of Jesus and the apostles. This is foundational to our faith. Anything that seeks to pull us away from an urgently watchful attitude should be refuted. If a teaching suggests that even one prophecy has yet to come to pass before Jesus can return for His Church, it does not conform to the doctrine of imminence.

You may have noticed that in the last few pages, I haven't mentioned the three different doctrinal positions regarding the Rapture of the Church (pre, mid, post). When we take imminence seriously, such debate becomes unnecessary. All views but one require many prophecies to be fulfilled before Jesus can return for His Church. In doing so, they rob us of imminence.

SUDDEN DEATH

There are those who say they can maintain an imminent attitude because they know they could die at any moment and meet Jesus after death. This is like trying to fix a car engine with duct tape. It may work, but not for long. This attitude unwittingly robs us of the exquisite diamond of the blessed hope of the Church and replaces it with the cubic zirconia of physical death. It is true that, should the Lord tarry, we will all meet death. The problem with death being our expectation is that according to the Scriptures I listed, Jesus didn't want us looking for death. He certainly didn't want us looking for the antichrist. *He wants us to look for Him!*

It only takes a few moments of fearless introspection to know why. Take some time to contemplate your death. Think of all the ways it could happen and what it would be like to die, to leave this world and to meet Jesus in Heaven. Keep in mind that even though death has been conquered through Christ's resurrection, it is still an enemy, and the last one to be destroyed, according to 1 Corinthians 15:26. In contrast to that, take a few moments to consider the fact that *at any moment,* Jesus could split the eastern sky and catch you up to meet Him in the clouds. There's a difference…the same kind of difference you would experience by taking a trip accompanied by an enemy or by a friend!

As mentioned earlier, the first-century Church was so full of expectation for Jesus's return that they greeted one another with the word *Maranatha*. It's a petition that every Christian had on the tip of their tongue. This is how they said *hello* and *goodbye*. If they thought they were so close to the appearing of Jesus, how much more should we be looking for it and expecting it?

ENOCH'S LOST PROPHECY

In the genealogies of Genesis, we can find hidden treasures that reveal profound truths. Consider the first ten generations from creation, a lineage where most of the patriarchs knew each other because of their long lifespans. Noah, for instance, lived to be 950 years old. Chuck Missler and many others have pointed out what happens when we look closely at the meanings of our early forefathers' names:

Adam = Man
Seth = Appointed
Enos = Mortal
Cainan = Sorrow
Mahalaleel = The Blessed God
Jared = Shall Come Down
Enoch = Teaching or Discipling
Methuselah = His Death Brings
Lamech = Powerful
Noah = Rest

When read together, these names form a prophetic sentence: "Man is appointed mortal sorrow, the Blessed God shall come down teaching; His death brings powerful rest."[1]

This hidden message speaks of God's redemptive plan, a plan that would unfold over millennia and culminate in Christ, who would bring ultimate rest and redemption. It also shows us that a name can hold great significance.

Enoch is a fascinating figure, often shrouded in mystery. Some have tried to mythologize him, associating him with occult practices or even claiming him as the founder of Freemasonry. However, the biblical account gives us a much different picture. Enoch lived just before the Flood, during a time when fallen angels mingled with the daughters of men and giants roamed the antediluvian world. In this chaotic and corrupt era, Enoch posed a significant threat to satan's kingdom.

The Bible tells us that only two people *"walked with God"*: Enoch and Noah. Both were supernaturally rescued from judgment, but Enoch's story holds special meaning.

Born when Adam was 622 years old, Enoch likely spent 300 years learning from him. Genesis 5:22 notes that Enoch *"walked with God after he begot Methuselah."* The name *Methuselah* means "his death brings," signifying that when *Methuselah* died, judgment would come. This anticipation must have weighed heavily on Enoch, as he knew that his son's death would bring the Flood.

THE BIRTH OF IMMINENCE

Methuselah's life represented the prophetic concept of imminence and the understanding that judgment could come at any moment. A.W. Pink vividly describes this in his book *Gleanings from Genesis*:

> Imagine God should say to you, the life of that little one is to be the life of the world. When that child dies the world will be destroyed. What would be the effect on you? Not knowing how soon that child might die... The world might perish at any time. Every time that child fell sick the world's doom would stare you in the face! Would you not realize as never before your urgent need for preparing to meet

God? Would you not at once begin to occupy yourself with spiritual things? ...It is difficult to escape the conclusion but from the time Methuselah was born, the world lost all its attractiveness for Enoch and from that time on he walked with God.[2]

This sense of urgency drove Enoch into a closer walk with God. Hebrews 11:5 (KJV) tells us that *"By faith Enoch was translated that he should not see death; and was not found, because God had translated him...."* Enoch's faith was rooted in God's Word, for *"faith comes by hearing, and hearing by the word of God"* (Romans 10:17 NKJV). His life exemplifies the kind of faith that pleases God, as Hebrews 11:6 (NKJV) states, *"But without faith it is impossible to please Him."*

Jude 1:14 (KJV) reveals that *"Enoch also, the seventh from Adam, prophesied...."* This prophecy is the earliest recorded from a man in the Bible and shows Enoch's insight into the future judgment. Living in a time of unimaginable wickedness, from the rise of the Nephilim to his own cousin Lamech's wicked polygamy, Enoch stood as a beacon of righteousness.

In the midst of all this evil and just before the worldwide judgment of the Flood came, Enoch was raptured. It's important to note here that the rapture of Enoch was not a secret event. Hebrews 11:5 notes that he was *"translated and was not found,"* indicating that a search was made for him. This mirrors the search party that went out for Elijah when he was taken up by a whirlwind (2 Kings 2:1–18). Will there be a similar search for us when we're gone? Nevertheless, Enoch's primary prophecy can be found in the naming of his son, Methuselah. What can we learn from this?

Methuselah died at the age of 969 years old, the longest lifespan recorded in the Bible. This longest living man just happens to be the one who's death declared judgment. This shows us the incredible longsuffering of God. As 1 Peter 3:20 (KJV) says, *"the longsuffering of*

God waited in the days of Noah," and 2 Peter 3:9 (KJV) reminds us, "*The Lord is not slack concerning his promise, as some men count slackness; but is longsuffering to us-ward, not willing that any should perish, but that all should come to repentance.*"

ENOCH GAVE BIRTH TO IMMINENCE

Enoch's life and the birth of Methuselah serve as a profound illustration of imminence. Just as Enoch lived with the knowledge that his son's death would bring judgment, we live with the understanding that Christ's return is imminent. This awareness should drive us to walk closely with God, to live in readiness, and to engage fully in the work of His Kingdom, knowing that *"the night is far spent, the day is at hand"* (Romans 13:12 KJV).

Enoch birthed "The Maranatha Mindset" into the earth, and his example calls us all to look up because our redemption draws nigh.

5

THE SECRET OF THE SEVENS

You are the *Revelation Generation*. No other group in history has needed to understand the last book of the Bible more than we do today, but the adversary has done an incredible job of keeping us from its truths. The book of Revelation is more than a mysterious prophecy about future events, it's a profound unveiling of Jesus Christ in His fullness. It's high time we open it, dive in, and receive the revelation God intended for us.

This is where we debunk another one of the biggest lies we've been told about the Rapture: *"We don't need to read and understand the book of Revelation because we're not going to be here."*

Many people avoid the book of Revelation, thinking, *I won't be here, so I don't need to know what it says.* But consider this: you weren't present for the first advent of Jesus revealed in the Gospels, yet you still find reading them essential for your faith. The same holds true for Revelation. Even if you believe you won't be here during the events described, it's critical to understand them. This book is not just about the end times; it's about Jesus, His character, His plan, and what He expects of His Church.

UNLOCKING THE POWER OF PROPHECY

From the beginning, satan has hated prophecy because it forecasts his ultimate defeat. The first prophetic word ever given was spoken over him, in Genesis 3:15, and it declared that his head would be crushed by the seed of the woman, Jesus Christ. This first mention of prophecy tells us how powerful it is and why the enemy despises it so much. Prophecy is a divine weapon, and throughout history, satan has tried to twist it into something that promotes confusion, fear, gloom, and doom. But biblical prophecy, especially the book of Revelation, shines light in the darkness. It's about hope, victory, and the ultimate triumph of Christ over all His enemies.

> *Blessed (happy, prosperous, to be admired) is he who reads and those who hear the words of the prophecy, and who keep the things which are written in it [heeding them and taking them to heart]; for the time [of fulfillment] is near*
>
> (Revelation 1:3 AMP).

In fact, Revelation is the only book in the Bible that gives us a detailed physical description of Jesus after His resurrection and ascension to the right hand of the Father. It shows us what He cares about and what He focuses on now that He has been exalted in Heaven. This book isn't just about the future; it's about the *present reign* of Jesus and how we, as His Church, are meant to live in the light of that reign.

WHAT IS APOCALYPSE?

The word *apocalypse* comes from the Greek word *apokalypsis*, which means "unveiling" or "revelation."

Apocalypse

(noun)

Etymology: From the Greek word *apokalypsis*, meaning "unveiling" or "revelation."

1. **The uncovering of something hidden**: The disclosure of knowledge or revelation, especially in a prophetic context.

2. **In biblical terms**: A specific reference to the book of Revelation, the final book of the Bible, which reveals the ultimate destiny of the world, the return of Christ, and the final judgment.

3. **Common usage**: Often misunderstood as referring to the end of the world or catastrophic destruction, but in its original meaning, it simply refers to a dramatic revealing or unveiling of truth.

Example: The *apocalypse* in the book of Revelation unveils the true nature of who Jesus is and what His plans are for His Church, Israel, and the world.

It does not mean the end of the world as many believe. Rather, it means "to reveal something that has been hidden." So, when we read Revelation, we are reading an unveiling of Jesus Christ, an exposure of His nature and His plan for humanity.

Now get this, the Holy Spirit's primary mission, as Jesus says in John 16:13 (KJV), is to reveal Christ to us: "*Howbeit when he, the Spirit of truth, is come, he will guide you into all truth: for he shall not speak of himself; but whatsoever he shall hear, that shall he speak: and he will shew you things to come.*"

Through this revelation, we gain a deeper understanding of the Father, for Jesus came to *reveal* the Father, and the Spirit *reveals* Jesus. Many believers don't realize that this is what the book of Revelation is all about: knowing Jesus more deeply. It is not about satisfying our curiosity regarding the future, nor is it meant to scare us with images of beasts, plagues, or judgments. The main point of the book is to reveal who Jesus is *now* as King of kings and Lord of lords.

THE MOST IMPORTANT SUBJECT
IN REVELATION

What is the most frequently mentioned topic in the book of Revelation, aside from Jesus? Take a minute right now to make a few guesses.

This is important because if you can understand this key, the purpose of the book will become clear to you. What do you think it is? Many assume it might be the antichrist, the plagues, or the final battle of Armageddon. But you might be surprised to learn that the most prominent theme in the book of Revelation is the number *seven*.

Throughout the 22 chapters of Revelation, the number seven appears at least 54 times. This repetition isn't accidental. Let's look at the significance of this number:

- *Seven Churches* (Revelation 1:4)
- *Seven Spirits of God* (Revelation 1:4)
- *Seven Golden Lampstands* (Revelation 1:12)
- *Seven Stars* (Revelation 1:16)
- *Seven Seals* (Revelation 5:1)
- *Seven Angels and Seven Trumpets* (Revelation 8:2)
- *Seven Thunders* (Revelation 10:3)
- *Seven Bowls* (Revelation 17:1)
- *Seven Kings* (Revelation 17:10)

The number seven in Scripture represents divine perfection or completeness. From Genesis to Revelation, the number seven marks the fulfillment of God's purposes. In Genesis, God completed creation in six days and rested on the seventh, marking the perfection of His work. In Revelation, seven signifies the completion of God's plan for redemption and judgment. It's the number of fulfillment, rest, and divine order.

In Revelation, the repeated use of the number seven is God's way of reminding us that what we are reading is not just about chaos or destruction. It is about the *completion* of His plan. Everything He started in Genesis, every promise and every prophecy, finds its fulfillment in this book. Revelation is the final word, the culmination of all that God has been working toward since the beginning of time.

THE FULLNESS OF CHRIST'S REVELATION

As you dive into Revelation, you will begin to see that the three dimensions of Jesus revealed in the New Testament are fully realized in this book. He is revealed as:

- **Savior**: In the Gospels, we encounter Jesus as the Savior, the One who rescues us from sin.
- **Lord**: In the Epistles, we are taught how to live under the lordship of Jesus, submitting to His authority.
- **King**: In Revelation, we see Jesus as the King of kings, the One who reigns over all. His rule is supreme, His authority final.

Understanding these dimensions helps us grasp the full picture of who Jesus is. He is not just our Savior and Lord; He is the rightful King who will return to set all things in order.

REVELATION: THE FINAL UNVEILING

It bears repeating that the book of Revelation was not written to satisfy our curiosity about the future. Nor is it just about creating a timeline of events. It's really about preparing us to recognize Him, to understand His plan, and to live in anticipation of His return. When we approach Revelation with this understanding, the mysteries begin to unravel. We see Jesus as He truly is: glorious, powerful, and victorious.

As you develop a *Maranatha Mindset*, you'll likely find a growing hunger to understand Bible prophecy. As you dive into the book of

Revelation, don't be discouraged by the complex imagery or symbolism you may encounter. You now understand that the one word summing up all New Testament eschatology is "Watch." You've also grasped the secret of the sevens, giving you a key to translate these passages. No matter how intricate the language appears, the underlying message is always the same: *Watch for Him to complete His work.* With that perspective, you have everything you truly need to guide you through Revelation's mysteries.

We must study this book in God's Word carefully and prayerfully. We are the generation that needs to know Revelation more than any generation that has come before us. The world is becoming darker, and as the day of Christ's return draws closer, the truths in this book will shine brighter, illuminating the path ahead for those who have *ears to hear.*

6

WHAT IS THE GREAT TRIBULATION?

The Bible has plenty to say about suffering, persecution, and tribulation. Why is it that some believers seem resigned to facing God's wrath, while others are holding onto the promise of a divine rescue? If we're going to expose the myths and lies surrounding the Rapture, we need to clear up the confusion about what The Tribulation actually is.

You'll never fully grasp why it's important for the Church to be absent from The Tribulation until you understand it's purpose.

I like to distinguish between three different types of tribulation.

1. General tribulation
2. The Tribulation
3. The Great Tribulation

GENERAL "TRIBULATION"

This is the lowercase "t" tribulation that every believer faces as part of their Christian walk; trials, persecutions, and spiritual battles. Jesus Himself warned us in John 16:33 (KJV), *"...In the world ye shall have tribulation: but be of good cheer; I have overcome the world."*

This kind of tribulation is not a sign of God's wrath but a reality that comes from living out our faith in a world that's hostile to it. We see it all throughout the New Testament. Believers are attacked, misunderstood, and persecuted for standing for Christ.

The apostle Paul echoed this reality in Acts 14:22 (KJV) when he said, *"...we must through much tribulation enter into the kingdom of God."* This is the kind of trouble that comes from satan's attacks, the curse of a fallen world, and opposition from those who reject the truth. It's unavoidable, and we're called to face it with courage and perseverance.

George Whitefield said, *"I was honored today with having a few stones, dirt, rotten eggs, and pieces of dead cat thrown at me."*[1] It was not uncommon for those opposed to Whitefield's message to throw rotten vegetables, eggs, or even dead animals, such as cats, at him while he preached. Whitefield once remarked that if he wasn't causing such a strong response, he might not be preaching as he should.

Leonard Ravenhill echoed this sentiment when he said, *"If Jesus had preached the same message that ministers preach today, He would never have been crucified."*[2] This underscores the need for bold, uncompromising preaching and that every believer must be prepared and equipped to stand under this kind of pressure. I believe that an understanding of the Pre-Tribulation Rapture, helps them to do just that.

THE TRIBULATION

This is where it starts to get specific. The Tribulation, with a capital "T," refers to a future seven-year period prophesied in Daniel and outlined in Revelation. It's a time when God's focus shifts back to dealing with Israel and pouring out judgment on a Christ-rejecting world. This is not just the typical suffering and hardships of life; this is God's direct intervention, unleashing His wrath to fulfill the prophetic timetable.

Daniel 9:27 (KJV) speaks of a seven-year covenant that will be broken, initiating a time of unprecedented suffering:

And he shall confirm the covenant with many for one week: and in the midst of the week he shall cause the sacrifice and the oblation to cease, and for the overspreading of abominations he shall make it desolate, even until the consummation, and that determined shall be poured upon the desolate.

Revelation further describes this period (beginning at chapter 6) with a sequence of judgments, involving the Seven Seals, Trumpets, and Bowls, concluding in an extraordinary outpouring of divine wrath.

THE GREAT TRIBULATION

The second half of the Tribulation, often called The Great Tribulation, is when all hell breaks loose…literally. Jesus warned in Matthew 24:21 (KJV) that this will be a time of suffering *"such as was not since the beginning of the world to this time, no, nor ever shall be."*

Another one of the lies propagated about the Rapture and the end times is that these prophecies have already been fulfilled. However, they can't explain when exactly this verse came to pass. This is a time that's historically catastrophic, marked by unprecedented judgments, global chaos, and the rise of the antichrist's reign of terror.

One of the biggest misconceptions out there is the idea that believers in the Rapture think they will escape all forms of tribulation. Critics argue that we're just naïve optimists who believe we'll get to float away before the world ever gets rough. But that's not what Rapture teaching says at all.

The Bible does teach that things will get darker and more difficult as the end approaches. We are not promised a free pass from hardship. In fact, the closer we get to the end, the more intense the spiritual battles and persecutions are likely to become. But here's the key difference: The Tribulation is not just a time of random chaos, it's a specific period of God's direct wrath being poured out. Scripture tells us that the Church is not appointed unto this wrath (1 Thessalonians 5:9).

Believing in the Rapture doesn't mean never facing adversity. It means believing in the promise that before God's wrath is unleashed in full measure, He will rescue His Bride from it. That's why Paul called it a *"comfort"* in 1 Thessalonians 4:18. It's a source of strength and encouragement. It is *the* blessed hope and it empowers us to stand strong in the face of darkness. We know it's going to get bad. We know we'll face tribulation in this world. But we also know when the time comes for God to pour out His judgment, He will make a clear distinction between His people and those who've rejected Him, just as He did in the days of Noah and Lot.

ARE WE ALL EXPERIENCING GOD'S WRATH ALREADY?

Some critics of the Pre-Tribulation Rapture suggest that we're all subject to the wrath of God, pointing out that every generation has faced it because we live in a cursed world that's still suffering the indirect punishment that came when Adam fell. This is the kind of flawed reasoning that only survives in the safety of an echo chamber and collapses the moment it meets any scrutiny.

Let's address the foundational point behind this argument. When someone brings this up, you need to ask them:

> "Are you willing to stake the credibility of your interpretation of Scripture on the claim that the indirect wrath of God, manifested through the curse, is the exact same thing as the direct, historic wrath of God poured out in the Day of the Lord, when He brings an end to the corrupt systems of this world in the most detailed event in the entire Bible?"

Of course, they're not willing to do that. The distinction between indirect and direct wrath alone pokes enough holes in this argument for it to sink like a stone, but we're not done yet.

Thankfully, there's a Bible story that lays all of this out for us, and it just happens to be one Jesus pointed to when describing the last days: *"as it was in the days of Lot..."* (Luke 17:28 KJV).

Lot lived in a world filled with indirect judgment, the curse of this fallen world, just like we do today. But there came a moment when God was about to pour out His direct wrath on Sodom. Abraham asks a crucial question, *"Shall not the Judge of all the earth do right?"* (Genesis 18:25 KJV). This question reveals something powerful: since God is righteous, He cannot pour out His direct wrath on a city that contains the righteous.

When it was time for God's wrath to fall, He made sure Lot was evacuated. As the angel is rushing Lot out of the city, he says, *"Haste thee, escape thither; for I cannot do anything till thou be come thither"* (Genesis 19:22 KJV). God's direct wrath could not fall until the righteous were safe. The difference here is obvious. Lot endured the indirect effects of living in a cursed world, but when God's direct wrath came, he had to be snatched out.

Now, how is that going to work during the Tribulation when God's direct wrath isn't confined to just one city but will cover the entire planet? The solution is simple. Take the righteous off the planet, into the Father's House, until the wrath is over. Here we have a biblical precedent. The righteous aren't meant to endure God's direct judgment. Just as Lot and his family had to be taken out of Sodom, so must the Church be taken up before the wrath of the Tribulation begins.

So when someone accuses Rapture teaching of promoting a "pie-in-the-sky" mentality, remind them that we're fully aware of the battles ahead. But we're also holding onto the promise that the King is coming and He's coming for His own.

THE WRATH OF GOD
OR MAN?

This is what the Bible calls the, "Time of Jacob's Trouble."

> *Alas! for that day is great, so that none is like it: it is even the time*
> *of Jacob's trouble; but he shall be saved out of it*
>
> (Jeremiah 30:7)

This is a period of time expressly designated for Israel and the unbelieving world, rather than the Church. This period is not just a time of human or satanic wrath but it is specifically characterized by the direct and intense outpouring of God's judgment upon the earth. It's vital for you to understand this. This coincides perfectly with what we read in Daniel 9:24 about "Daniel's Seventieth Week." This is a time set aside to bring about the fulfillment of God's promises to Israel and to address the final rebellion against God before the establishment of His Kingdom.

There are those who claim that the first part of the Tribulation is just the wrath of man or satan. Let's take a look at this and ask:

- Where is the wrath coming from?
- Who is responsible?
- What role does the Church have in it?

To understand why the Tribulation is the outpouring of God's wrath, it is crucial to recognize that it is a period meant to fulfill specific prophetic purposes as stated.

> *Seventy weeks are determined upon thy people and upon thy*
> *holy city, to finish the transgression, and to make an end of sins,*
> *and to make reconciliation for iniquity, and to bring in everlasting*

righteousness, and to seal up the vision and prophecy, and to anoint the most Holy

(Daniel 9:24 KJV).

Here we see the entire purpose of the Tribulation summarized:

- The finish transgression
- To make an end of sins
- To make reconciliation for iniquity
- To bring in everlasting righteousness
- To seal up the vision and the prophecy
- To anoint the Most Holy Place

Here is the same passage from the Amplified Bible:

Seventy weeks [of years, or 490 years] have been decreed for your people and for your holy city (Jerusalem), to finish the transgression, to make an end of sins, to make atonement (reconciliation) for wickedness, to bring in everlasting righteousness (right-standing with God), to seal up vision and prophecy and prophet, and to anoint the Most Holy Place.

Let's break this down simply so it's easy to understand. Here in Daniel, we see a prophecy about something big God is planning, notably for the people of Israel and their holy city, Jerusalem, and that God has set aside seventy weeks of time to accomplish this plan. But these aren't weeks as we normally think of them (a period of seven days). Here, each "week" actually represents seven years. So if we multiply 70 by 7, we get 490 years.

The seventieth week is the last seven years of this period and it's known as the time of intense judgment and purification. This is what we've been referring to when we say, "The Tribulation" and this is how we know it lasts seven years.

There are several other verses in Daniel that deal with timing as well. When you study this subject you'll run across the phrase, "time, times, and half a time."

> *And he shall speak great words against the most High, and shall wear out the saints of the most High, and think to change times and laws: and they shall be given into his hand until a time and times and the dividing of time*
> (Daniel 7:25 KJV).

> *And I heard the man clothed in linen, which was upon the waters of the river, when he held up his right hand and his left hand unto heaven, and sware by him that liveth for ever that it shall be for a time, times, and an half; and when he shall have accomplished to scatter the power of the holy people, all these things shall be finished*
> (Daniel 12:7 KJV).

Time, times, and a half a time is just an antiquated way of saying three and a half years. In prophecy, this phrase helps us understand that the second half of the Tribulation, called The Great Tribulation, will last for three and a half years, or 42 months (Revelation 12:14, Daniel 7:25). The Bible talks about this in several ways by referencing 1,260 days, 42 months, or time, times, and half a time, but they all refer to the same three-and-a-half-year period.

This is how we know it's not just a symbolic period of time. God not only gives us the analogy of Daniel's seventieth week and the reference to "time, times, and half a time," but He also breaks it down into months and even exact days. It's as if He wants to eliminate any possibility of confusion. By giving these precise timeframes, God makes it clear that this is a literal and specific period, leaving no room for doubt.

These references suggest a total period of seven years, with significant events occurring at the midpoint, such as the breaking of the covenant by the antichrist and the abomination of desolation. The entire Tribulation lasts for seven years, but the most intense part, The Great Tribulation, lasts for three and a half years. All of this happens as part of God's plan to bring an end to sin and set everything right.

THE BEGINNING OF GOD'S WRATH

The first half of the Tribulation is no walk in the park. I talk with people all the time who think that this season will be a time of peace. They often quote 1 Thessalonians 5:3 (KJV): *"For when they shall say, Peace and safety; then sudden destruction cometh upon them, as travail upon a woman with child; and they shall not escape."*

This doesn't mean the world will actually be at peace. It means that those who control the levers of power will claim there's peace and safety. We see this even now with politicians continually declaring peace and stability when they're in office, despite the chaos around us. Sadly, with the rise of censorship, it's becoming more and more difficult to challenge these narratives, and it may soon become illegal to openly disagree with them. The illusion of peace will be upheld, and those who dissent will face serious consequences. This could also refer to the fact that there's peace in Israel but does not speak to the condition of the rest of the world.

The first three and a half years of the Tribulation, often referred to as the *"beginning of sorrows"* (Matthew 24:8), will be a time of increasing global instability, marked by both natural and supernatural events. This period will bring severe judgment upon the earth, but it is just the beginning of the full outpouring of God's wrath.

EVENTS OF THE FIRST THREE AND A HALF YEARS

RISE OF THE ANTICHRIST:

The antichrist will emerge as a global political leader, likely appearing as a man of peace. He will initially seem to solve many of the world's crises, particularly brokering a peace agreement with Israel (Daniel 9:27). This covenant will signal the start of the seven-year Tribulation.

THE FOUR HORSEMEN (REVELATION 6):

- *First Seal:* The antichrist rides out on a white horse, symbolizing conquest through diplomacy and deception.

- *Second Seal:* War breaks out as the red horse of conflict emerges. Peace is taken from the earth and nations turn against one another, leading to widespread violence and bloodshed.

- *Third Seal:* The black horse of famine follows, likely the result of wars and economic collapse, causing massive food shortages.

- *Fourth Seal:* The pale horse brings death through war, famine, plague, and wild animals.

There are three more seals after this but the Fourth Seal of judgment alone will result in *the death of 25 percent of the global population.* With today's population of around eight billion people, that would mean *two billion deaths* just within this first part of the Tribulation. This staggering loss of life will come from a combination of war, famine, disease, and chaos caused by the breakdown of society. This does not even account for the additional lives lost through other seals, persecutions, natural disasters, and famines. The world will be experiencing the most severe time of death and destruction in history, with massive numbers of people suffering under these judgments.

THE FOUR HORSEMEN - REVELATION 6:1-8

Events of the First 3½ Years

THE WHITE HORSE

The Antichrist rides out on a white horse, symbolizing conquest through diplomacy and deception.

THE RED HORSE

War breaks out as the red horse of conflict emerges. Peace is taken from the earth, and nations turn against one another, leading to widespread violence and bloodshed.

THE BLACK HORSE

The black horse of famine follows, likely the result of wars and economic collapse, causing massive food shortages.

THE PALE HORSE

The pale horse brings death through war, famine, plague, and wild animals. This seal alone is responsible for the death of one-quarter of the world's population.

Note: When reading about these deaths, it's important to notice that these catastrophes are impacting the entire world. Those on the earth who believe in God are not spared.

WHERE IS THIS JUDGMENT COMING FROM?

They called to the mountains and the rocks, "Fall on us and hide us from the face of him who sits on the throne, and from the wrath of the Lamb! For the great day of their wrath has come, and who can withstand it?"

(Revelation 6:16-17 NIV)

This wrath is coming directly from the Lamb. Jesus is the One who breaks the seals, and it is His wrath from which men and women are desperately trying to hide. Before we dive into the details of what's to come, it's important to understand that the Bible makes it clear that this entire seven-year period is the wrath of Jesus.

This is a key reason why we know the Tribulation is not meant for the Church. The focus is on Israel and the nations, a time of intense purification and judgment. Jesus has already taken the full wrath of God upon Himself for His Church, which is why we are exempt from experiencing it. For believers, the penalty has been paid, and there is no longer any wrath left for us.

During this seven-year period, God's wrath will be unleashed through three distinct series of judgments (three cycles of seven), each one becoming progressively more severe: the *Seal Judgments*, the *Trumpet Judgments*, and the *Bowl Judgments*. Let's break down each of these to grasp the intensity of what will unfold during this time.

THE SEAL JUDGMENTS

(Revelation 6:1-17, 8:1-5)

These are the first judgments unleashed at the start of the Tribulation, symbolized by seals being broken from a scroll in Heaven. Each broken seal brings a new form of judgment upon the earth:

- *First Seal:* The White Horse - The rise of the antichrist, symbolizing conquest and deception.

- *Second Seal:* The Red Horse - War breaks out around the earth, causing widespread bloodshed.

- *Third Seal:* The Black Horse - Famine strikes, leading to severe food shortages and economic collapse.

- *Fourth Seal:* The Pale Horse - Death and Hades follow, killing one-fourth of the world's population through war, famine, plague, and wild beasts.

- *Fifth Seal:* Martyrs - Souls of those martyred for their faith cry out for justice.

- *Sixth Seal:* Cosmic Disturbances - Earthquakes, the sun turns black, the moon turns red, stars fall, and mountains and islands are moved from their places, causing mass terror.

- *Seventh Seal:* Silence in Heaven - As this seal is opened, there is silence in Heaven for half an hour, preparing for the upcoming trumpet judgments.

THE TRUMPET JUDGMENTS

(Revelation 8:6-13, 9:1-21, 11:15-19)

Following the Seal Judgments, the Trumpet Judgments are sounded by angels and bring even greater devastation upon the earth:

- *First Trumpet:* Hail, fire, and blood rain down, burning up a third of the earth's vegetation.

THE SEAL JUDGMENTS
(REVELATION 6:1-17, 8:1-5)

FIRST SEAL:
The White Horse - The rise of the Antichrist, symbolizing conquest and deception.

SECOND SEAL:
The Red Horse - War breaks out across the earth, causing widespread bloodshed.

THIRD SEAL:
The Black Horse - Famine strikes, leading to severe food shortages and economic collapse.

FOURTH SEAL:
The Pale Horse - Death and Hades follow, killing a fourth of the world's population through war, famine, plague, and wild beasts.

FIFTH SEAL:
Martyrs - Souls of those martyred for their faith cry out for justice.

SIXTH SEAL:
Cosmic Disturbances - Earthquakes, the sun turns black, the moon turns red, stars fall, and mountains and islands are moved from their places causing mass terror.

SEVENTH SEAL:
Silence in Heaven - As this seal is opened, there is silence in heaven for half an hour preparing for the upcoming trumpet judgments.

THE TRUMPET JUDGMENTS
(REVELATION 8:6-13, 9:1-21, 11:15-19)

FIRST TRUMPET:

Hail, fire, and blood rain down, burning up a third of the earth's vegetation.

SECOND TRUMPET:

A huge mountain, burning with fire, is thrown into the sea, turning a third of the sea to blood, killing a third of the sea creatures, and destroying a third of the ships.

THIRD TRUMPET:

A great star called Wormwood falls from the sky, poisoning a third of the rivers and freshwater, causing many people to die.

FOURTH TRUMPET:

A third of the sun, moon, and stars are struck, darkening a third of the day and night.

FIFTH TRUMPET:

First Woe - Locust-like creatures with the power to torment people for five months are released from the abyss.

SIXTH TRUMPET:

Second Woe - Four angels are released to kill a third of humanity using an army of 200 million.

SEVENTH TRUMPET:

Third Woe - The kingdom of the world becomes the kingdom of Christ, marking the end of this period and signaling the final set of judgments.

THE BOWL (VIAL) JUDGMENTS
(REVELATION 16:1-21)

FIRST BOWL:
Sores break out on all who have the mark of the beast and worship his image.

SECOND BOWL:
The sea turns completely to blood, killing every living thing in the ocean.

THIRD BOWL:
Rivers and springs turn to blood, further polluting the freshwater supply.

FOURTH BOWL:
The sun scorches people with intense heat, but they refuse to repent and curse God.

FIFTH BOWL:
The kingdom of the beast is plunged into darkness, causing pain and suffering, yet people still refuse to repent.

SIXTH BOWL:
The Euphrates River dries up, preparing the way for the kings of the East to gather for the battle of Armageddon.

SEVENTH BOWL:
A massive earthquake shakes the earth, flattening cities, and huge hailstones weighing about 100 pounds fall from the sky. The destruction is so severe that it causes global devastation.

- **Second Trumpet:** A huge mountain, burning with fire, is thrown into the sea, turning a third of the sea to blood, killing sea creatures, and destroying ships.

- **Third Trumpet:** A great star called Wormwood falls from the sky, poisoning a third of the rivers and freshwater, causing many people to die.

- **Fourth Trumpet:** A third of the sun, moon, and stars are struck, darkening a third of the day and night.

- **Fifth Trumpet:** First Woe - Locust-like creatures with the power to torment people for five months are released from the abyss.

- **Sixth Trumpet:** Second Woe - Four angels are released to kill a third of humanity using an army of 200 million.

- **Seventh Trumpet:** Third Woe - The kingdom of the world becomes the Kingdom of Christ, marking the end of this period and signaling the final set of judgments.

THE BOWL (VIAL) JUDGMENTS

(Revelation 16:1-21)

The Bowl Judgments are the final and most intense of God's wrath, poured out in rapid succession at the very end of the Tribulation:

- **First Bowl:** Sores break out on all who have the mark of the beast and worship his image.

- **Second Bowl:** The sea turns completely to blood, killing every living thing in the ocean.

- **Third Bowl:** Rivers and springs turn to blood, further polluting the freshwater supply.

- **Fourth Bowl:** The sun scorches people with intense heat, but they refuse to repent and they curse God.

- *Fifth Bowl:* The kingdom of the beast is plunged into darkness, causing pain and suffering, yet people still refuse to repent.

- *Sixth Bowl:* The Euphrates River dries up, preparing the way for the kings of the East to gather for the battle of Armageddon.

- *Seventh Bowl:* A massive earthquake shakes the earth, flattening cities, and huge hailstones weighing about 100 pounds fall from the sky. The destruction is so severe that it causes global devastation.

These judgments show the relentless and increasing severity of God's wrath during the Tribulation. Through the Seal, Trumpet, and Bowl Judgments, God brings judgment upon a rebellious world and prepares the way for the Second Coming of Christ. And we can see these events unfold in a clear sequence because John repeatedly uses time markers such as "after this" and "then I saw." This wording indicates a deliberate, step-by-step progression, supporting the idea that the seals, trumpets, and bowls are revealed in chronological order.

Again, where does all of this come from and who is responsible? This is an important question especially when considering many of the precious promises given by God to His Church. Fortunately, these are not hard questions to answer based on what we've learned so far.

At the onset of the Tribulation, the intensity of God's wrath is so palpable and obvious that even the heathen recognize it and are crying out for death. It is a tragic irony when the world, despite its distance from God, recognizes the unmistakable hand of divine judgment, while many within the Church remain oblivious to it and say it's just the wrath of man or satan. This disconnection reveals a profound misunderstanding of the gravity and scope of what the Scriptures describe as The Tribulation, leading to a failure to grasp the urgency and seriousness of the times in which we are living. Just to review:

Where does this wrath originate?
Answer: It comes from Heaven.
Who is administering this wrath?
Answer: Jesus Christ.

In Revelation 6, the opening of the Tribulation is unmistakably portrayed as an outpouring of divine wrath. This period is so catastrophic that some estimates suggest that up to half of the world's population could be annihilated in the first three and a half years alone (see Revelation 6:8; 9:16).

Some Christians imagine themselves as heroes during the Tribulation, picturing a "Rocky-style" training montage where they're getting ready for the battle ahead, running up the steps in Philadelphia, doing endless pushups, "Eye of the Tiger" blaring in the background. But here's the hard truth: there's no amount of physical training, no motivational preaching, and certainly no Hollywood mashup that can prepare you for the level of devastation and darkness that's coming. This isn't a fight you can win. The only preparation that matters is spiritual, and the only real escape is the one Jesus promised. It's not about being a hero, it's about trusting in the ultimate Hero, Jesus Christ, and recognizing that He already fought the battle and won the victory for you.

While it is essential for Christians to be prepared for persecution and personal tribulation, The Tribulation represents something far more dire. It is the pure wrath of God, and no amount of personal preparation or spiritual readiness can fully equip anyone to endure it.

THE WRATH OF SATAN OR THE WRATH OF THE LAMB?

Some don't understand how satanic opposition can equal divine wrath. This is why they will ignore the plain meaning of Revelation 6:17

and assume this is the wrath of man or satan. However, throughout Scripture, we see a pattern of divine judgment where God employs foreign nations and enemies as devices of judgment against His people. These instances reveal how God uses external forces to execute His will and bring His people to repentance. Again, the purpose of the Tribulation is to wake up Israel and shake up the earth.

One notable example is found in the history of Israel with the Assyrians. In 2 Kings 17:6, the Assyrian Empire, under the leadership of Tiglath-Pileser III, invaded and conquered the northern kingdom of Israel. This military action led to the dispersion of the ten tribes of Israel. The Assyrians were not merely conquerors, but instruments of divine judgment against a nation that had persistently engaged in idolatry and rejected God's commands.

Assyria was referred to as *"the rod of My anger"* (Isaiah 10:5 NKJV), indicating that even though these nations acted according to their own desires, God was sovereignly using them to execute His judgment.

Similarly, the *Babylonian* conquest of Judah highlights another instance of divine judgment. In Jeremiah 25:9, God speaks through the prophet, proclaiming that He would use Babylon as a means of executing judgment against Judah. The Babylonians, led by King Nebuchadnezzar, besieged Jerusalem, destroyed the temple, and exiled the Jewish people. This devastating period of exile was a direct result of Judah's continual disobedience and failure to heed God's warnings. This was the wrath of God.

The *Philistines* also played a role in God's judgment. In Judges 13:1, the Israelites faced oppression from the Philistines during the time of the Judges. This oppression was not simply a military conflict but a form of divine discipline intended to bring the Israelites back to God. The Philistines' dominance served as a consequence of Israel's unfaithfulness and disobedience.

Another example is the *Midianites'* oppression of Israel, described in Judges 6:1-6. The Midianites exerted severe hardship on the Israelites as a form of divine correction. This period of oppression was meant to address Israel's infidelity and to prompt the people to return to a faithful relationship with God. Gideon's rise as a deliverer demonstrated both God's judgment and His mercy.

Even in spiritual warfare, we see examples of demonic spirits being unleashed as instruments of God's judgment. One striking example is found in 1 Kings 22:19-23, where God permits a "lying spirit" to deceive the prophets of King Ahab. The scene reveals a divine council where God asks who will persuade Ahab to go to battle and ultimately fall at Ramoth-gilead. A spirit steps forward, volunteering to deceive Ahab's prophets, and God grants permission:

> *And the Lord said, Who shall persuade Ahab, that he may go up and fall at Ramothgilead? And one said on this manner, and another said on that manner. And there came forth a spirit, and stood before the Lord, and said, I will persuade him. ...And* [the Lord] *said, Thou shalt persuade him, and prevail also: go forth, and do so*
>
> (1 Kings 22:20-22 KJV).

I would be lying if I said that I fully understood every nuance of this interaction, but this account does show how even demonic forces can be used to fulfill God's purposes in judgment.

Another example of God allowing an evil spirit to execute His judgment is in the life of King Saul. After Saul's repeated disobedience, we read in 1 Samuel 16:14 (KJV): *"But the Spirit of the Lord departed from Saul, and an evil spirit from the Lord troubled him."*

Because of Saul's failure to obey God's commands, the Spirit of the Lord left him, and God permitted an evil spirit to torment him. God only allowed this because of Saul's rebellion and disobedience to the instructions he had been given through the prophet Samuel. God rejected Saul as king and allowed him to be tormented by episodes of severe distress and irrational behavior as a direct act of judgment for his failure as Israel's king.

In both instances, we see how God, can allow demonic forces to operate as part of His divine judgment, even using evil spirits as tools of judgment to carry out His purposes in the face of rebellion and disobedience. They reflect a recurring theme concerning God's sovereignty over the nations and His ability to use worldly entities to fulfill His divine purposes. During the Tribulation, part of the Lamb's wrath is the release of man's inhumanity to man as war breaks out worldwide. Though it may be performed by carnal beings, it is the result of the hand of God.

THE CHRISTIAN AND THE TRIBULATION

Now that we understand the true meaning and source of the Tribulation, it's essential to ask, "What role does the Christian play in all of this?" The Bible provides a clear answer:

And to wait for his Son from heaven, whom he raised from the dead, even Jesus, which delivered us from the wrath to come

(1 Thessalonians 1:10 KJV).

Because thou hast kept the word of my patience, I also will keep thee from the hour of temptation, which shall come upon all the world, to try them that dwell upon the earth

(Revelation 3:10 KJV).

For God did not appoint us to wrath, but to obtain salvation through our Lord Jesus Christ

(1 Thessalonians 5:9 NKJV).

These verses make it abundantly clear that believers are not destined to experience the wrath of God that will be poured out during the Tribulation. Instead, they are promised deliverance and salvation, aligning with the expectation of the Rapture.

To further grasp this truth, let's turn back to Genesis 18 and 19, where we find an important precedent in the story of Lot and Sodom. I want us to revisit this because when Jesus described the last days, He compared them to the days of Lot (Luke 17:28). In Genesis 18, Abraham pleads with God to spare the righteous from the destruction of Sodom, saying, *"Would You also destroy the righteous with the wicked?"* (Genesis 18:23 NKJV). God assures Abraham that He would not destroy the city if even ten righteous people were found. But when they couldn't be found, God did something significant... He removed Lot and his family before He unleashed His judgment on the city because: *"...I cannot do anything till thou be come thither"* (Genesis 19:22 KJV).

God's judgment **cannot** be poured out on a city where His covenant people live. If this was true for Lot in the Old Covenant, how much more is it true for the body of Christ in the New Covenant?

Through Lot, we see a biblical precedent being set for God's deliverance. He doesn't pour out His wrath while the righteous are still present. Similarly, 2 Thessalonians 2:6-7 talks about the "Restrainer," a force that holds back the antichrist until it is time for judgment. Many scholars believe this restraining force is the presence of the Holy Spirit within the Church. Once the Church is removed, through the Rapture, the full weight of God's wrath will be unleashed during the Tribulation.

From the opening of the seals to the blowing of the trumpets and the pouring out of the bowls of judgment, each phase demonstrates God's direct hand in these events. Therefore, it is essential to understand that the Rapture is not just an escape from difficult times but a fulfillment of God's promise to keep His people from His divine wrath.

Look at the question that Abraham poses to God: *"Far be it from You to do such a thing as this, to slay the righteous with the wicked, so that the righteous should be as the wicked; far be it from You!* **Shall not the Judge of all the earth do right?"** (Genesis 18:25 NKJV)

The suggestion is that it would be *unjust* for God to pour out His wrath on the righteous. God affirms this to be true and removes Lot and his family before He releases His judgment. The same will be true in the last days.

Paul commissions us to *"...wait for His Son from heaven, whom he raised from the dead, even Jesus, who delivers us from the wrath to come"* (1 Thessalonians 1:10 NKJV). God's pattern of deliverance is clear throughout Scripture.

Understanding these distinctions provides clarity and reinforces the hope we have in Christ. The Rapture is the fulfillment of God's covenant to protect His people from the unprecedented wrath that will unfold during the Tribulation. By grasping this, we can look toward the end times not with fear, but with confidence in God's promise of deliverance.

"WHAT MAKES YOU SO SPECIAL?"

Imagine for a moment if the Church, as the body of Christ, were called to endure the full fury of God's wrath during the Tribulation. This notion isn't just challenging, it's nearly blasphemous. If we, the body of Christ, were subjected to the wrath of the Tribulation, it would be like crucifying Jesus a second time. Such a proposition would make light of the profound sacrifice He made on the Cross. Jesus has already taken God's wrath upon Himself for all who trust in Him. To suggest that His body should now bear that same wrath is an affront to the very core of our faith.

It's not uncommon to hear voices challenge the Rapture with a sense of smugness. "Who do you think you are?" they scoff. "Every Christian in history has faced persecution. Do you really think you'll be spared while others have had to suffer?" These critics misrepresent the doctrine, dismissing it as a fantasy. It's just another straw man.

Yes, it's true that every generation of believers has faced tribulation and persecution. We aren't promised an easy life free from hardship. However, no generation of believers has ever been subjected to the specific, direct, end-time wrath of God described in Revelation. That kind of wrath is a different matter altogether. It's one thing to endure the trials and tribulations that come from living in a fallen world and facing persecution for our faith, but it's entirely different to face this wrath.

This flips the critics' argument on its head. What makes this current generation of believers so special that it would be destined to endure God's wrath, a wrath that no other generation of Christians has ever had to face? Why should we believe that we are the exception to God's established pattern of delivering His people before pouring out His wrath? The critics, not those who hold to the hope of the Rapture, are the ones who must answer this question.

The Rapture is not a fantasy but a glorious fulfillment of God's promise to His Church. It's not about escaping hardship, but rather about being spared from the very wrath that Jesus already bore for us on the Cross.

ARE GOD'S PEOPLE PROTECTED DURING THE TRIBULATION?

The question of whether Christians are protected during the Tribulation hinges on understanding who is referred to in the term "Christians." For those who come to faith after the Rapture, during the Tribulation, their situation is different. These believers will endure intense persecution under the antichrist, and there is no blanket promise of physical protection for them. In fact, Revelation 13:7 (KJV) clearly states that the antichrist is given power to *"make war with the saints, and to overcome them."* Many of these Tribulation saints will be martyred for refusing to take the mark of the beast or worship the antichrist.

There is a unique group, though, that does receive a specific form of protection: the 144,000 Jewish evangelists mentioned in Revelation chapter 7. These individuals are sealed by God and appear to be protected from certain judgments, such as the demonic plague of locusts described in Revelation 9:4 (KJV). The locusts are commanded to harm only *"those men which have NOT the seal of God in their foreheads,"* which suggests that the 144,000 are supernaturally shielded during certain parts of the Tribulation. However, beyond this group and this specific judgment, there is no promise of protection from the plagues or persecutions that come during this period.

WHO ARE BEING MARTYRED IN THE TRIBULATION?

If the Rapture is true, then who are the ones being martyred during the Tribulation, and why do they have to endure it? Who are the "saints" mentioned in Revelation that the antichrist is given power over? These are all crucial questions.

Let's first tackle the martyrs. The people who are martyred during the Tribulation are those who come to faith after the Rapture. Revelation 7:14 (NKJV) refers to them as those who have *"come out of great tribulation,"* meaning they came to faith during the intense persecution of that time. These individuals weren't part of the *Ecclesia* (the Church) as we know it. After the Church is removed from the earth, many people will realize the truth of the Gospel and give their lives to Christ. Unfortunately, following Jesus during the Tribulation will come at an incredibly high cost. They will refuse to take the mark of the beast and will face brutal persecution, even to the point of death.

There's something very different about how the Gospel is presented and received during the Tribulation, and it becomes evident as you read through the book of Revelation. In the first three chapters of Revelation, the Church is undeniably the focal point. The Church is mentioned 19 times, front and center in the narrative. But then something dramatic happens. From chapter 4 onward, any direct mention of the Church on earth seems to disappear. Instead, the focus pivots entirely to the Jewish people and the nation of Israel.

Many scholars would argue, and I wholeheartedly agree, that during this time, the Church is seen in Heaven, receiving rewards at the Judgment Seat of Christ, enjoying the presence of the Savior, and experiencing the promises made to overcomers, but they are not directly mentioned. In Revelation 19, we do see the Bride in Heaven, already prepared, rejoicing at the Marriage Supper of the Lamb.

It's important to note that while we don't see direct mention of the Church on earth or explicitly in Heaven after chapter 3, we do see the Bride already with Jesus when He returns in Revelation 19. This visual of the Bride in Heaven suggests the Church is no longer part of the unfolding events on earth.

What makes the shift in focus even more striking is that after the Church disappears from the narrative, we are introduced to 144,000 Jewish evangelists from the twelve tribes of Israel (Revelation 7:4-8). These are Jewish believers who are sealed and set apart for a special purpose during this time. In addition to them, we see two powerful prophets raised up to preach the truth, only to be martyred in the streets of Jerusalem (Revelation 11:3-12). But that's not all, angels themselves are now declaring the everlasting Gospel (Revelation 14:6).

This marks a significant change in how the Gospel is spread. In the Church Age, the primary mission of evangelism belongs to the Church, the body of Christ. But during the Tribulation, after the Rapture has removed the Church, the evangelistic responsibility is given to the 144,000 sealed Jewish witnesses and the two prophets who serve as a testimony to the Israel and the nations. Additionally, angels are commissioned to proclaim the Gospel as well.

This change underscores God's focus on Israel and the nations during this time of preparation and judgment. Furthermore, it is a signal that God's full attention is concentrated on fulfilling His promises to Israel, while still offering salvation to all who would believe, even in this dark time.

We need to be thankful for the hour we're living in today. During this time we have the unique privilege to connect with God the Father as part of the body of Christ. Those who will remain and believe after the Rapture are part of a different group of believers who will be honored in their own, very special way. They endure the Tribulation not because God is punishing them, but because they are living in a time of final judgment, and their newfound faith in Christ comes with a high earthly cost. Their martyrdom will serve as a powerful witness during this period, and they will be rewarded for their faithfulness.

WHO ARE THE "SAINTS" IN REVELATION?

Now, let's deal with the "saints" mentioned in Revelation. Revelation 13:7 (KJV) says, "*And it was given unto him* [the antichrist] *to make war with the saints, and to overcome them: and power was given him over all kindreds, and tongues, and nations.*"

But wait…didn't Jesus say in Matthew 16:18, "*the gates of hell shall not prevail against it* [the Church]"? What are we to make of this?

The key lies in understanding that the "saints" mentioned in Revelation are not the same as the Church. The Church, made up of believers from the Day of Pentecost to the Rapture, has already been removed from the earth before the Tribulation begins. The Tribulation "saints" in Revelation are those who come to faith after the Rapture, during the time of the antichrist's reign.

OLD TESTAMENT SAINTS AND TRIBULATION SAINTS

The term "saints" is not exclusive to the Church. Throughout the Old Testament, we see references to saints as God's holy ones. For example, in Deuteronomy 33:3 (NKJV), Moses speaks of God's love for His people, saying, *"Yes, He loves the people; all His saints are in Your hand."*

In Psalm 30:4 (KJV), David says, *"Sing unto the Lord, O ye saints of his, and give thanks at the remembrance of his holiness."*

In these contexts, saints refers to the faithful of Israel, God's covenant people, long before the Church was ever established at Pentecost.

This might surprise you but even *angels* are sometimes referred to as saints in certain translations. One example often cited is Deuteronomy 33:2 (KJV), which says:

> *And he said, The Lord came from Sinai, and rose up from Seir unto them; he shined forth from mount Paran, and he came with ten thousands of saints: from his right hand went a fiery law for them.*

In this verse, the term "saints" (or "holy ones") is understood by many theologians to refer to angels accompanying the Lord. Though I may not agree with this understanding, it's certainly a possibility. However, this is not the usual application in the New Testament, where "saints" almost exclusively refers to human believers, whether they are Old Testament faithful, members of the Church, or Tribulation saints.

So when Revelation refers to saints, it's not slam-dunk proof that the Church is present during this time. The antichrist is given power to *"make war with the saints, and to overcome them"* (Revelation 13:7 KJV). The only way this is not a contradiction to Jesus's promise that the gates of hell would not prevail against the Church is if this is a different group of people.

The Church is a unique group, starting from the Day of Pentecost and ending with the Rapture. The Church was promised deliverance from the wrath to come, as seen in 1 Thessalonians 5:9 KJV): *"For God hath not appointed us to wrath, but to obtain salvation by our Lord Jesus Christ."* The Church will not experience the wrath of God during the Tribulation. This does not mean God has abandoned those who believe on Him during the Tribulation; they will be gloriously rewarded for their faithfulness.

It's important to recognize that no generation of the Church has ever been exempt from facing martyrdom or suffering. Every believer, no matter the time or place, must be ready to stand firm against persecution. Jesus warned that in this world we would have tribulation (John 16:33), and throughout history, many have laid down their lives for the faith.

However, the persecution we see during the Tribulation is different. While believers during the Tribulation will face persecution from the antichrist and his followers, the broader context is that they are living during a time when God's judgment is unfolding and they are not exempt from the drought, famine, scorching heat, and yet, even for those who come to faith during the Tribulation, there remains the promise of eternal life. Though they may endure unimaginable trials, their reward will be great as they stand before the throne of God.

The Tribulation may be a time of incredible darkness, but the light of Christ's ultimate victory shines through, giving hope to all who look to Him. In the end, God's justice will prevail, and His people will reign with Him in glory forever.

The Judge of all the earth will do what's right!

7

THE PHILADELPHIA EXPERIMENT

In 1943, under the veil of wartime secrecy, something extraordinary was said to have happened in the naval yard of Philadelphia. Known as the *Philadelphia Experiment*, it was rumored that the U.S. Navy had managed to make a battleship vanish. According to reports, the *USS Eldridge* didn't just disappear from view, it vanished from reality, transported across time and space, only to reappear miles away. Witnesses claimed crew members were left disoriented, some even embedded in the ship's hull, shaken by the unexplainable forces that tore them from one dimension and cast them into another.[1]

The details remain shrouded in mystery, but the imagery is undeniable; a vessel vanishing into thin air, leaving confusion and chaos in its wake. Whether this particular incident is fact or fiction, there is another event coming that will make this look like a Sunday school picnic.

Like the sudden vanishing of that ship, the Rapture will take place in an instant, a supernatural event that will leave the world in shock. One moment, the believers will be here, living among the nations; and the next, they will be gone. Gone, without a trace. The Bible describes this event as occurring in the "blink of an eye" before the Tribulation, before judgment falls. In one instant, the world's conscience will be gone.

Imagine the world scrambling for answers, the media reporting on millions missing, and the planet left grappling with an event they cannot comprehend. The Rapture is not science fiction or a conspiracy theory, like what happened to the *USS Eldridge*, it is prophetic truth. Much like the unsettling rumors surrounding the Philadelphia Experiment, people will find themselves asking the same haunting question: "What just happened?"

As we look at the message Jesus gave to the church of Philadelphia in the book of Revelation, we find a chilling yet thrilling promise. This faithful church will be kept from the "hour of trial" that is coming upon the whole world. Like the *USS Eldridge* supposedly disappearing into another dimension, the Church will be swept away, taken before the storm of judgment hits. What you're about to read is not a metaphor nor an allegory, it is the ultimate disappearing act, foretold by the One who controls time itself.

THE PHILADELPHIAN CHURCH

Around AD 95, more than 60 years after the Day of Pentecost, the apostle John, who at this point was pastoring in Ephesus and overseeing the churches of Asia Minor, is now exiled on the island of Patmos. Patmos was no ordinary prison. It was one of the harshest places to be exiled, a barren rock with little fresh water and barely any trees. This rugged, desolate landscape became the home of many political prisoners banished by Roman emperor Domitian. To make matters worse, the temple of Diana towered over the island, and John found himself living in a cave just beneath it. Yet, it was in this cave, of all places, where Jesus stepped in and revealed to John what no other eye had seen before. This is a comforting reminder that God can reach you no matter where you are.

John saw an apocalyptic vision of the last days, which culminates in the return and the reign of Jesus Christ. This moment could very well be the answer to what Jesus meant in Matthew 16:28 (NKJV), where He says, *"There are some standing here who shall not taste death till they see the Son of Man coming in His kingdom."* While some point to the transfiguration as the fulfillment of this, another explanation could be what John witnessed in his extraordinary vision of the coming Kingdom.

John dictated seven letters from Jesus to the Church at large. I often refer to these as the seven hidden epistles because they are often unnoticed or ignored. These letters are among the most profound portions of Scripture and are considered by many to be the most important two chapters in the New Testament for the modern believer. Each church represents not only a historical body of believers but also stages in the Church's spiritual journey throughout time. They also represent the different kinds of churches and Christians on earth today.

I always find it amusing when I hear ministers speculate about what Jesus would think about this or what He would say about that. The truth is, we don't have to guess! The letters John wrote in the book of Revelation are packed with insights into the nature and character of Jesus. If we took the time to really understand them, it could clear up much of the confusion surrounding so many of the assumptions floating around in the modern Church. Instead of imagining what Jesus might think, we can look directly at what He has already said, and those words speak volumes.

This is not a book about the seven churches, so we won't take time here to explore each of these epistles in great detail. However, if you're interested in learning more, I encourage you to check out my teachings on YouTube or visit www.encountertoday.com for a deeper exploration. That being said, I do want to pause and unpack what Jesus had to say to the church at Philadelphia, because it's deeply relevant to us today.

THE SECRET OF THE SEVEN

At the time of this writing, there were hundreds of churches scattered throughout the region, yet Jesus chose only seven to receive these letters. These seven churches were representative, meaning what was written to them applies to all churches, in all places, and in all times, including ours. This is why Jesus ended each message with the same powerful statement: *"Whoever has ears, let them hear what the Spirit says to the churches"* (Revelation 3:13 NIV).

This was not a throwaway line or a mere rhetorical flourish. It was an urgent call for discernment, inviting all who would listen to pay attention. Jesus is saying, "If you're able to hear this, then it's for you." What He said to these seven churches is what He's saying to us today.

Jesus uttered these words seven times during His earthly ministry and then seven times again to the churches in Revelation. As we discussed in the last chapter, you already understand the meaning and significance of the number seven. Each church represents an important aspect of the Church and epoch of its existence.

I believe that this church is representative of the Church that will be raptured before The Tribulation. If we look at the details of this hidden epistle, we may find some key traits that will prepare us for what's coming and help us to thrive in the these last days.

Here's what Jesus had to say to them in Revelation 3:7-13 (KJV):

> *And to the angel of the church in Philadelphia write; These things saith he that is holy, he that is true, he that hath the key of David, he that openeth, and no man shutteth; and shutteth, and no man openeth; I know thy works: behold, I have set before thee an open door, and no man can shut it: for thou hast a little strength, and hast kept my word, and hast not denied my name.*
>
> *Behold, I will make them of the synagogue of Satan, which say they are Jews, and are not, but do lie; behold, I will make them to come and worship before thy feet, and to know that I have loved thee. Because thou hast kept the word of my patience, I also will keep thee from the hour of temptation, which shall come upon all*

the world, to try them that dwell upon the earth. Behold, I come
quickly: hold that fast which thou hast, that no man take thy crown.

Him that overcometh will I make a pillar in the temple of my
God, and he shall go no more out: and I will write upon him the
name of my God, and the name of the city of my God, which is
new Jerusalem, which cometh down out of heaven from my God:
and I will write upon him my new name. He that hath an ear, let
him hear what the Spirit saith unto the churches.

Philadelphia represents the Bible-believing, revived Church. Jesus
has nothing but praise for this congregation, offering no rebuke or
condemnation. This is the Church that has turned back to the Word
of God with passion and conviction.

Situated at the heart of Greek civilization, Philadelphia earned the
nickname "Little Athens" due to its cultural and architectural resem-
blance to the great city of Athens. Strategically fortified, it served as
a defense against enemies trying to advance toward larger and more
prominent cities like Ephesus and Smyrna.

Philadelphia also had its share of struggles. I took a trip to Turkey
and was able to tour the locations of each of the seven churches. I
learned that Philadelphia was frequently rocked by devastating earthquakes, which made people hesitant to live there. While they would
conduct business in the city, many avoided making it their permanent home for fear of being trapped by collapsing buildings. The
inhabitants lived with the constant fear of imminent destruction. It's
no coincidence that Jesus offered them the concept of an imminent
blessed hope.

Because thou hast kept the word of my patience, I also will keep
thee from the hour of temptation, which shall come upon all the
world, to try them that dwell upon the earth

(Revelation 3:10 KJV).

Philadelphia, a church known for its unwavering devotion to Scripture, is the one congregation that Jesus specifically promises to protect from the coming tribulation and wrath. But it's not just the wrath itself that they will be spared from. Jesus promises to protect them from *"the hour of temptation."* In other words, this faithful church won't just be shielded from the trials; they will be kept from the very time in which those trials take place. What an incredible promise!

HOW CAN WE JOIN?

I don't know about you but I want to be part of this church. Remember that what Jesus promises this church is available to anyone who has ears to hear. Jesus describes Himself to this church as *"He who is Holy."* The Philadelphia church knew Jesus as holy and pursued holiness in their own lives. This is a crucial distinction that often gets blurred in today's world. People confuse righteousness with holiness. Righteousness is what God has done for us through the sacrifice of His Son. It's a gift we receive by faith, not something we earn. Holiness, however, is what we do in response to that righteousness. While righteousness makes us look like Jesus, holiness is when we act like Jesus.

Jesus also identifies Himself as *"He who is true"* (Revelation 3:7 NKJV). This speaks of His genuineness, His perfection, and His completeness. He's the true bread from Heaven, as mentioned in John 6:32-35. Everything about Jesus is authentic, and He calls His Church to live in that same genuineness. I encourage you to mediate on the entirety of this message for this church in your personal prayer time.

Then, Jesus says He holds *"the key of David,"* which is a symbol of authority (Revelation 3:7). He is the One who opens doors that no one can shut and shuts doors that no one can open. In this, He reassures His followers that He is in control of every opportunity, every ministry, and every challenge. If we understand this, we won't be tempted to compromise for opportunities that aren't from Him.

I want you to understand this; Jesus is not limited in His ability to open doors for you!

THE OPEN DOOR

Jesus says to the church of Philadelphia, *"I know thy works: behold, I have set before thee an open door, and no man can shut it…"* (Revelation 3:8 KJV).

Opportunities to serve and support your local church are all open doors Jesus provides. Whether it's serving in children's ministry, cleaning the church, or helping in worship, these are the doors Jesus opens for us. Remember, when He opens a door, He expects us to move forward and step through it.

Additionally, one must wonder if this open door is similar to the one mentioned in Revelation 4:1 (KJV): *"After this I looked, and, behold, a door was opened in heaven: and the first voice which I heard was as it were of a trumpet talking with me; which said, Come up hither, and I will shew thee things which must be hereafter."*

Jesus continues by acknowledging that this was a small, humble church, with *"a little strength"* (Revelation 3:8). This wasn't a church with grand buildings or vast resources, but they were rooted in the Word of God. Despite their size, their faithfulness allowed Christianity to spread into distant places like India. The size of the congregation doesn't determine its strength…God's power does. Little is much when God is in it!

Jesus commends this church for keeping His Word. To *"keep"* means to guard and protect, much like how people today treat their cell phones, where if it falls, they panic; if someone else touches it, they wipe it off. The believers in Philadelphia treated the Word of God with care and reverence. This is a far cry from today's culture, where biblical illiteracy is rampant. Many people can't name the four Gospels or define the Great Commission. A growing number of Christians don't even understand the core message of the Bible.

WATCH OUT FOR FAKE JEWS?

Jesus also warns about those who *"say they are Jews and are not"* (Revelation 3:9 KJV). This speaks to those who claim a spiritual identity they do not possess. As Paul says in Romans 9:6 (NLT), *"for not all who are born into the nation of Israel are truly members of God's people!"* Not everyone who claims to follow God truly does, and the time will come when those who have merely a form of godliness will be revealed.

For the faithful, however, Jesus promises in Revelation 3:10 (KJV), *"Because thou hast kept **the word of my patience**, I also will keep thee from the hour of temptation, which shall come upon all the world, to try them that dwell upon the earth."* This is not a small promise. It's a guarantee that the faithful will be spared from The Tribulation, the time of God's judgment on the earth.

WHAT IS THE "WORD OF MY PATIENCE"?

> *Be patient therefore, brethren, unto the coming of the Lord. Behold, the husbandman waiteth for the precious fruit of the earth, and hath long patience for it, until he receive the early and latter rain. Be ye also patient; stablish your hearts: for the coming of the Lord draweth nigh*
>
> (James 5:7-8 KJV).

> *Looking for that blessed hope, and the glorious appearing of the great God and our Saviour Jesus Christ*
>
> (Titus 2:13 KJV).

Watch therefore: for ye know not what hour your Lord doth come. But know this, that if the goodman of the house had known in what watch the thief would come, he would have watched, and would not have suffered his house to be broken up. Therefore be ye also ready: for in such an hour as ye think not the Son of man cometh

(Matthew 24:42-44 KJV).

But if we hope for that we see not, then do we with patience wait for it

(Romans 8:25 KJV).

For ye have need of patience, that, after ye have done the will of God, ye might receive the promise. For yet a little while, and he that shall come will come, and will not tarry

(Hebrews 10:36-37 KJV).

It's easy to see from these verses that when we talk about patience, we're not merely talking about being able to tolerate an annoying coworker. This kind of patience has to do directly with the coming of the Lord.

WHAT IS "THE HOUR OF TEMPTATION"?

The phrase *"the hour of temptation"* in Revelation 3:10 (KJV) is one that few seem to truly and thoroughly understand. So, what exactly is this "hour of temptation," and what will it entail?

We know from Scripture that God rewards those who diligently seek Him (Hebrews 11:6), but we often fail to connect this reward with the protection from the coming hour of temptation even though it's easily seen in the context. Take a look at the framework surrounding this familiar verse for yourself:

By faith Enoch was translated that he should not see death; and was not found, because God had translated him: for before his translation he had this testimony, that he pleased God. But without faith it is impossible to please him: for he that cometh to God must believe that he is, and that he is a rewarder of them that diligently seek him

(Hebrews 11:5-6 KJV).

Here, we see a connection between faithfulness, pleasing God, and being spared from coming judgment. Enoch was taken up, removed from earth because he walked with God in faith. This parallels the promise in Revelation 3:10, where Jesus assures the faithful Church that they will be kept from the hour of temptation that is coming upon the whole world.

But what exactly is the hour of temptation? Some translations use the word *trial* instead of *temptation*, but in this context, both refer to the same thing; a time of severe testing and tribulation. This isn't merely about everyday challenges or temptations, it's about a specific, unprecedented period of global trial sent by God. Jesus describes this in Matthew 24:21-22 (KJV):

For then shall be great tribulation, such as was not since the beginning of the world to this time, no, nor ever shall be. And except those days should be shortened, there should no flesh be saved: but for the elect's sake those days shall be shortened.

This hour of temptation refers to The Great Tribulation, a time of unparalleled suffering, testing, and judgment. The test will likely involve monumental decisions centering on the mark of the beast, as Revelation later reveals. The world will face a choice: align with the forces of the antichrist or remain faithful to God.

The church of Philadelphia is promised protection from this *"hour of temptation,"* indicating that the faithful will be removed, just as Enoch was, before the testing begins. This promise is for all who have kept Christ's word and have not denied His name.

The verse emphasizes the *"hour,"* highlighting that it is a set period of time, not merely the events of judgment themselves. This is significant because it speaks of being spared from the very *time* in which these trials will occur.

The Greek word used for *temptation* in this verse is *peirasmos* (πειρασμός), which typically means a trial or a test. It is not necessarily a moral temptation to sin, but rather a severe test or trial meant to prove and judge. In this context, it indicates a period of global upheaval and judgment. This further underscores the promise Jesus made to the church at Philadelphia that they will be spared from the entire time period of testing that is to come upon the whole world.

The following are some verses that show how the *"hour of temptation"* correlates with the coming of the Lord:

*The Lord knoweth how to deliver the godly out of **temptations**, and to reserve the unjust unto **the day of judgment** to be punished* (2 Peter 2:9 KJV).

*And take heed to yourselves, lest at any time your hearts be overcharged with surfeiting, and drunkenness, and cares of this life, and so that day come upon you unawares. For as a snare shall it come on all them that dwell on the face of the whole earth. **Watch ye therefore, and pray always, that ye may be accounted worthy to escape all these things that shall come to pass**, and to stand before the Son of man*

(Luke 21:34-36 KJV).

BEHOLD, I COME QUICKLY

When Jesus says in Revelation 3:11 (KJV), *"Behold, I come quickly,"* He isn't necessarily talking about timing, but rather about suddenness. His return will be swift and unexpected. He follows this with a warning: *"Hold fast what you have, that no one may take your crown"* (Revelation 3:11 NKJV). This suggests that our reward can be taken if we let go of our faithfulness.

In Philadelphia today, there's still one remaining pillar hidden among cedar and laurel trees. The original church is long gone, destroyed over the centuries, but that lone pillar still stands as a powerful symbol of endurance and faithfulness. In Revelation 3:12, Jesus promises that those who remain faithful will be like pillars in God's temple, standing firm for eternity.

The church of Philadelphia, the one holding fast to the true Word of God, isn't just a reflection of one particular group or denomination. In our time, it represents any church or believer, regardless of size or label, that remains faithful to God's Word. This is the Church Jesus is coming back for, a Church that has kept His Word, lived in holiness, stood strong in faith, and is occupying when He comes.

8

PROBLEMS WITH POST-TRIBULATION

Navigating the topic of the Rapture's timing can be quite the adventure, can't it? With so many interpretations and passionate perspectives, it's essential to approach this subject with humility. Allow me to re-emphasize that this isn't about playing "gotcha." I have many cherished friends who hold to varied end-time views, including the Post-Tribulation position, and they are dedicated, insightful believers. We're all on this journey together, seeking to understand the marvelous plans God has laid out in Scripture.

We should never let differences in eschatological views divide us. Instead, these discussions can strengthen our faith and deepen our appreciation for the richness of God's Word. After all, iron sharpens iron, and exploring these topics can lead us to greater clarity and unity. With that in mind, let's look more closely at some of the challenges associated with the Post-Tribulation position. Our goal isn't to diminish this viewpoint but to thoughtfully examine certain aspects that raise questions.

The Pre-Tribulation position has often been the subject of intense debate, especially since the 1980s. It's been somewhat of a popular whipping post, with many alternative viewpoints hurling questions our way without facing the same level of scrutiny themselves. It's as if the spotlight has been fixed on one side, leaving the others comfortably in the shadows.

Differing views on the end times should never fracture our fellowship.

In this chapter, we're going to turn the tables a bit. We'll cross-examine the Post-Tribulation view and take a closer look at its potential flaws. Again, this isn't about winning an argument or proving someone wrong, it's about seeking clarity and understanding. By examining these challenges, we hope to shed light on areas that may have been overlooked and encourage a more balanced discussion on this significant topic.

I know that some will look at the chapter titles and skip to this chapter but I encourage you to read the book all the way through first. I will reiterate some things here, but not everything. You need to read the book in its entirety to get the full case.

LIES, MYTHS, AND MISREPRESENTATION

One of my primary issues with the Post-Tribulation camp is their persistent habit of misrepresenting what Pre-Tribulationists actually believe and teach. I truly don't believe it's intentional, but it's certainly blatant. When I'm trying to respond to someone else's position, I strive to "steelman" their argument; meaning, I try to understand it in its strongest and most convincing form. This way, I can ensure that I'm addressing their actual beliefs, not some "straw man" version of them. But more often than not, I see Post-Tribulation arguments doing just the opposite.

Recently, I picked up a book by a well-known Post-Tribulation theologian, eager to engage with the views. Unfortunately, I couldn't even get through the first chapter without encountering more than half a dozen blatant misrepresentations of what Pre-Tribulationists believe, and that's not even counting the errors in their own doctrinal claims. If you're going to argue a point, you should at least engage with what your opponent actually believes, not a caricature.

These inaccuracies represent such a basic lack of understanding that they lead me to question the value of the rest of their arguments. If you're a Post-Tribulation believer, here are just a few of the false claims that make us question whether you're being intellectually honest in approaching this subject:

- "Pre-tribbers think they'll escape before things get bad." This is simply not true.

- "Every generation has faced tribulation, and yet they expect to escape it."

- "The word *rapture* is not in the Bible."

- "The rapture was never taught until the 1800s."

- "Pre-tribulation encourages people to hide their heads in the sand instead of engaging in the culture."

These are just a few examples, and they're all addressed in this book, but they represent a fundamental misunderstanding of the Pre-Tribulation views and history. If Post-Tribulation believers want to take part in meaningful dialogue, it's vital that they understand what Pre-Tribulationists actually believe, not some watered-down version meant to dismiss us out of hand.

By the way, this can be done on both sides and I don't expect them to get it right every time. I certainly miss it in my attempts to understand their position from time to time. Let's strive for accuracy, mutual respect, and honest representation. Only then can we have a truly productive discussion about the timing of the Lord's return.

THE CASE OF THE MISSING CHURCH

Those who oppose the concept of the Pre-Tribulation Rapture often say it's not in the Bible and challenge us to provide one verse communicating this truth. I have provided many verses already and I normally go even further than that by giving them a book: 1 Thessalonians. However, few fail to turn that question around on the Post-Tribber. Where's your verse? If the Post-Tribulation position is correct, then why is there an apparent absence of the Church during the detailed descriptions of the Tribulation in the book of Revelation? This observation isn't just a minor footnote. Remember that the Tribulation and the Day of the Lord is the most discussed event in the entirety of the Bible. We have more details about this event than any other, and yet there's not one verse that places the Church in this period of time.

Now, why is this significant? If the Church were to go through the Tribulation, as the Post-Tribulation position suggests, we'd expect to see some mention of it during these critical chapters. After all, the Church is a central figure in God's plan, and guidance or encouragement would be essential for believers facing such unprecedented trials. However, instead of the Church, we see 144,000 Jewish evangelists being used by God.

Why do the first three chapters of Revelation focus so heavily on the Church, and then suddenly, after John is caught up to Heaven in Revelation 4:1, the narrative shifts to a distinctly Jewish context? This abrupt change isn't just a mere "argument from silence."

An argument from silence occurs when someone draws a conclusion based on the absence of statements rather than the presence of evidence. In many cases, such arguments are weak because the lack of mention doesn't necessarily indicate non-existence or irrelevance. For example, if a historical document doesn't mention a particular event, it doesn't conclusively prove that the event didn't happen, it might have been omitted for various reasons.

However, in the case of Revelation, the silence regarding the Church during the detailed accounts of the Tribulation (chapters 6 through 18) is striking and significant. When a text that previously emphasized the Church suddenly stops mentioning it, especially during a period where its presence would be expected, the absence becomes a form of evidence in itself. Combine that with the fact that the focus shifts dramatically to Israel and Jewish themes, such as the 144,000 from the twelve tribes of Israel (Revelation 7:4-8) and the rebuilding of the temple (Revelation 11:1-2).

While arguments from silence are typically considered weak in other contexts, when the central issue revolves around the absence of the Church, this silence assumes greater evidentiary significance.

It's worth noting that while the Church isn't mentioned, the term *saints* does appear during the Tribulation (Revelation 13:7). These "saints" refer to individuals who come to faith during the Tribulation period, often called "Tribulation Saints," rather than the Church as we know it today. As we learned in previous chapters, the term *saints* is used in both the Old and New Testaments to describe God's people but is not specifically God's Church.

The fact that the word *ecclesia* is not mentioned during the Tribulation is only part of our argument. It's not just that the term *church* is absent, there is no reference to the Church in any form throughout the entire Tribulation period on earth. When we point out this argument from silence, some critics claim that the Church is also not specifically mentioned as being in Heaven during this time. However, this isn't true.

When faced with this counter-argument, I often ask, "Are you saying that no part of the Church is in Heaven during this period?" Even those who hold a Post-Tribulationist view must admit that many believers are present in Heaven at this point, so the absence of the word *ecclesia* in Heaven is really a moot point. In fact, there are compelling reasons to believe that the Church is present in Heaven during the Tribulation, even if not explicitly called by that name.

Consider, for instance, the 24 elders described in Revelation chapters 4 and 5. These elders are often seen as representative of the Church, clothed in white robes, crowned, and worshipping God before His throne, symbols that align with believers who have already received their rewards. Moreover, in Revelation 19, we clearly see the Bride of Christ, which is unmistakably the Church, already in Heaven, prepared and ready for the marriage supper of the Lamb. The language there is not future tense; it depicts the Bride already glorified, not still on earth enduring the horrors of The Tribulation. This is powerful evidence that the Church is present with Jesus in Heaven while God's judgments unfold upon the earth.

So while critics may try to suggest otherwise, the reality is that the absence of the word *church* during the Tribulation is significant. It underscores the difference in God's focus during this period while showing us that the true Bride is safe in the presence of her Savior.

The fact remains that there is not one verse that places the Church within the time of the tribulation.

NO TIME FOR THE JUDGMENT SEAT OF CHRIST

One of the biggest challenges for the Post-Tribulation view is finding a place for the Judgment Seat of Christ. The Bema Seat, where believers will stand before Jesus and be rewarded for their faithfulness, service, and obedience, is a fundamental event in God's prophetic timeline. We've already addressed this in a previous chapter, but it's an important point.

The Post-Tribulation view leaves no clear moment for this judgment to take place. If believers are raptured at the end of the Tribulation, meeting Christ in the air only to immediately turn around and descend with Him to establish His Kingdom, when exactly are we to be judged and rewarded? There is simply no time slot available in this scenario for the necessary evaluation of the believer's life and the dispensing of rewards.

In the Pre-Tribulation framework, believers are raptured before the Tribulation begins, and it is during this time in Heaven that the Bema Seat Judgment takes place. This period allows for the full assessment of each believer's life, providing rewards for faithful service before returning to earth with Christ for the Millennial Kingdom. This fits perfectly with the narrative represented in Revelation where we see believers in Heaven already possessing their white robes and rewards.

In contrast, the Post-Tribulation view awkwardly forces believers to skip over this event or to believe that it somehow happens in a rush during the descent, which diminishes its importance. The Post-Tribulation position struggles to provide a plausible place for this event, highlighting another fundamental flaw in its eschatological framework.

THE CASE OF THE MISSING RESURRECTION

The absence of any mention of the glorious event of the Rapture in the detailed description of Christ's return in Revelation 19 and 20 is a significant issue for the Post-Tribulation view. If the Rapture, arguably the pinnacle of Christ's redemptive work for believers, were to occur simultaneously with His Second Coming, we would expect it to be explicitly described at that pivotal moment. Instead, we see Jesus descending, defeating His enemies, binding satan, and then, only afterward, the resurrection of the Tribulation saints. The lack of any mention of the Church's resurrection or Rapture during this momentous sequence seems odd and makes the Post-Tribulation timeline feel inconsistent with the actual flow of events presented in Scripture.

The silence here speaks volumes, making it clear that the glorification of the Bride must have already taken place, in perfect alignment with the Pre-Tribulation view.

I dive deeper into this when I answer more questions in Chapter 9 where we explore what the Bible means when it refers to the "First Resurrection." For now, the critical takeaway is this:

> Nowhere in Scripture do we see the Rapture, or the resurrection, or the glorification of the Church happening after the Tribulation, nor do we see it when Jesus comes to the earth.

We aren't waiting for wrath...we are waiting for Jesus.

POST-TRIBULATION TIMELINE

The Post-Tribulation position faces a significant problem with its timeline when we examine the order of events described in Revelation 19 and 20. According to Post-Tribulation proponents, believers are caught up, resurrected, and glorified as we meet Jesus in the air while He descends to earth. After this, they say, we immediately follow Him as He defeats His enemies and establishes His Kingdom.

However, in Revelation 19, Jesus descends and defeats His enemies, the antichrist, and the armies gathered against Him. Then, in Revelation 20, an angel binds satan for a thousand years. Only after these events do we see the resurrection of the Tribulation saints who were martyred.

If the Post-Tribulation timeline were correct, we would expect to see the Rapture and resurrection of the Church happening alongside Jesus's return, before He defeats His enemies. The Bible's timeline contradicts the order proposed by the Post-Tribulation view. Rather than harmonizing with Scripture, their argument creates an inconsistency that weakens their case.

NO SHEEP OR GOATS?

Here's another timeline issue. One of the challenges for the post-tribulation view lies in reconciling the Judgment of the Sheep and the Goats as described by Jesus in Matthew 25:31-46 with the idea of a single, end-of-Tribulation Rapture. If all believers are raptured at the conclusion of the Tribulation, who exactly are the "sheep" and "goats" standing before Christ to be separated?

Let's break this down: according to the Post-Tribulation view, Jesus returns at the end of the Tribulation, rapturing all believers (even though there's no mention of this resurrection in Revelation 19). Following this, the Millennial Kingdom begins. But there's an immediate problem…if all believers are glorified in their resurrected bodies at the Rapture, and the unbelievers are judged, why does there need to be a follow up "Sheep and Goats" judgment. The glorification of the saints would have already done the separating.

The Bible also says that there will be a population of people inhabiting the Millennial Kingdom who have natural bodies. There will be a continuation of natural life including, marriage, childbirth, work, and even death. Here's what the Bible says:

> *They shall not labour in vain, nor bring forth for trouble; for they are the seed of the blessed of the Lord, and their offspring with them*
>
> (Isaiah 65:23 KJV).

Isaiah describes the reign of the Messiah as a time when death in childbirth will no longer occur, a period marked by health and longevity (Isaiah 65:20-23). This prophecy cannot be referring to resurrected believers, who will have glorified bodies. Instead, it's referring to those who survived the Tribulation and entered the Millennial Kingdom in their natural, mortal state.

Isaiah 65:21-22 (KJV) goes on to describe normal human activities: *"And they shall build houses, and inhabit them; and they shall plant vineyards, and eat the fruit of them. They shall not build, and another inhabit; they shall not plant, and another eat...."* Glorified saints wouldn't need to farm or eat, so these verses must refer to mortal humans engaging in normal life activities.

Ezekiel 47:12 (KJV) speaks of leaves that are for healing during this time:

> *And by the river upon the bank thereof, on this side and on that side, shall grow all trees for meat, whose leaf shall not fade, neither shall the fruit thereof be consumed: it shall bring forth new fruit according to his months, because their waters they issued out of the sanctuary: and the fruit thereof shall be for meat, and the leaf thereof for medicine.*

Glorified bodies wouldn't need healing, so this verse implies the presence of mortal humans who do.

Death, though rare, will also be present. *"There shall be no more thence an infant of days, nor an old man that hath not filled his days: for the child shall die an hundred years old; but the sinner being an hundred years old shall be accursed"* (Isaiah 65:20 KJV). This verse not only proves the presence of death (albeit at advanced ages) but also indicates natural human lifespans, though greatly extended.

There will be blessings for those who worship God with their offerings and curses for those who refuse:

> *And it shall come to pass, that every one that is left of all the nations which came against Jerusalem shall even go up from year to*

year to worship the King, the Lord of hosts, and to keep the feast of
tabernacles. And it shall be, that whoso will not come up of all the
families of the earth unto Jerusalem to worship the King, the Lord
of hosts, even upon them shall be no rain

(Zechariah 14:16-17 KJV).

It's clear that believers in glorified bodies during the Millennial Kingdom won't need rain for crops, nor will they face judgment due to disobedience. These needs are irrelevant for those whose nature has been transformed. Instead, these verses are directed at new generations born during this period, living in natural bodies. These people will still be subject to the natural order and the laws of obedience, and, in the end, their loyalty to God will be tested. It's this group that must rely on rain for their crops and is subject to discipline if they fail to worship the King as commanded. The Millennial Kingdom isn't just about peace, it's about giving humanity one last opportunity to live under Christ's perfect rule, with their faithfulness being tested before eternity begins.

And when the thousand years are expired, Satan shall be loosed out
of his prison, and shall go out to deceive the nations which are in the
four quarters of the earth, Gog and Magog, to gather them together
to battle: the number of whom is as the sand of the sea

(Revelation 20:7-8 KJV).

Notice how the population of the earth, heavily decimated during the Tribulation and then further reduced at the judgment of the nations, is miraculously restored during the Millennial Reign of Christ. The earth becomes teeming with life once again. This period is marked by prosperity, health, and longevity. Now, if the post-tribulation position is true, the question is: about whom do they believe these verses are talking?

If all believers are raptured and glorified at the Second Coming, and the wicked are judged, who is left in natural bodies to repopulate the earth during the Millennium? Without the Tribulation survivors entering the Millennium, there's no one left to fulfill these prophecies, and the Post-Tribulation position struggles to provide a coherent explanation for this reality.

The Sheep and Goats Judgment is described as a separation of the righteous ("sheep") from the wicked ("goats") at the return of Christ. No sinner will enter this Kingdom (1 Corinthians 6:9-10). The sheep are allowed to enter into the Kingdom, while the goats are cast away. If all believers are raptured and glorified, there would be no "sheep" left in natural bodies to enter the Millennial Kingdom in their current state. The Post-Tribulation position essentially collapses in on itself here because it leaves no clear candidates for those who populate the Kingdom in natural bodies.

WARNING: SERIOUS DOCTRINAL PROBLEMS AHEAD

Because this is so clearly laid out in Scripture, some defenders of the Post-Tribulation position try to argue that those who were simply "nice to Israel" will be the ones permitted to enter the Millennial Kingdom. But have they truly considered the implications of this argument? If that were the case, it would imply that salvation is not required to enter Christ's Kingdom and you can bypass faith in Jesus altogether. Should we then alter our entire approach to evangelism and proclaim that there are actually two ways to salvation? One: trust in Jesus for eternal life, or Two: just be kind to the Jewish people, and you're in. It's absurd. This line of thinking completely contradicts the core of the Gospel message and undermines the exclusive nature of salvation through Christ. The idea that merely being nice to Israel could earn someone a place in Christ's Kingdom falls apart when you take a serious look at the doctrinal ramifications.

In the Pre-Tribulation view, however, this puzzle has a clear solution. After the Rapture, many people will come to faith during the Tribulation period, and they are referred to as "Tribulation Saints." At the return of Christ, these believers are not raptured or glorified but enter the Millennial Kingdom in their natural bodies as the "sheep." This allows them to marry, have children, and fulfill the prophecies of a growing population throughout the thousand-year reign of Christ.

On a side note, these new generations born during the Millennial Reign of Christ are the reason why the devil is released for a short time at the end of that period. These individuals will have only known life under Christ's perfect rule, where righteousness and peace prevail. Satan's release serves as a test and an opportunity for them to make their own choice, to decide whether to follow Christ or to be deceived by satan. It underscores God's respect for free will, giving these people the chance to choose whom they will serve, just as other generations before them. God so values freedom that He gives all of us the opportunity to choose against Him.

This question alone should be enough to rule out Post-Tribulationism as a valid possibility, and it also highlights the Pre-Tribulation Rapture as a more coherent framework for interpreting the biblical narrative.

GLORIFIED REBELS?

We are dealing with mysteries that have been hidden since the foundation of the world, and I don't believe that any of us can claim a perfect eschatology exists on earth today. Every position has its share of seemingly unanswered questions. So instead of aiming for absolute certainty, we should ask ourselves: *Which interpretation checks the most boxes and resolves the most questions?*

The Pre-Tribulation position stands out because it doesn't require ignoring or downplaying critical points that would otherwise cause major theological issues. Once we begin dismissing these key aspects as insignificant, we end up with proposals that only create more problems. For instance, some who hold to a Post-Tribulation perspective have gone as far as suggesting that everyone in the Millennium will have resurrected bodies. They think this settles the issue; but in reality, it makes things even worse.

At the end of the Millennial Reign of Christ, there will be a mass rebellion led by satan (as described in Revelation 20:7-9). Are we to believe that those who have already trusted in Christ, been born again, and received glorified bodies will then turn and rebel against God? This implies a form of "eternal insecurity" that contradicts everything we know about the glorified state of the redeemed. It simply doesn't fit with the biblical promise of eternal life. This kind of idea isn't just inconsistent, it shatters the idea of "Blessed Assurance."

THE FATHER'S HOUSE

Jesus's promise to His disciples in John 14:1-3 provides a compelling challenge to the Post-Tribulation perspective. The heart of every Christian leaps when they read these words:

> *Let not your heart be troubled: ye believe in God, believe also in me. In my Father's house are many mansions: if it were not so, I would have told you. I go to prepare a place for you. And if I go and prepare a place for you, I will come again, and receive you unto myself; that where I am, there ye may be also*
>
> (John 14:1-3 KJV).

Jesus here makes a direct and specific promise. He tells His followers that He is leaving to prepare a place for them and that He will return to receive them to Himself, so that they can be where He is. This language is clear, comforting, and filled with expectation. There is no ambiguity; Jesus is emphasizing His personal return to take His followers to a place He has prepared, in His Father's house.

If we take this promise literally, which is the natural reading of the text, it becomes difficult to reconcile it with the Post-Tribulational view. According to Post-Tribbers, Jesus comes back at the end of the Tribulation to establish His Kingdom on earth and then rules with His saints. We have no time to see this promised fulfilled. However, in John 14, Jesus promises to *"receive you unto myself"* and take His followers to a place He has prepared, which clearly refers to Heaven. The language here points to a removal of believers from earth to be with Jesus in the dwelling He has prepared above. It describes an intimate gathering of believers to be brought into the presence of God, not a triumphant descent to earth to fight alongside Jesus.

The Post-Tribulation view requires believers to meet Jesus in the air, only to make a U-turn and come back to earth with Him for judgment and His Millennial Reign. However, that's not what Jesus describes here.

So why is this promise in John 14 important? It underscores the Pre-Tribulation position that believers will be caught up to be with the Lord before the Tribulation begins, where they will be in the presence of God as Christ fulfills His promise. It's not about Jesus coming to earth and setting up His Kingdom immediately. Instead, it's about taking His Bride away, bringing them to a prepared place before the events of judgment unfold.

The key difference here is how we approach Scripture. A Pre-Tribulation view respects the literal interpretation of these words from Jesus. It allows the Bible to say what it means without forcing a spiritualized or symbolic meaning where one isn't necessary. The

Post-Tribulation perspective, however, has to reinterpret this promise to make it fit its timeline, either by suggesting it's symbolic or by reshaping its plain meaning.

This is why what you believe about the Rapture matters. It's not just a doctrinal debate; it's a reflection of how we approach God's Word. Do we take Jesus's words at face value? Do we believe that He means what He says and that He is preparing a real place for His followers, intending to come back and take us to be with Him? Or do we dismiss these clear promises as mere allegory or figurative language?

John 14 stands as a clear, unambiguous promise from the One who always keeps His Word.

CHRISTIANS WILL BE PROTECTED?

Another significant problem with the Post-Tribulational perspective is the notion that believers will be protected supernaturally during the outpouring of God's wrath on earth, much like Moses and the children of Israel were protected when God poured out the plagues on Egypt. On the surface, this comparison might seem plausible, but it doesn't hold up under closer scrutiny for a couple of crucial reasons.

First, when Jesus spoke about the end times, He did not compare it to the time of Moses and the plagues in Egypt. Instead, He specifically compared the last days to the times of Noah and Lot. Jesus said, *"As it was in the days of Noah, so it will be also in the days of the Son of Man"* (Luke 17:26 NKJV) and *"Likewise also as it was in the days of Lot…"* (Luke 17:28 KJV). In both of these cases, God removed the righteous before pouring out His judgment. Noah and his family were lifted above the floodwaters, and Lot was taken out of Sodom before fire and brimstone rained down. God ensured their removal before judgment, a pattern that stands in stark contrast to the Post-Tribulation view of believers enduring God's wrath while being shielded from harm, like during the Exodus. Jesus's chosen analogies clearly point to a removal of the righteous before judgment falls.

Second, the idea that believers will be supernaturally preserved during the outpouring of God's wrath is not supported by Scripture. Yes, there is an instance of divine protection, but it specifically refers to the 144,000 Jewish evangelists sealed by God:

> *And I saw another angel ascending from the east, having the seal of the living God: and he cried with a loud voice to the four angels, to whom it was given to hurt the earth and the sea, Saying, Hurt not the earth, neither the sea, nor the trees, till we have sealed the servants of our God in their foreheads*
>
> (Revelation 7:2-3 KJV).

The sealing of the 144,000 is a clear promise of protection for them alone. Beyond this, there is no other specific promise that believers will be divinely shielded during the Tribulation. In fact, the Bible paints a different picture altogether, clearly stating that the antichrist will be given power to overcome the saints:

> *And it was given unto him to make war with the saints, and to overcome them: and power was given him over all kindreds, and tongues, and nations*
>
> (Revelation 13:7 KJV).

This directly contradicts the idea that believers will be safely protected throughout the Tribulation. Instead, Scripture speaks of a time when believers will face unprecedented persecution, with the antichrist given the authority to wage war against the saints and even prevail over them.

In addition to the persecution of the antichrist, the saints during the Tribulation are not guaranteed any supernatural protection from the plagues and judgments that God pours out on the world. They will face the scorching heat from the sun (Revelation 16:8-9), endure the waters turned to blood (Revelation 16:4-6), and experience the agony of widespread darkness (Revelation 16:10-11). If believers were divinely protected from these catastrophic events, they would likely fare much better than the unrepentant world, and the Christian population would quickly outnumber the wicked as the followers of the antichrist perish by the billions. This makes the Post-Tribulation idea of supernatural preservation untenable, as the Bible clearly depicts a world consumed by unimaginable suffering with no such guarantees for those who come to faith during this time.

So when we look at these arguments, we see that the idea of supernatural preservation during the Tribulation simply doesn't hold up. Beyond the 144,000, there is no scriptural evidence that believers will be immune from harm.

IMMEDIATELY *AFTER* THE TRIBULATION...

*Immediately after the tribulation of those days shall the sun be darkened, and the moon shall not give her light, and the stars shall fall from heaven, and the powers of the heavens shall be shaken: And then shall appear the sign of the Son of man in heaven: and then shall all the tribes of the earth mourn, and they shall see the Son of man coming in the clouds of heaven with power and great glory. And he shall send his angels with a great sound of a trumpet, and they shall gather together his **elect** from the four winds, from one end of heaven to the other*

(Matthew 24:29-31 KJV).

The argument that Matthew 24:29-31 refers to the Rapture is common, but a careful examination of the context and language reveals something different. The passage begins with the phrase *"Immediately after the tribulation of those days."* This timing is crucial as well as who he's speaking to.

In Rapture passages, it is Jesus who calls His Church to Himself. The gathering here by angels is more consistent with a gathering of the surviving Tribulation saints rather than the Rapture, especially since no resurrection is mentioned.

The term "elect" in Matthew 24:31 can lead to some confusion, as it is often used to refer to the Church. However, in this context, the "elect" refers to the faithful remnant of Israel. Throughout Matthew 24, Jesus is speaking from a Jewish perspective, mentioning the Sabbath (verse 20) and the abomination of desolation (verse 15), which are especially significant to Israel. The context leans heavily toward addressing Israel and those who would come to faith during the Tribulation.

Matthew 24:29-31 is not a description of the Rapture but rather of the Second Coming of Christ. The timing, context, and role of angels all point toward the gathering of those who have survived the Tribulation while trusting in God.

9

MORE QUESTIONS

In this chapter, I delve into some of the most frequently asked questions and common objections surrounding the Rapture of the Church. We will examine:

- Did Darby invent the Rapture?
- What about the Last Trump?
- Are there two second comings?
- Which comes first, the wheat or the tares?
- What is the First Resurrection?
- When was the book of Revelation written?
- Will the world get better or worse?
- Is the Rapture in Matthew 24?

Let's dive right in!

DID DARBY INVENT THE RAPTURE?

For me, the claim that John Nelson Darby invented the Pre-Tribulation Rapture serves as a kind of litmus test. When someone trots this out, I know they probably got their information from someone else's YouTube video or an echo chamber of bad theology. You know how easy it is to spot when someone's perspective has been shaped solely by one political news source, leaving them out of touch with

THEY LIED TO YOU ABOUT THE RAPTURE

reality? The same principle applies to the claim that Darby invented the Rapture: it's a misconception that's remarkably simple to disprove.

The concept of the Pre-Tribulation Rapture is not a new idea cooked up in the 1800s. The evidence proves otherwise. There's some incredible research out there that puts this lie to bed once and for all. If you want to further explore the history of these doctrines, pick up and read: *Dispensationalism Before Darby: Seventeenth-Century and Eighteenth-Century English Apocalypticism* by William C. Watson.

Watson meticulously lays out how Pre-Tribulation and dispensational beliefs were very much present well before Darby came on the scene, quoting ministers of those eras in their own words and in full context. Two additional great resources: *Pre-Trib Findings in the Early Church Fathers* by Lee W. Brainard and *The Rapture: The Pretribulational Rapture of the Church Viewed From the Bible and the Ancient Church* by Ken Johnson.

The evidence is out and the verdict is in. The idea that God will take His people out before the outpouring of His wrath has been present in every century of the Church. To assert that the Pre-Tribulational Rapture is something Darby dreamed up is like looking at the ocean and saying water doesn't exist. It's ignoring the facts.

Now some might say that Christians throughout history didn't always articulate the Rapture the way we do today. That's fair. But to suggest the essence of this belief, the anticipation of Christ's return, and the transformation of the faithful before the tribulation wasn't there is simply false. The early church fathers, medieval theologians, and even the reformers spoke of this hope in various forms.

The way the conversation normally goes is that these detractors say, "There is zero evidence that a rapture of any kind was taught before Darby." Then once you show them evidence, they say, "Well in context they weren't really pre-tribbers, they were more pre-wrath." Now they're moving the goalpost. To be clear, the only main difference between Pre-Tribulation and Pre-Wrath is when they say the wrath of God starts. They both teach that the Church is not appointed to wrath, which is the heart of Pre-Tribulation theology and what the critics attack. They started this by saying that the concept of being delivered from the wrath of the tribulation was not taught throughout church history, and they can't squirm out of it now that history is not on their side. This idea was only able to survive as long as we didn't have internet and people couldn't research this on their own.

THE DARBY DECEPTION

The story that Darby was influenced by a young Scottish girl named Margaret MacDonald is another one of those baseless myths that somehow refuses to die. According to this narrative, MacDonald had a supposed prophetic vision in the 1830s about the Pre-Tribulation Rapture, which some claim was demonic, and that this is where Darby got his idea. But when you dig into the historical documents and her writings, her vision doesn't even match what we understand today as the Pre-Tribulation Rapture. In fact, it leans more toward a Mid or even Post-Tribulation view, with believers enduring tribulation and facing the antichrist. There's also no evidence that Darby ever even met her or drew from her vision. It's simply a lie that's been repeated so often that people take it as fact.

What Darby did was systematize Dispensationalism, organizing and articulating a framework that helped believers understand the sequence of end-time events more clearly. He provided a theological lens through which we could view the Rapture, Tribulation, and the Millennial Reign. He actually got this from his pastors who got it from theirs and it wasn't new. Darby simply helped to popularize it.

Keep in mind that those who insist there is *no* reference to anything resembling the Pre-Tribulation Rapture are actually boxing themselves into a corner. They bear a much higher burden of proof compared to those who believe in the Pre-Tribulation Rapture. It's like someone trying to argue that there's no gold in China. They would have a much harder task than someone claiming there is. Why? Because proving there's no gold would require scouring all of China, every mine, every jewelry box, every bank vault, every corner. But the person who claims there is gold only needs to find one earring to prove his point.

In the same way, those denying any Pre-Tribulation references have set an impossible standard for themselves. All I need is a single quote, clearly in context, that supports what we believe about the Rapture, and suddenly, their sweeping argument crumbles.

Let's look at a few quotes from church history:

PRE-DARBY WRITINGS

Ephraem the Syrian, writing in the fourth century, said: For all the saints and elect of God are gathered, prior to the tribulation that is to come, and are taken to the Lord, lest they see the confusion that is to overwhelm the world because of our sins.

—Pseudo-Ephraem (4th Century)[1]

And therefore, when in the end the Church shall be suddenly caught up from this, it is said, "There shall be tribulation such as has not been since the beginning, neither shall be."

—Irenaeus of Lyon (AD 120–202)[2]

Go therefore and declare to the elect of the Lord his mighty deeds and say to them that this beast is a type of the great tribulation which is to come. If you therefore prepare yourselves and with your whole heart turn to the Lord in repentance, then shall ye be able to escape it, if your heart is pure and blameless....

—The Shepherd of Hermas (AD 150)[3]

After this, [is] our gathering together unto Christ at His coming... [that is, the] saints being translated into the air... [so that] they may be preserved during the conflagration of the earth, and the works thereof: 2 Pet. 3.10. that as Noah and his family were preserved from the deluge by being lifted up above the waters in the ark, so should the saints at the conflagration be lifted up in the clouds, unto their ark, Christ, to be preserved there from the deluge of fire, wherein the wicked shall be consumed.

—Joseph Mede (1586-1639) as cited by William Watson in
Dispensationalism Before Darby[4]

In a commentary on Revelation 6:14, Victorinus of Petrovium (AD 250-300) said, "And the heaven withdrew as a scroll that is rolled up.] For the heaven to be rolled away, that is, that the Church shall be taken away."[5]

The saints shall be caught up into the air, and so escape the conflagration of the world.

—Increase Mather (1600s)[6]

The Souls of the glorified Saints shall descend and be united to their own Bodies, and then ascend to meet the Lord in the Air, and the wicked are left behind on their dunghill the earth. These congregated Saints shall be admitted into one place, and state of Glory: They are before the throne of God...there is room enough in heaven for all the saints, In my Father's house, saith Christ, are many mansions.

—Oliver Haywood (1700)[7]

The report of these things does not disturb us, nor the spectacle itself. For the elect shall be gathered prior to the tribulation, so they shall not see the confusion and the great tribulation coming upon the unrighteous world.

—Ephraem the Syrian (AD 372)[8]

The point is, this isn't some newfangled doctrine. The Rapture has always been part of the Church's hope. Dismissing it as a 19th-century invention is, frankly, lazy scholarship. The historical record is rich with examples of believers who held to this view, long before Darby ever penned a word.

It's important to note that there were seasons in church history when teaching Pre-Millennialism, or even mentioning the Rapture of the Church, would be considered outright heresy. During these times, preaching or publishing such teachings could lead to severe persecution, even death. The reason for this suppression was the rise of the state church. The idea of a coming Kingdom posed a direct threat to those in power. A message that encouraged believers to look toward a future divine Kingdom, rather than submitting entirely to the authority of the earthly regime, was dangerous. The state church needed people focused on the here and now, under their control, not looking up with hopeful anticipation of Christ's reign. They aimed for complete control over the masses, and the concept of an impending Kingdom, where God would ultimately take over, was a narrative they could not afford to let spread. So, they stamped it out wherever possible, silencing those who dared to lift the eyes of the faithful toward a hope beyond earthly power.

Ultimately, it doesn't really matter what the early church fathers taught or how popular a doctrine has been throughout history. The real question is, "What does the Bible say?" This same line of reasoning could be applied to doctrines like *justification by faith*. Before Martin Luther nailed his 95 Theses to the door of the Wittenberg church, this wasn't a widely understood or emphasized doctrine.

Often when we discuss these topics, someone will challenge us, asking, "Why are you talking about the early church fathers? Why don't you just quote Scripture?" They argue that no early church fathers taught this doctrine, and when we prove that they did, they suddenly pivot and ask why we're bothering to bring them up in the first place. The reality is, the early church fathers held some unusual beliefs and many hadn't yet systematized certain doctrines that we consider foundational today, like the Trinity. But there's no denying that some of them held to views that align with what we would now call Pre-Tribulation beliefs.

So the next time someone brings out the Darby myth, you will be ready. The evidence out there is clear, historical, and undeniable, for anyone who takes the time to look. Let them know that the truth isn't hiding; it's simply waiting for those willing to take an honest look at the facts.

WHAT ABOUT THE LAST TRUMP?

Behold, I shew you a mystery; We shall not all sleep, but we shall all be changed, In a moment, in the twinkling of an eye, at the last trump: for the trumpet shall sound, and the dead shall be raised incorruptible, and we shall be changed

(1 Corinthians 15:51-52 KJV).

When we talk about the *"last trump"* in 1 Corinthians 15, there's often a leap to connect it to the Seventh Trumpet in Revelation 11, as though Paul had this in mind while writing to the Corinthians. But here's the problem with that: Paul wrote his letter to the Corinthians around AD 53, while John received the Revelation of the Seven Trumpets roughly 40 years later, during his exile on the island of Patmos in AD 95.

Imagine if someone in 2025 is watching an old Monty Python skit about SPAM and thinks they're referring to spam emails. We all know that back in 1980, SPAM had nothing to do with the junk cluttering our inboxes, it was just salty, delicious canned meat. This is the mistake people are making by retroactively applying the Seventh Trumpet to Paul's earlier reference.

Paul wasn't talking about John's trumpet because it would have been impossible for him to do so. That would be like hearing someone in a video from 1980 mention "The Cloud" thinking they meant a data storage method instead of a fluffy thing in the sky. The same applies to terms like *virus, stream,* or *tablet*. These words carry different meanings today, and trying to apply a modern revelation to an old conversation just doesn't work.

So what could the "last trump" refer to? The context points us in a different direction. It's very likely tied to Jewish traditions because Paul expects them to know exactly what he's talking about. Some suggest that this is specifically referring to the Feast of Trumpets, known as Rosh Hashanah. During this feast, the shofar is blown a total of 100 times. The final blast, called the *Tekiah Gedolah* or Great Blast, is known as the last trump. It's the culmination of a series of trumpet calls intended to awaken and gather God's people, symbolizing the completion of God's plan and heralding the coming of the Messiah.

The shofar is blown throughout the Rosh Hashanah service in four segments:

- **30 Blasts** after the Torah Reading: These represent a call to repentance and reflection, as the people of God align themselves with His Word.

- **30 Blasts** during the Musaf Service: Symbolizing the additional offerings given during the Holy Days, they represent an extra measure of devotion, going beyond the norm to seek God's face.

- **30 Blasts** at the End of the Musaf: These blasts symbolize spiritual breakthrough and God's intervention in the lives of His people.

- **The Final 10 Blasts** (Tekiah Gedolah): The culmination of the entire series, this final trumpet sound is seen as the "last trump," signaling the ultimate arrival of the Messiah.

The last trump in Jewish tradition signifies an ending and a beginning. It's a divine wake-up call, a final proclamation that God's purposes are reaching their ultimate fulfillment. When Paul references *"the last trump"* in 1 Corinthians 15:52, it could be that he was pointing to this idea of the culmination of believers being gathered and transformed. The Church is being called home, and the last trump is the heavenly signal for that glorious event.

Ken Johnson, a respected scholar in the study of the Feasts of God, notes in his book *The Rapture,* that Pentecost was historically referred to as the Feast of the First Trumpet, whereas Rosh Hashanah was known as the Feast of the Last Trumpet.[9] This distinction offers deep prophetic significance, connecting the biblical feasts with God's redemptive timeline and helping us understand why Paul referred to the last trump in 1 Corinthians 15:52.

Others suggest that the last trump could be a reference to Numbers 10:1-3, where two silver trumpets were used to call the people together, signaling an assembly or a warning for war. In other places including Joel 2:1 and Jeremiah 4:5-6, the blowing of the trumpet also had the dual purpose to gather God's people and to sound an alarm. In this context, the last trump can be seen as God calling His people to gather, while signaling a final spiritual battle.

Whatever the last trump is, it is certain that it's not the Seventh Trumpet of Revelation. The thought that Paul was referring to a prophetic detail yet to be revealed to John decades later just doesn't align. Rather, this trumpet is most likely deeply tied to the Jewish

THE FEASTS OF GOD

The Feasts of God are viewed by some as prophetic symbols outlining God's redemptive plan. *The first four feasts—Passover, Unleavened Bread, First Fruits, and Pentecost—are believed by many to represent Jesus' crucifixion, burial, resurrection, and the outpouring of the Holy Spirit. We are said to be in the Church Age, seen as an intermission before the final feasts. Some suggest that the Feast of Trumpets points to the Rapture, the Day of Atonement signifies Christ's Second Coming, and Tabernacles foreshadows His Millennial Reign on Earth. Together, these feasts are thought to reflect God's plan from Christ's first coming to His future return.*

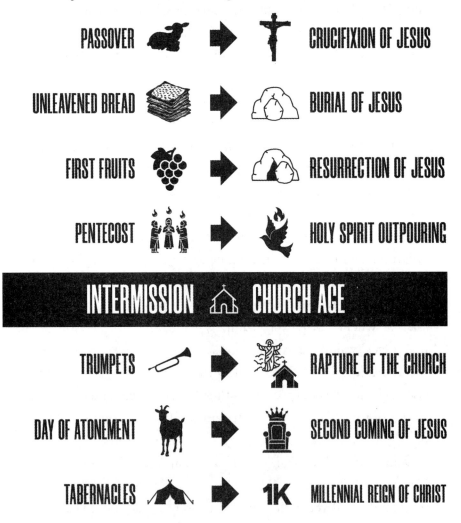

PASSOVER ➡ CRUCIFIXION OF JESUS

UNLEAVENED BREAD ➡ BURIAL OF JESUS

FIRST FRUITS ➡ RESURRECTION OF JESUS

PENTECOST ➡ HOLY SPIRIT OUTPOURING

INTERMISSION CHURCH AGE

TRUMPETS ➡ RAPTURE OF THE CHURCH

DAY OF ATONEMENT ➡ SECOND COMING OF JESUS

TABERNACLES ➡ 1K MILLENNIAL REIGN OF CHRIST

understanding of culmination and divine gathering, a truth that resonates not only with ancient prophecy but with our blessed hope in Christ's imminent return and the Rapture of His Church.

The last trump is a call to readiness, a call to victory, and ultimately, a call to be in the presence of our Lord forever. So whether we hear that final blast today or tomorrow, one thing is certain: it will be a sound unlike any other, and it will be a sound of completion, a sound of hope, and a sound that will change everything.

ARE THERE TWO SECOND COMINGS?

It seems like every decade or so, attacking the concept of the Rapture becomes a trendy hobby for critics. It's like a fad that comes in waves of popularity. When these attacks surface, one of the go-to arguments is to flippantly say, "There aren't going to be two second comings of Jesus." Statements like these get applause, laughter, and everyone nodding in agreement, but nobody ever stops to actually examine whether this clever quip holds any truth. So, let's take a closer look.

First, is anyone really claiming that there are two second comings? I don't know of any teacher or preacher who advocates for that. This is what you call a "straw man fallacy," which is a rhetorical tactic where someone misrepresents their opponent's argument just to easily knock it down. No one is teaching there are two "second advents." What we're saying is that the Bible teaches one Second Coming, but it happens in phases, almost like bookends.

When I hear someone make that claim, I often like to ask them, "How many first advents were there?" Usually, they seem caught off guard that anyone's actually questioning their bold statement. They stammer, "Just one." And that's when I respond, "Really? Are you sure about that? When exactly did that first advent occur? Was it when Jesus was conceived in Mary's womb? Was it when He was born in

Bethlehem? Or maybe it was when He amazed the teachers in the temple at age 12? Or perhaps it was at His baptism in the Jordan River when the heavens opened and the Father spoke?"

The point is, we never think of these separate moments as "multiple advents." They were all parts of His one First Coming, unfolding in stages.

Take the moment with Mary Magdalene after Jesus's resurrection: He told her not to touch Him because He hadn't yet ascended to the Father. Later, He invited Thomas to touch Him. So, did Jesus ascend and return between those moments? Of course He did. Was that His second coming or were there two first comings? These seem like silly questions because they are. We know that this was one advent that happened in phases. He revealed Himself first to Mary and then to a remnant before being made known to the masses.

There is one Second Coming that will unfold in phases. First, He comes for His Church, His remnant, and then to the masses. There's no contradiction here, just the unfolding plan of the God who operates beyond our simple timelines.

We must tread carefully when it comes to this particular argument and way of thinking because it resembles, almost eerily, the misconceptions many Jews hold about the Messiah. The reason many Jews rejected Jesus as Messiah is that they say, "There aren't going to be two comings of the Messiah." They can't fathom how the Old Testament prophecies could refer to two separate advents. In their minds, all these messianic prophecies would happen in one fell swoop and honestly, you can't blame them for thinking that way. Look at Isaiah 61:1-2 (KJV), which says:

> *The Spirit of the Lord God is upon me; because the Lord hath anointed me to preach good tidings unto the meek; he hath sent me to bind up the brokenhearted, to proclaim liberty to the captives, and the opening of the prison to them that are bound; to proclaim the*

*acceptable year of the Lord, and the day of vengeance of our God;
to comfort all that mourn.*

Jesus quoted this exact passage during His first sermon, recorded in Luke 4:18-21 (KJV):

The Spirit of the Lord is upon me, because he hath anointed me to preach the gospel to the poor; he hath sent me to heal the brokenhearted, to preach deliverance to the captives, and recovering of sight to the blind, to set at liberty them that are bruised, To preach the acceptable year of the Lord. And he closed the book....

Did you notice that Jesus closed the book in the middle of the prophecy? Isaiah continues by saying, *"To proclaim the acceptable year of the Lord, and the day of vengeance of our God"* (Isaiah 61:2 KJV). Jesus stopped short, leaving out the part about the *"day of vengeance,"* which points to His Second Coming and the judgment that will come with it.

Think about how there is zero indication in that verse that a 2,000-year gap would exist between these two events. It flows directly from *"...the acceptable year of the Lord..."* into *"...the day of vengeance..."* as if they happen back-to-back. It seems that a veil has existed over prophecies like this that keeps people from recognizing that these were two completely separate events wrapped up in one prophecy. With the benefit of hindsight, we see the distinction clearly, but sometimes it's difficult to see the forest for the trees when you're standing in it. Could the same thing be happening now with people who mock the idea of the Rapture and the Second Coming being separate phases of one glorious event?

When you start to unfold the details of the Second Coming, some stark differences become evident:

- In the Rapture, Jesus comes for His saints; whereas, at the Second Coming, He returns with His saints (1 Thessalonians 4:16-17 versus Revelation 19:14).

- The Rapture is a meeting in the air: believers are caught up to meet the Lord in the clouds. In contrast, the Second Coming involves Jesus's feet physically touching the Mount of Olives, splitting it in two (Zechariah 14:4).

- At the Rapture, the event is described as sudden, *"like a thief in the night"* (1 Thessalonians 5:2 NIV). The Second Coming, however, is an event that happens over time and *"every eye shall see"* (Revelation 1:7 KJV).

- At the Rapture, Jesus gathers His own (1 Thessalonians 4:16-17) while at the Second Coming, angels gather the elect (Matthew 24:31).

- Paul called the Rapture a mystery (1 Corinthians 15:51), not revealed in the Old Testament, while the Second Coming and resurrection of God's people is predicted in the Old Testament.

- During the Rapture, Jesus takes believers to be with Him in Heaven (John 14:2-3). In the Second Coming, He returns to rule and reign on earth (Revelation 20:4).

- The Rapture is a rescue mission for the Church, delivering believers from the wrath to come (1 Thessalonians 1:10). The Second Coming is a judgment mission, bringing wrath and vengeance upon those who oppose God (Revelation 19:15).

These differences are significant, which should cause us to be cautious about dismissing them, especially since history has already shown that misunderstanding the timing and sequence of God's plans can lead to monumental errors, like missing the Messiah altogether.

WHICH COMES FIRST, THE WHEAT OR THE TARES?

Matthew 13:30 presents a parable that often gets cited by Post-Tribulation believers as a stumbling block for the Pre-Tribulation perspective. Let's read it now:

> *Let both grow together until the harvest: and in the time of harvest*
> *I will say to the reapers, Gather ye together first the tares, and bind*
> *them in bundles to burn them: but gather the wheat into my barn*
> (Matthew 13:30 KJV).

On the surface, it might seem that Jesus is saying the wicked (the "tares") are taken up first before the righteous (the "wheat"). Post-Tribulation proponents often use this to argue that the Pre-Tribulation Rapture is invalid, implying that the judgment of the wicked must come first. But there's more here than meets the eye.

First, we need to understand that this passage is not actually about the Rapture. It is about the Final Judgment at the end of the age, when Jesus separates the wicked from the righteous, not when He gathers His Church to Himself. The context of Matthew 13 makes it clear that this parable isn't about the snatching away of the Bride of Christ. It's a broad parable meant to teach us about the ultimate separation of good and evil.

Furthermore, the Post-Tribulation position is itself contradicted when we cross-reference Jesus's own teachings later in the same chapter. In Matthew 13:48-50, He shares another parable about a dragnet and the separation of fish:

> *Which, when it was full, they drew to shore, and sat down, and*
> *gathered the good into vessels, but cast the bad away. So shall it be*

> *at the end of the world: the angels shall come forth, and sever the*
> *wicked from among the just, and shall cast them into the furnace of*
> *fire: there shall be wailing and gnashing of teeth*
>
> (Matthew 13:48-50 KJV).

Here, Jesus is teaching about the good and bad fish. Interestingly, it is the good fish that are gathered first, and then the bad are separated and cast away. This seems to directly contradict the interpretation of the previous parable, if one were to use it to argue for a Post-Tribulation Rapture. In fact, this entire chapter highlights that there are distinct and different gatherings at different points in time.

Both parables describe God's final sorting process and His ultimate justice. Just as a farmer deals with the harvest, or a fisherman sorts out the catch, Jesus describes an end-time gathering in which each individual is judged.

Finally, it's important to note that even the Post-Tribulation time-line does not support the gathering of the wicked before the righteous. In their framework, the righteous are taken up to meet Jesus in the air and then make an immediate U-turn to return to earth for the judgment of the wicked. In other words, according to the Post-Tribulation position, the righteous are gathered first, which directly contradicts the very point they often try to make using Matthew 13:30.

So if Post-Tribulation advocates bring up this argument, they're actually arguing against their own position. They say the tares are taken up first, yet their timeline has the righteous being caught up before judgment. It's an inconsistency that reveals the fundamental weakness of this view and further affirms the coherence of the Pre-Tribulation position.

WHAT IS THE FIRST RESURRECTION?

Let's take a close look at Revelation 20:4-6 (KJV):

And I saw thrones, and they sat upon them, and judgment was given unto them: and I saw the souls of them that were beheaded for the witness of Jesus, and for the word of God, and which had not worshipped the beast, neither his image, neither had received his mark upon their foreheads, or in their hands; and they lived and reigned with Christ a thousand years.

But the rest of the dead lived not again until the thousand years were finished. This is the first resurrection. Blessed and holy is he that hath part in the first resurrection: on such the second death hath no power, but they shall be priests of God and of Christ, and shall reign with him a thousand years.

According to these verses, we see a resurrection that clearly takes place after the Second Coming of Christ, as it describes the beheaded martyrs from the Tribulation. These saints are raised to reign with Christ during His Millennial Kingdom. This is described as the first resurrection.

The phrase "first resurrection" used in Revelation 20:4-6 has caused some confusion, especially because we see other resurrections in the Bible that occurred before this event. So, what does it mean by "first"? The key to understanding this lies in recognizing that the first resurrection refers to a category of resurrections, specifically, those who are righteous. There are two resurrections: the resurrection of the righteous and the resurrection of the wicked.

We know that this isn't referring to the first resurrection ever because Jesus was raised from the dead. Jesus was the first to be resurrected in a glorified body, becoming the *"firstfruits of them that slept"* (1 Corinthians 15:20 KJV). His resurrection marks the beginning of God's plan to raise all of His people. Furthermore, in Matthew 27:52-53, after Jesus rose from the dead, many bodies of the saints came out of the graves and appeared to many. This was another resurrection, though limited in scope, occurring right after Christ's victory over death.

So if these resurrections occurred before Revelation 20, how can the resurrection of the Tribulation martyrs be called the first resurrection? The answer is that the first resurrection refers to the category of all resurrections unto life and those who belong to Christ.

THE JEWISH HARVEST ANALOGY

To better understand the first resurrection, it helps to compare it to the Jewish agricultural cycle, which had two main harvests. The first harvest included three stages:

First Fruits: This was the initial portion of the harvest, representing the best and earliest part. In the context of resurrection, this refers to Jesus Christ. He is the first fruits of the resurrection (1 Corinthians 15:20-23).

Main Harvest: This represents the resurrection of the Church, or those who are "in Christ" at the time of the Rapture (1 Thessalonians 4:16-17). This includes believers who have died in Christ and those alive at His coming, who will be caught up to meet Him in the air.

Gleanings: In Jewish agriculture, the gleanings were the leftovers gathered at the end. Prophetically speaking, the gleanings include the resurrection of the Tribulation martyrs and Old Testament saints. The Tribulation martyrs are those who come to faith during the Tribulation and die for their testimony, while the Old Testament saints are those who trusted in God's promise before Christ's first coming.

All of these stages form the first harvest or the first resurrection which is a collective term that encompasses all resurrections of the righteous.

In contrast, the second resurrection is the resurrection of the unrighteous. This occurs at the Great White Throne of Judgment described in Revelation 20:11-15. This is the resurrection of those who rejected God, and it is a resurrection unto judgment and condemnation.

THE 1ˢᵀ RESURRECTION

THE RESURRECTION OF THE RIGHTEOUS

THE 2ᴺᴰ RESURRECTION

THE RESURRECTION OF THE UNRIGHTEOUS

THE GREAT WHITE THRONE JUDGMENT

STAGE 1

FIRST FRUITS: RESURRECTION OF CHRIST

STAGE 2

HARVEST: RESURRECTION & TRANSLATION OF THE CHURCH

STAGE 3

GLEANINGS: TRIBULATION MARTYRS & O.T. SAINTS

THE MILLENNIUM (1,000 YEARS)

NEW HEAVENS & NEW EARTH

ETERNITY

So, much like the Jewish agricultural harvest, the first resurrection takes place in the phases just listed. All these phases make up the first resurrection, which is why Revelation 20 can describe the resurrection of the Tribulation martyrs as part of the first resurrection. It's not the first resurrection ever, but it belongs to the first kind a resurrection to eternal life and glory.

The Post-Tribulation view often presents the idea that the Rapture and the Second Coming are a simultaneous event, with believers caught up and immediately brought back with Jesus as He comes to judge the earth. However, Revelation 20 seems to contradict this. If the Rapture took place at the same time as the Second Coming, with all the righteous being caught up, then there would be no need for this specific resurrection of Tribulation martyrs after Jesus's return.

The Pre-Tribulation perspective, on the other hand, makes sense of this sequence. In this view, the Rapture occurs before the Tribulation, taking up the Church. Then, during the Tribulation, many come to faith and suffer martyrdom under the antichrist. These Tribulation martyrs are part of this subsequent resurrection in Revelation 20, where they receive their glorified bodies and reign with Christ.

WHEN WAS THE BOOK OF REVELATION WRITTEN?

The dating of the book of Revelation plays a significant role in interpreting eschatology, particularly for those holding to a preterist view. Preterists argue that Revelation was written before AD 70, around AD 65, because their eschatology depends on interpreting the events described in Revelation as having already been fulfilled in the past, specifically with the destruction of Jerusalem and the temple in AD 70. Without an early date, their entire theological framework falls apart.

In contrast, Pre-Tribulationists are not reliant on either an early or late dating for Revelation. Whether the book was written earlier or later, the Pre-Tribulationist view still holds. However, there is strong evidence supporting a later date during the reign of the Roman Emperor Domitian.

Some suggest that Revelation had to be written before the destruction of the temple in AD 70 because the text makes no mention of this significant event. But this argument can be easily dismissed when we consider a few important factors:

1. **Revelation is about the future, not the past**: The book primarily deals with events yet to come, so the omission of the temple's destruction is not unusual.

2. **John wrote only what he was shown**: John was not free to write whatever he wished. He was instructed to write down only what he saw and heard in the vision (Revelation 1:19).

3. **The temple's destruction was irrelevant by AD 95**: If the book was written in AD 95, the destruction of the temple would have occurred a quarter-century earlier, and over 800 miles away. It would not have been relevant to the immediate concerns of the readers in Asia Minor.

Others argue that the words *soon* or *near* found in Revelation must refer to AD 70, implying an early writing date. However, they overlook the fact that these same words are also used to refer to the coming of the Lord, an event that is still future.

Now, let's look at some key points that strongly support the view that Revelation was written during the reign of Domitian, around AD 95:

- **Irenaeus** (c. AD 130–202): One of the earliest and most authoritative sources on the subject, Irenaeus wrote in *Against Heresies* that John's vision occurred "almost in our day, towards the end of Domitian's reign" (which ended in AD 96). This is significant because Irenaeus was raised in Smyrna, one of the churches mentioned in Revelation, and would have had direct knowledge of these events.

- **Other early church fathers**: Clement of Alexandria (c. AD 150–215), Eusebius of Caesarea (c. AD 260–340), and Victorinus of Pettau (late 3rd century) also affirmed that John was exiled to Patmos under Domitian, supporting the later date.

- **The condition of the seven churches**: The letters to the seven churches in Revelation 2–3 reflect a period of time that had passed since the early church was established. For example, Laodicea is described as wealthy and self-sufficient (Revelation 3:17), but this would not have been the case immediately following the earthquake that devastated the city in AD 60. By Domitian's reign, the city had recovered and regained its wealth, fitting the timeline of a later date.

- **Antipas' martyrdom**: In Revelation 2:13, Jesus mentions Antipas, a martyr killed in Pergamum for his faith. Historical records suggest that Antipas was martyred around AD 92, during Domitian's reign, further supporting the later date.

- **John's exile to Patmos**: Revelation 1:9 mentions John's exile to the island of Patmos, which aligns with Domitian's practice of exiling political and religious dissidents.

- **The early-date theory started centuries later**: The idea that Revelation was written as early as AD 65 didn't surface until about 400 years later. The earliest sources, closest to the time of John, uniformly support the later date.

While preterists rely heavily on an early date for Revelation, the overwhelming historical and contextual evidence points to the book being written around AD 95 during the reign of Domitian. This later date aligns with the conditions of the churches, historical events, and the testimonies of early church leaders.

WILL THE WORLD GET BETTER OR WORSE?

Is the world getting better or worse? It seems odd to even ask this question when the Bible provides such a clear answer. I never fail to be surprised by how many in the Church attempt to view the world through rose-tinted glasses, boldly declaring, "No, the world is getting better."

Honestly, the madness of such a statement makes you want to say, "Bless their heart." Yet, somehow this view that we are inching closer and closer to Heaven on earth is gaining prominence.

I can't help but think of that line from Chico Marx: **"Who ya gonna believe? Me or your own eyes?"**

Truth be told, anyone who claims that the world is on an upward trend is clearly not paying attention. They're ignoring both Scripture and reality. For a moment, let's take this idea seriously and examine why it matters and how it impacts a Christian's walk with God.

FOR BETTER OR WORSE?

Some folks argue that the world is improving. They point to technological advances, medical miracles, and improvements in quality of life and life expectancy. Sure, technology is making our lives more comfortable. Medicine has made diseases that once devastated humanity a thing of the past. By that definition, one could argue that we're doing better. But hold on a minute, we need to ask the *right* question first.

175

Instead of asking, "Is the world getting better or worse?" we need to ask, "*What is God's definition of better and worse?*" His answer, "*For the Lord does not see as man sees; for man looks on the outward appearance, but the Lord looks at the heart*" (1 Samuel 16:7 NKJV).

To God, "better" is not about having Wi-Fi in every home or a cure for polio. "Better" is about a heart turned toward righteousness. It's about holiness, purity, and obedience to Him. And by that definition, it's not even close…things are getting worse.

THINGS WERE "BETTER" BEFORE THE FLOOD

Let's go back to Genesis, to the days before the Flood. Genesis 6 paints a vivid picture of the world and God's opinion of it: "*The Lord saw how great the wickedness of the human race had become on the earth, and that every inclination of the thoughts of the human heart was only evil all the time*" (Genesis 6:5 NIV).

This was a time of tremendous technological advancements. Life spans were *better* than they are now, with people living for centuries. But that's not what God saw when He looked at humanity. He didn't look at the tech, the medicine, or the human comfort levels. He looked at the wickedness of their hearts. It wasn't about quality of life, it was about the *quality of the soul.* The Bible says that humankind's wickedness was "great" and that every thought was *only evil all the time, continually.* That's how God defined "worse."

A GRIM FORECAST FROM SCRIPTURE

The Bible tells us exactly what will happen in the last days, and it's anything but sunshine and roses. Here's a glimpse of the future, according to God's Word:

Now the Spirit expressly says that in latter times some will depart from the faith, giving heed to deceiving spirits and doctrines of demons

(1 Timothy 4:1 NKJV).

While evildoers and impostors will go from bad to worse, deceiving and being deceived

(2 Timothy 3:13 NIV).

This know also, that in the last days perilous times shall come

(2 Timothy 3:1 KJV).

Therefore rejoice, O heavens, and you who dwell in them! Woe to the inhabitants of the earth and the sea! For the devil has come down to you, having great wrath, because he knows that he has a short time

(Revelation 12:12 NKJV).

For then shall be great tribulation, such as was not since the beginning of the world to this time, no, nor ever shall be

(Matthew 24:21 KJV)

BY NO DIVINE STANDARD IS THE WORLD GETTING BETTER

We're living in a time when **perversion** has never been more accessible, where false religions and cults are growing at an unprecedented rate, where the sanctity of the family is under siege. Technology, for all its wonders, has also made sin easier to access, easier to hide, and more widespread. We have the power, with our weapons, to destroy the planet many times over, and we call this progress?

By **God's standard**, the world is not improving. Not even close.

A DANGEROUS DOCTOR'S VISIT

Imagine a scenario where you're horribly sick and deteriorating quickly, so you get an appointment with one of the world's finest doctors. He listens to your symptoms, nods his head, and then instead of making a diagnosis or providing a cure he says, "You know, it may seem bad, but just think, at least you're not living in the 1700s! Back then, they didn't even have this kind of air conditioning or advanced medical equipment. You're really lucky to be alive today!" He keeps talking about how much "better" things are now compared to then, as your vision starts to blur and your symptoms worsen. *And then... you die.*

Sure, things are "better" in some ways. But you're still dying. The problem is right in front of you, and ignoring it because things are supposedly "better" is foolish. Progress is relative, it's not absolute. Sometimes, looking at the bright side keeps us from seeing the immediate danger. As Nesrine Malik says in her article, "Why the World Can Get Worse by Constantly Saying It's Getting Better," the unintended consequence of always looking on the bright side is that we become blind to the darkness creeping in.[10]

WHY DOES IT MATTER?

You might be wondering, "So what if people believe things are getting better?" Here's why it matters: Jesus predicted a mass deception in the last days (Matthew 24). Without a correct understanding of biblical eschatology, believers risk being lulled into complacency or worse, into false hope. When you think the world is getting better, you may not feel the urgency to evangelize, to pray, or to stay vigilant. You're in danger of getting too comfortable, of forgetting that we're in a battle, not a garden party.

The world will get worse, but that's no reason to give up. How many of us know we're going to die one day? Every single one of us, unless Jesus returns first. Just because we're getting older and weaker, does that mean we should give up on eating healthy, exercising, or taking care of ourselves? Of course not!

Likewise, just because the world is spiraling toward judgment doesn't mean we stop being salt and light. We keep sharing the Gospel. We keep praying. We keep fighting the good fight, because we know that God is not willing that any should perish, but that all should come to repentance (2 Peter 3:9).

The belief that the world is getting better through the Church taking over every aspect of society may sound "victorious" to some, but it is a dangerous delusion. True victory doesn't come from taking over the world. It comes from being faithful to Jesus in a world that's falling apart.

The Bible is explicit in its predictions that the world is *not* heading for some golden age before Jesus returns. It's heading for judgment. Things are getting worse, and they will continue to do so until the day Christ steps back onto this earth to set things right. So, be vigilant. Don't be fooled by empty promises that tell you everything's going to get better. We do know how the story ends, and we know Who is coming back to make all things new.

Until then, we won't give up, or let up, but we will take up our cross, and follow Him.

IS THE RAPTURE IN MATTHEW 24?

First and foremost, it's critical to note that the Pre-Tribulation view does not hinge on the Rapture being explicitly taught in Matthew 24. Our assertion is that the Rapture was a mystery hidden until Paul revealed it, as noted in 1 Corinthians 15:51-52 (NKJV): *"Behold, I tell you a mystery: We shall not all sleep, but we shall all be changed—in a moment, in the twinkling of an eye, at the last trumpet...."*

This idea of the Church being "caught up" was unknown to the disciples and wasn't explicitly laid out by Jesus in His earthly teachings. Paul's revelation stands as the defining teaching on the Rapture, which means we don't have to hang our doctrinal hat on finding it within Matthew 24. Nevertheless, there are certain passages that some believe could indirectly refer to the Rapture but there's an honest divide within the Pre-Tribulation community on whether Matthew 24 is one of those references.

THE DEBATE ABOUT "LEFT BEHIND"

Another significant point of debate centers on the phrase "left behind." Is it appropriate to use this phrase based on the context of Matthew 24? Even among Pre-Tribulation believers, there's debate on whether being "left" in this passage means left to face judgment or left to live in the Millennial Kingdom. Some argue that those taken are removed in judgment, while the faithful remnant is left to inherit the Kingdom. There are many brilliant Pre-Tribulation scholars who hold this view, noting the distinctly Jewish context of the passage.

I'd argue that regardless of how you interpret the "taken" and "left" in Matthew 24, there's nothing wrong with using the phrase "left behind" as an appropriate term to describe those who remain on earth after the Rapture. It's entirely in line with how biblical terminology has been used in other contexts throughout Scripture. For example, Paul quotes Deuteronomy 25:4 (KJV), *"Thou shalt not muzzle the ox when he treadeth out the corn,"* to support the principle of paying ministers for their labor (1 Corinthians 9:9). While the original passage literally refers to oxen, Paul extends the application to the treatment of church workers. Similarly, using "left behind" to describe those missing the Rapture is both fitting and evocative, even if it might be borrowed from another context.

WHAT DOES MATTHEW 24 ACTUALLY SAY?

Let's revisit Matthew 24:40-41 (KJV): "*Then shall two be in the field; the one shall be taken, and the other left. Two women shall be grinding at the mill; the one shall be taken, and the other left.*"

The context of Matthew 24 is crucial here. After Jesus completes His instruction on the Tribulation (Matthew 24:21), He transitions into a different segment of His teaching: "*Now learn a parable of the fig tree; When his branch is yet tender, and putteth forth leaves, ye know that summer is nigh*" (Matthew 24:32 KJV).

Following this, Jesus shifts to comparing this period to the days of Noah:

> *But as the days of Noah were, so also will the coming of the Son of man be. For as in the days before the flood, they were eating and drinking, marrying and giving in marriage, until the day that Noah entered the ark, and did not know until the flood came and took them all away, so also will the coming of the Son of man be*
> (Matthew 24:37-39 NKJV).

COULD THIS BE A REFERENCE TO THE RAPTURE?

In this teaching, Jesus describes a time when people will be going about their daily lives, eating, drinking, marrying, and working. This portrayal has led many of us to consider whether there's an allusion to the Rapture here. It's notable that Jesus is describing a time when life is functioning normally, people are working side by side and living together in peace.

Contrast this description with what the Bible reveals about the conditions during the Tribulation. The Tribulation is characterized as a time of unparalleled upheaval. Economically, believers and unbelievers won't be side by side because the mark of the beast has been instituted, and believers will be systematically cut out of public society.

It's described as a time when families are torn apart, with children betraying parents and vice versa. People are well aware of God's judgment during the Tribulation and are crying out for the rocks to fall on them. The carefree, oblivious daily living described in Matthew 24 simply does not align with the chaos of the Tribulation.

This stark contrast in the tone of these two periods is one reason why I lean toward the idea that Jesus may indeed be alluding to the Rapture. It is a period of unexpected departure before the onset of God's judgment, much like Noah's entrance into the ark where he was supernaturally sealed in for seven days before the flood came.

At the end of the day, whether Matthew 24 in any way describes the Rapture or not doesn't alter the fact that we are commanded to be ready for His return and to *occupy till He comes* (Luke 19:13 KJV). We're watching for Him and we're working for Him, sharing the Gospel and striving to ensure as few people as possible are left behind.

10

PROOFS FOR THE PRE-TRIBULATION RAPTURE

Imagine standing in a long security line at the airport, watching the clock tick closer to your departure time. Tension rises as the line barely moves, and you start to wonder if you'll make it to the gate on time. Suddenly, an airline agent walks up, scans your boarding pass, and says, "Follow me." Before you know it, you're bypassing the chaos, stepping into a fast lane, and boarding the plane with time to spare. Relief washes over you as you settle into your seat, leaving behind the frustration and stress of the line.

The Pre-Tribulation Rapture is a bit like that divine fast pass. It's not an escape from responsibility but a promise to remove believers from the chaos of the coming Tribulation. As we step into this chapter, we'll explore the case for this blessed hope, piece by piece, proving that it's an essential part of God's prophetic plan. It's a chance to solidify what we've covered throughout the book while introducing a few fresh insights that add even more depth to the discussion. By the end, you'll have a clear and compelling understanding of why the Rapture matters and why its timing is so significant.

THE DOCTRINE OF IMMINENCE

Only the Pre-Tribulation view can truly honor this concept. When you read the New Testament, the consistent message to believers is to be ready because the Lord could come at any time. In Titus 2:13, Paul refers to the return of Jesus as the *"blessed hope,"* something we eagerly anticipate. This makes it clear that we should be looking for the Savior, not for signs of judgment or the coming of the antichrist. By contrast, those who hold to a Mid-Tribulation or Post-Tribulation view are necessarily waiting for specific events during the Tribulation, making the return of Jesus something that is predictable, rather than imminent.

Tribulation believers are warned to look for specific signs, while the Church is directed to live in a state of expectation of the Savior. *"Therefore you also be ready, for the Son of Man is coming at an hour you do not expect"* (Matthew 24:44 NKJV).

THE CHURCH IS PROMISED DELIVERANCE FROM WRATH

Another proof is God's promise to deliver His Church from His wrath. In 1 Thessalonians 1:10 (NKJV), Paul makes it clear that we are *"to wait for His Son from heaven, whom He raised from the dead, even Jesus, who delivers us from the wrath to come."* Once again, in 1 Thessalonians 5:9 (NKJV), he writes, *"For God did not appoint us to wrath, but to obtain salvation through our Lord Jesus Christ."*

Jesus says to the church in Philadelphia, *"Because you have kept My command to persevere, I also will keep you from the hour of trial which shall come upon the whole world, to test those who dwell on the earth"* (Revelation 3:10 NKJV).

The Pre-Tribulation view is the only one that takes these promises seriously and ensures that believers are spared from the very wrath they were promised to escape.

THE PURPOSE OF THE TRIBULATION

The Tribulation, referred to in Jeremiah 30:7 as *"the time of Jacob's trouble,"* is specifically focused on Israel and the nations, not on the

Church. The goal of the Tribulation is twofold: to bring Israel to a place of repentance and to execute judgment on an unbelieving world. It is the final week of Daniel's 70 weeks (Daniel 9:24-27), which is God's determined dealing with the people of Israel and Jerusalem.

Throughout all of the New Testament passages concerning the Tribulation, there is no mention of the Church on earth during that time.

HONORING SCRIPTURE WITH A LITERAL INTERPRETATION

A critical strength of the Pre-Tribulation Rapture view is its commitment to honoring Scripture with a literal interpretation. Pre-Tribulationism allows us to read the Bible as it is written, without resorting to over-spiritualizing or allegorizing prophetic texts. If you begin to spiritualize or allegorize the clear teachings of the Bible regarding eschatology, where do you draw the line? If the promises of deliverance from God's wrath are not literal, then how do we know which promises to take literally? The danger of allegorizing prophecy is that it can lead to the erosion of confidence in the entirety of God's Word.

Only the Pre-Tribulation view allows you to consistently remain faithful to the plain meaning of the text, while honoring God's promises to His Church and His distinct plan for Israel. The idea that God has a separate plan for Israel and the Church is not something invented by dispensationalists; it's a truth that emerges naturally from a literal reading of the Bible.

THE CHURCH'S ABSENCE IN THE TRIBULATION

In the first three chapters, the Church (the *Ecclesia*) is mentioned 19 times and is clearly the focal point. But after John is called up

to Heaven in Revelation 4:1—a possible picture of the Rapture—
the Church is conspicuously absent from the narrative here on earth
while simultaneously present in Heaven as represented by the 24
elders. The Church reappears in Revelation 19, not on earth, but as
the Bride of Christ, returning with Him from Heaven.

THE RESTRAINER IN 2 THESSALONIANS 2

In 2 Thessalonians 2:6-8, Paul speaks of a restrainer that must be *"taken
out of the way"* before the antichrist can be revealed. Many prominent
Bible scholars maintain that the "restrainer" is the Holy Spirit working through the Church. The Holy Spirit's unique restraining influence operates through the Church, and once the Church is caught
away, the path is cleared for the "man of sin" to be revealed. This fits
perfectly with a Pre-Tribulation understanding of the end times.

TIME NEEDED FOR THE JUDGMENT
SEAT OF CHRIST

Also known as the Bema Seat, this is the moment when believers will
be judged for their works and faithfulness (2 Corinthians 5:10). If the
Rapture occurs after the Tribulation, when exactly would this take
place? The Pre-Tribulation Rapture allows believers to be caught up,
judged, and rewarded, making it possible for them to return with
Christ at His Second Coming.

PURPOSE FOR THE SEPARATION
OF THE SHEEP AND THE GOATS

Described in Matthew 25:31-46 at the end of the Tribulation, Jesus
will judge the nations, separating individuals into two groups. Those

who are fit to enter His Millennial Kingdom are in one and those who are not in the other. If the Rapture occurred at the end of the Tribulation, with all believers being caught up and transformed, then there would be no need for this separation of the sheep and goats, because the righteous would have already been separated. The Pre-Tribulation Rapture provides the answer, as it allows those who come to faith during the Tribulation (and survive it) to be identified and enter into Christ's Millennial Kingdom.

WHO WILL POPULATE THE MILLENNIUM?

A frequently overlooked aspect of eschatology is the question of who will populate the earth during the Millennial Kingdom. The Bible speaks of the Millennial Reign of Christ as a time when people will be living and repopulating the earth (Isaiah 65:20-23). If the Rapture were to occur after the Tribulation, with every believer being transformed and glorified, there would be no one left in a carnal state to enter the Millennium and repopulate the earth. Only the Pre-Tribulation view accounts for this scenario, as it teaches that there will be survivors of the Tribulation who come to faith during that time and then go on to populate the earth during Christ's thousand-year reign.

DIFFERENCES BETWEEN THE RAPTURE
AND THE SECOND COMING

The Bible presents distinct differences between the Rapture and the Second Coming, which can only be reconciled by viewing them as two separate events or two bookends of the same event. We've listed some of these previously. The Pre-Tribulation view allows these distinctions to remain intact, whereas the Post-Tribulation view creates contradictions in how these events are described.

BENEFITS BELIEVERS

Finally, the Pre-Tribulation Rapture is unique in the way it benefits believers. It instills hope and a sense of urgency, inspiring us to live in readiness and expectation of Christ's return. The Pre-Tribulation view, unlike other eschatological perspectives, carries this profound benefit, encouraging believers as they put on this helmet of the hope of salvation (1 Thessalonians 5).

CONCLUSION

In the end, regardless of the timeline you believe in, as long as you're watching for Him and helping His Bride do the same, we're on the same page. The heart of our faith should always be rooted in eager anticipation of His return. The main purpose of this book is to address errors and misconceptions within my own camp, while inspiring hearts to fall in love with the reality of His appearing. Our differences should never overshadow the glorious truth that our Savior is coming back, and He's coming back for a Bride who is awake, prepared, and deeply in love with Him.

This kind of unity around the return of Jesus will be more powerful than any timeline or interpretation, making us truly ready for the day when we finally meet Him face-to-face.

Maranatha!

APPENDIX

MARANATHA MINDSET BIBLE VERSES

Following is a list of powerful verses to strengthen your hope, renew your mind, and help you put on the helmet of salvation as we look forward to the coming of the Lord. Maranatha!

Genesis 18:23-26 (KJV): *And Abraham drew near, and said, Wilt thou also destroy the righteous with the wicked? Peradventure there be fifty righteous within the city: wilt thou also destroy and not spare the place for the fifty righteous that are therein? That be far from thee to do after this manner, to slay the righteous with the wicked: and that the righteous should be as the wicked, that be far from thee: Shall not the Judge of all the earth do right? And the Lord said, If I find in Sodom fifty righteous within the city, then I will spare all the place for their sakes.*

Genesis 19:22 (KJV): *Haste thee, escape thither; for I cannot do anything till thou be come thither. Therefore the name of the city was called Zoar.*

Psalm 27:5 (KJV): *For in the time of trouble he shall hide me in his pavilion: in the secret of his tabernacle shall he hide me; he shall set me up upon a rock.*

Psalm 50:3-5 (KJV): *Our God shall come, and shall not keep silence: a fire shall devour before him, and it shall be very tempestuous round about him. He shall call to the heavens from above, and to the earth, that he may judge his people. Gather my saints together unto me; those that have made a covenant with me by sacrifice.*

Isaiah 26:19-21 (KJV): *Thy dead men shall live, together with my dead body shall they arise. Awake and sing, ye that dwell in dust: for thy dew is as the dew of herbs, and the earth shall cast out the dead. Come, my people, enter thou into thy chambers, and shut thy doors about thee: hide thyself as it were for a little moment, until the indignation be overpast. For, behold, the Lord cometh out of his place to punish the inhabitants of the earth for their iniquity: the earth also shall disclose her blood, and shall no more cover her slain.*

Daniel 12:1-2 (KJV): *And at that time shall Michael stand up, the great prince which standeth for the children of thy people: and there shall be a time of trouble, such as never was since there was a nation even to that same time: and at that time thy people shall be delivered, every one that shall be found written in the book. And many of them that sleep in the dust of the earth shall awake, some to everlasting life, and some to shame and everlasting contempt.*

Zephaniah 2:3 (KJV): *Seek ye the Lord, all ye meek of the earth, which have wrought his judgment; seek righteousness, seek meekness: it may be ye shall be hid in the day of the Lord's anger.*

Matthew 24:27 (KJV): *For as the lightning cometh out of the east, and shineth even unto the west; so shall also the coming of the Son of man be.*

Matthew 24:29-31 (KJV): *Immediately after the tribulation of those days shall the sun be darkened, and the moon shall not give her light, and the stars shall fall from heaven, and the powers of the heavens shall be shaken: And then shall appear the sign of the Son of man in heaven: and then shall all the tribes of the earth mourn, and they shall see the Son of man coming in the clouds of heaven with power and great glory. And he shall send his angels with a great sound of a trumpet, and they shall gather together his elect from the four winds, from one end of heaven to the other.*

Matthew 24:42 (KJV): *Watch therefore: for ye know not what hour your Lord doth come.*

Mark 13:32 (KJV): *But of that day and that hour knoweth no man, no, not the angels which are in heaven, neither the Son, but the Father.*

Luke 12:40 (KJV): *Be ye therefore ready also: for the Son of man cometh at an hour when ye think not.*

Luke 17:34-37 (KJV): *I tell you, in that night there shall be two men in one bed; the one shall be taken, and the other shall be left. Two women shall be grinding together; the one shall be taken, and the other left. Two men shall be in the field; the one shall be taken, and the other left. And they answered and said unto him, Where, Lord? And he said unto them, Wheresoever the body is, thither will the eagles be gathered together.*

Luke 19:12-13, 15-17 (KJV): *He said therefore, A certain nobleman went into a far country to receive for himself a kingdom, and to return. And he called his ten servants, and delivered them ten pounds, and said unto them, Occupy till I come. ...And it came to pass, that when he was returned, having received the kingdom, then he commanded these servants to be called unto him, to whom he had given the money, that he might know how much every man had gained by trading. Then came the first, saying, Lord, thy pound hath gained ten pounds. And he said unto him, Well, thou good servant: because thou hast been faithful in a very little, have thou authority over ten cities.*

John 14:1-4 (KJV): *Let not your heart be troubled: ye believe in God, believe also in me. In my Father's house are many mansions: if it were not so, I would have told you. I go to prepare a place for you. And if I go and prepare a place for you, I will come again, and receive you unto myself; that where I am, there ye may be also. And whither I go ye know, and the way ye know.*

Romans 10:9 (KJV): *That if thou shalt confess with thy mouth the Lord Jesus, and shalt believe in thine heart that God hath raised him from the dead, thou shalt be saved.*

1 Corinthians 15:51-52 (KJV): *Behold, I shew you a mystery; We shall not all sleep, but we shall all be changed, In a moment, in the twinkling of an eye, at the last trump: for the trumpet shall sound, and the dead shall be raised incorruptible, and we shall be changed.*

Philippians 3:20-21 (KJV): *For our conversation is in heaven; from whence also we look for the Saviour, the Lord Jesus Christ: Who shall change our vile body, that it may be fashioned like unto his glorious body, according to the working whereby he is able even to subdue all things unto himself.*

1 Thessalonians 4:13-17 (KJV): *But I would not have you to be ignorant, brethren, concerning them which are asleep, that ye*

sorrow not, even as others which have no hope. For if we believe that Jesus died and rose again, even so them also which sleep in Jesus will God bring with him. For this we say unto you by the word of the Lord, that we which are alive and remain unto the coming of the Lord shall not prevent them which are asleep. For the Lord himself shall descend from heaven with a shout, with the voice of the archangel, and with the trump of God: and the dead in Christ shall rise first: Then we which are alive and remain shall be caught up together with them in the clouds, to meet the Lord in the air: and so shall we ever be with the Lord.

1 Thessalonians 5:2-6 (KJV): *For yourselves know perfectly that the day of the Lord so cometh as a thief in the night. For when they shall say, Peace and safety; then sudden destruction cometh upon them, as travail upon a woman with child; and they shall not escape. But ye, brethren, are not in darkness, that that day should overtake you as a thief. Ye are all the children of light, and the children of the day: we are not of the night, nor of darkness. Therefore let us not sleep, as do others; but let us watch and be sober.*

1 Thessalonians 5:9 (KJV): *For God hath not appointed us to wrath, but to obtain salvation by our Lord Jesus Christ.*

2 Thessalonians 2:3-7 (KJV): *Let no man deceive you by any means: for that day shall not come, except there come a falling away first, and that man of sin be revealed, the son of perdition; Who opposeth and exalteth himself above all that is called God, or that is worshipped; so that he as God sitteth in the temple of God, shewing himself that he is God. Remember ye not, that, when I was yet with you, I told you these things? And now ye know what withholdeth that he might be revealed in his time. For the mystery*

of iniquity doth already work: only he who now letteth will let, until he be taken out of the way.

Hebrews 9:27-28 (KJV): *And as it is appointed unto men once to die, but after this the judgment: So Christ was once offered to bear the sins of many; and unto them that look for him shall he appear the second time without sin unto salvation.*

Revelation 3:10 (KJV): *Because thou hast kept the word of my patience, I also will keep thee from the hour of temptation, which shall come upon all the world, to try them that dwell upon the earth.*

END-TIME GLOSSARY OF TERMS

A

ABADDON

Abaddon is a term used in Revelation 9:11 to describe the angel of the bottomless pit, whose name in Hebrew means "destruction" and in Greek is *Apollyon*, meaning "destroyer." This figure is associated with the release of demonic locusts during the Fifth Trumpet Judgment in the Tribulation. Abaddon is not merely a place of destruction but a powerful spiritual being who leads the forces of darkness in unleashing torment upon humanity. This symbolizes a significant phase of God's judgment upon the earth during the Tribulation, as His wrath is poured out on the unrepentant.

ABOMINATION OF DESOLATION

This term is found in Daniel 9:27, Matthew 24:15, and Mark 13:14 and refers to a future event when the antichrist will desecrate the rebuilt Jewish temple by placing an object of blasphemy in the Holy of Holies. This act will mark the midpoint of the seven-year Tribulation and initiate The Great Tribulation (the final 3.5 years). It is a pivotal moment that signals the unleashing of God's wrath upon the world. This blasphemous act will be a clear sign to those living during the Tribulation that the antichrist has revealed his true intentions.

Some believe that the abomination of desolation was fulfilled in 168 BC when Antiochus Epiphanes desecrated the second temple by sacrificing a pig on the altar and erecting an idol of Zeus. Others argue that it was fulfilled in AD 70 with the destruction of the temple by the Romans. However, both of these events fail to align with Jesus's specific prophecy in Matthew 24:15, which was given after Antiochus Epiphanes's time. Jesus spoke of this abomination as a future event, not something that had already occurred. Furthermore, the book of Revelation, written approximately in AD 95, describes a similar act of desecration as yet to come (Revelation 13:14-15). The ultimate fulfillment must be during the end times, involving the antichrist, who will demand worship in a rebuilt temple, marking the midpoint of the Tribulation. Therefore, these historical desecrations are merely foreshadows, not the final fulfillment, of what Jesus and Daniel described. (See Dual Fulfillment)

AGE (OR DISPENSATION)

In biblical terms, an "Age" refers to a distinct period or era in God's redemptive plan for humanity. Each age represents a unique phase of God's unfolding purposes, marked by different responsibilities and expectations for humanity. For instance, the Bible speaks of *"this present evil age"* (Galatians 1:4 NKJV) and "the age to come" (Ephesians 1:21), both highlighting different periods in God's overarching timeline.

Throughout Scripture, the concept of ages points to God's progressive revelation and interaction with mankind. Consider Ephesians 3:9-11, where Paul speaks of God's eternal purpose being unveiled across different times, as well as Hebrews 1:1-2 (KJV), where it is made clear that God spoke in different ways *"at sundry times and in diverse manners"* through the prophets, but ultimately through His Son. The word *dispensation* is also used to describe this idea in passages including Ephesians 1:10 (NKJV), which speaks of the *"dispensation of the fullness of times,"* the culmination of God's plan to bring all things together under Christ.

The belief that God has divided human history into distinct ages or dispensations, each with unique expectations and responsibilities can be found in the way God clearly changes His approach throughout Scripture while maintaining His unchanging nature. For instance, during the Age of Innocence (Genesis 1–3), Adam and Eve were responsible for keeping God's command not to eat from the tree of the knowledge of good and evil. After the Fall, humanity entered a new dispensation, often referred to as the Age of Conscience, where mankind was to live according to their understanding of right and wrong (Genesis 4–8). Later, the Age of Law brought the clear, codified laws of God given to Moses (Exodus 19–20), marking a new period of God's dealings with humanity.

Perhaps the most compelling defense of this comes from the Age of Grace, often referred to as the Church Age (Ephesians 3:2-6), when salvation by faith through grace was fully revealed in Jesus Christ. This distinct period contrasts with the future Millennial Kingdom (Revelation 20:1-6), when Jesus will physically reign on earth. Understanding these shifts helps to make sense of biblical events and God's purposes, showing how His redemptive plan is progressively revealed.

The concept of ages helps believers understand that God's dealings with humanity are not random but purposeful, leading toward the ultimate fulfillment of His Kingdom. Each age adds a layer to the grand narrative, culminating in the eternal state (Revelation 21–22), when God will dwell with humanity in perfect unity forever.

AGE OF GRACE (OR CHURCH AGE)

The Age of Grace, also known as the Church Age, is the period of time from Pentecost (Acts 2) until the Rapture of the Church. It is called the Age of Grace because it is the era in which God's grace is offered freely through faith in Jesus Christ, providing salvation to all who believe. This is the time when the Church is actively proclaiming the Gospel to the world, and the Holy Spirit works powerfully through the Church to fulfill the Great Commission. During this time, God's primary focus has been on the Gentiles, though He has never forsaken His covenant with Israel. After the Rapture, the focus shifts back to Israel and the final fulfillment of prophetic events.

AMILLENNIALISM

Amillennialism is the belief that there will not be a literal 1,000-year reign of Christ on earth, as described in Revelation 20. Instead, proponents believe the "Millennium" is symbolic and refers to Christ's spiritual reign from Heaven, which began at His ascension and continues until His Second Coming. This view dismisses a literal future kingdom where Christ rules on earth. Amillennialism misinterprets key prophetic passages, particularly in Revelation and Daniel, and overlooks the clear promise of a literal, earthly Kingdom where Christ will physically reign.

ANGELS

Angels are spiritual beings created by God, often serving as His messengers and agents of divine intervention. Throughout the Bible, angels play a critical role in both delivering messages from God and executing His judgments. In the context of end-time prophecy, angels are central figures, especially in the book of Revelation, where they blow trumpets, pour out bowls of wrath, and oversee various judgments upon the earth (Revelation 8:2, Revelation 16:1). Additionally, angels are seen gathering the elect of Israel and protecting God's people.

While angels serve God and His purposes, it's important to note that believers are warned not to worship them (Revelation 22:8-9).

In Revelation chapters 2 and 3, each of the seven churches is addressed by a letter that begins with a message to the "angel" of that particular church. These "angels" are commonly understood to be the messengers or pastors of the churches. The Greek word used for "angel" is *angelos*, which means "messenger," and in this context, it likely refers to the human leaders responsible for delivering God's message to their congregations. These pastors, or spiritual overseers, were held accountable for guiding their churches in truth, warning them of dangers, and encouraging faithfulness.

ANTICHRIST

The antichrist is the future world leader prophesied in Daniel 7, 2 Thessalonians 2, and Revelation 13 who will rise to power during the Tribulation. He will deceive the nations, demand to be worshipped, and institute global tyranny under his rule. He is empowered by satan and will make a peace treaty with Israel, which he will break at the midpoint of the Tribulation, committing the abomination of desolation. The Church will be raptured before the antichrist is revealed, as 2 Thessalonians 2:7 indicates that the *"restrainer"* will be removed before the antichrist can come to power.

The antichrist is referred to by several different names throughout Scripture, each highlighting different aspects of his character and role in the end times. In 1 John 2:18, he is explicitly called the antichrist, meaning "against Christ" or "in place of Christ." In 2 Thessalonians 2:3 (NKJV), he is referred to as the man of sin and the son of perdition, emphasizing his lawlessness and ultimate destruction. Daniel 7:8 and Daniel 9:26 describe him as the little horn and the prince that shall come, focusing on his rise to power and destructive influence. Revelation 13:1 calls him the beast, symbolizing his brutal and tyrannical reign during the Tribulation. Additionally, in Daniel 8:23 (KJV), he is referred to as a king of fierce countenance, illustrating his ruthless leadership and ability to deceive. These titles paint a comprehensive picture of the antichrist as the ultimate opponent of Christ and God's people in the final days.

The Bible warns us that the spirit of the antichrist is not just a future concern, but a present reality. First John 2:18 (KJV) says, *"Little children, it is the last time: and as ye have heard that antichrist shall come, even now are there many antichrists; whereby we know that it is the last time."* Furthermore, 1 John 4:3 (KJV) declares, *"And every spirit that confesseth not that Jesus Christ is come in the flesh is not of God: and this is that spirit of antichrist, whereof ye have heard that it should come; and even now already is it in the world."* This tells us that the spirit of deception and opposition to Christ is active today, working to undermine the truth. However, the most important thing to remember is found in 1 John 4:4 (NKJV), *"You are of God, little children, and have overcome them, because He who is in you is greater than he who is in the world."* No matter how powerful the spirit of the antichrist may seem, the power of Christ within us is far greater. We're not afraid of the antichrist, the antichrist is afraid of us.

ANTIOCHUS EPIPHANES

Antiochus Epiphanes was a Hellenistic Greek king notorious for his intense persecution of the Jewish people. His desecration of the second temple in Jerusalem, where he sacrificed a pig on the altar and set up a statue of Zeus, is considered a foreshadowing or type of the antichrist who will desecrate a future temple during the Tribulation. This event, known as the abomination of desolation, is referenced in Daniel 11:31 and later by Jesus in Matthew 24:15, where it is linked to future events. Antiochus Epiphanes serves as a historical and prophetic figure, embodying the kind of evil and sacrilege that the future antichrist will manifest on a global scale. His actions provide a glimpse of what the world will face in the end times, particularly in relation to the desecration of sacred things.

Prophecy is pattern, and we frequently see multiple or double fulfillments of prophetic events. This concept means that a prophecy may have an initial, partial fulfillment in history, followed by a greater or ultimate fulfillment in the future.

For examples:

- The abomination of desolation in Daniel 11:31, the desecration of the Jewish temple by Antiochus Epiphanes is a clear historical event, but Jesus refers to this same concept in Matthew 24:15 as something yet to happen in the future, pointing to the antichrist's actions during the Tribulation.

- The Day of the Lord: In many instances, prophecies of God's judgment have had a near fulfillment, such as the fall of Jerusalem in AD 70, but the ultimate fulfillment still awaits at the end of days with the final Day of the Lord, described in Revelation and other prophetic books.

These patterns and double fulfillments highlight the layered nature of biblical prophecy, where God weaves together past, present, and future in His unfolding plan for humanity

APOSTASY

Apostasy refers to a great falling away from the Christian faith, as prophesied in 2 Thessalonians 2:3. This widespread rejection of biblical truth is seen as a precursor to the rise of the antichrist. This apostasy will become increasingly evident as the world moves toward the Tribulation, and we already see signs of it today in the moral and spiritual decline of society and even within the Church.

Some scholars suggest that the "apostasy" mentioned in 2 Thessalonians 2:3, typically interpreted as a spiritual falling away, could actually refer to a physical departure, potentially alluding to the Rapture of the Church. While this interpretation is certainly possible given the context of the chapter, it doesn't need to be true to support the Pre-Tribulation Rapture view. The idea that the Church will be taken before the antichrist is revealed is still clearly stated in 2 Thessalonians 2:7-8 (NKJV), which says, *"For the mystery of lawlessness is already at work; only He who now restrains will do so until He is taken out of the way. And then the lawless one will be revealed...."* This passage shows that the restraining force (widely interpreted as the Holy Spirit working through the Church) must be removed before the antichrist can come to power, solidifying the belief that the Rapture occurs before the antichrist is revealed. An interesting case can be made for this "apostasy" being an actual physical departure, but we'll not take the time to go down that rabbit hole here.

Whether this verse refers to a doctrinal falling away or a physical departure, we know that a great spiritual apostasy will take place based on other Scriptures. First Timothy 4:1 (NKJV) clearly states, *"Now the Spirit expressly says that in latter times some will depart from the faith, giving heed to deceiving spirits and doctrines of demons."* This passage confirms that many will abandon the truth and be led astray by false teachings in the last days, aligning with the broader biblical warning about apostasy. Regardless of how 2 Thessalonians 2:3 is interpreted, the falling away from the faith is a prophetic certainty.

ARMAGEDDON

Armageddon is the location of the final battle between the forces of good and evil, mentioned in Revelation 16:16. This battle will take place in the Valley of Megiddo, where the antichrist and his armies will gather to make war against Christ at His Second Coming. This battle occurs at the end of the Tribulation, after the Church has been raptured and after the antichrist has ruled the world for seven years. Christ will return *with* His saints and defeat the antichrist and his armies, ushering in the Millennial Kingdom. This event underscores the complete victory of Christ and the ultimate defeat of satan's forces.

ATONEMENT (DAY OF)

Yom Kippur, or the Day of Atonement, is one of the holiest days in the Jewish calendar, marked by repentance and reconciliation with God. In eschatological terms, some view this day as foreshadowing the final atonement for Israel at the Second Coming of Christ. Zechariah 12:10 describes a future moment when Israel will recognize Jesus as the Messiah and mourn for the One they pierced. The Church, having already been raptured, will return with Christ at this moment, witnessing Israel's national repentance and redemption.

B

BABYLON

In the book of Revelation, Babylon is used symbolically to represent a corrupt system of political, economic, and religious power that stands in opposition to God. Revelation 17–18 portrays Babylon as a *"great harlot"* and a *"city"* that will fall under God's judgment during the Tribulation. There is much debate about whether Babylon refers to a literal city, such as Rome or a rebuilt city in the Middle East, or if it symbolizes the United States of America or the world's collective rebellion against God. Babylon represents the culmination of humanity's rebellion, which will face ultimate destruction in the final days of the Tribulation. The fall of Babylon marks the end of satan's reign of deception before Christ establishes His Kingdom. Some commentators have suggested that the Bible is a tale of two cities—Babylon and Jerusalem, and only one will live on for eternity.

BEAST

The term *beast* refers to two figures in Revelation 13: the first beast is the antichrist, and the second is the false prophet. The first beast rises out of the sea and is a political leader empowered by satan to rule the world during the Tribulation. He demands worship, blasphemes God, and persecutes the saints. The second beast, the false prophet, performs miraculous signs and compels people to worship the antichrist, even instituting the infamous "mark of the beast." The rise of the beast represents the height of satan's influence on earth, but his reign is short-lived, as Christ will defeat him at the Second Coming.

BEMA SEAT

This is discussed at length in the first part of the book. The Bema Seat is the Judgment Seat of Christ where believers will be evaluated for their works and service after the Rapture (2 Corinthians 5:10). This is not a judgment for sin—since Christ has already taken the punishment for believers' sins—but rather a judgment for rewards based on how believers lived out their faith. The term *bema* refers to the raised platform where athletes in ancient Greece would receive their prizes; and in the context of the end times, it represents the place where Christ will reward His followers for their faithfulness, obedience, and service. Those who stand before the Bema Seat will receive crowns and other rewards, which they will lay at the feet of Jesus in worship. This judgment is distinct from the Great White Throne judgment, which deals with the final judgment of the wicked.

BLASPHEMY

In the context of the end times, blasphemy will be a hallmark of the antichrist's reign. Revelation 13:5-6 says that the beast (the antichrist) will be given authority to speak great things and blasphemies, directly attacking the name of God and those who dwell in Heaven. Blasphemy against God will be a key characteristic of the global rebellion during the Tribulation, with the antichrist and his followers exalting themselves above God. This blasphemy will culminate in the abomination of desolation, where the antichrist will enter the temple and declare himself to be God.

Blasphemy has been defined by some to mean attributing the works of God to the devil or attributing the works of the devil to God.

BLESSED HOPE

The *blessed hope* refers to the joyful expectation of the return of Jesus Christ to take His Church to be with Him. This phrase comes from Titus 2:13 (KJV), where the apostle Paul writes, *"Looking for that blessed hope, and the glorious appearing of the great God and our Savior Jesus Christ."*

I believe that the *"blessed hope"* is also referred to as the *"helmet of salvation"* mentioned by Paul in Ephesians 6:17 and 1 Thessalonians 5:8. This helmet symbolizes the protection of our minds and the assurance of our salvation, reminding us of the hope we have in Christ's return. The anticipation of Jesus's coming serves as a mental safeguard against despair and discouragement, helping us keep an eternal perspective as we navigate the trials of this world. The blessed hope not only encourages us but also fortifies our minds with the certainty of Christ's ultimate victory and our future with Him.

Paul emphasizes that this blessed hope is meant to encourage and comfort believers, as seen in 1 Thessalonians 4:18 (KJV), *"Wherefore comfort one another with these words,"* referring to the promise of Christ returning for His Church.

BRIDE OF CHRIST

The Bride of Christ, which refers to the Church, is currently in the betrothal stage. This means that while we are spiritually pledged to Jesus, we await the consummation of this union. In biblical times, betrothal was a binding contract, a promise that led to a future marriage. Likewise, as the Bride of Christ, we have entered into a covenant relationship with Jesus, secured by His sacrifice and the indwelling of the Holy Spirit. Paul describes this promise in 2 Corinthians 11:2 (KJV), saying, *"For I am jealous over you with godly jealousy: for I have espoused you to one husband, that I may present you as a chaste virgin to Christ."*

The wedding will take place in Heaven, marking the union of Jesus and His Church after the Rapture. The Marriage Supper of the Lamb, some suggest, will occur when Jesus returns to earth with His Bride to reign for a thousand years, as mentioned in Revelation 19:7-9. This beautiful event celebrates the ultimate fulfillment of God's redemptive plan and the everlasting joy of being united with Christ. During His Millennial Reign the Bride will rule with Him, sharing in His glory and bringing about His righteous Kingdom on earth.

As the Bride, we are to prepare ourselves by growing in holiness, keeping our lamps full of oil, and eagerly waiting for the day when we will be united with our Bridegroom in perfect love and fulfillment.

BRIDEGROOM

Bridegroom is a term used to refer to Jesus Christ in His relationship with the Church, which is called the Bride of Christ. Jesus Himself used this analogy during His ministry on Earth, indicating that He is the Bridegroom who will come for His Bride (the Church) when the time is right. In Matthew 25:1-13, Jesus tells the parable of the ten virgins, portraying Himself as the Bridegroom arriving at midnight, which points to His return being both imminent and unexpected.

In biblical times, the bridegroom would prepare a place for his bride after the betrothal and then come unexpectedly to bring her to the home he had prepared. In John 14:2-3 (NKJV), Jesus tells His disciples, *"I go to prepare a place for you. ...I will come again and receive you to Myself."* This is the language of the Bridegroom speaking of His return to bring His beloved to their eternal home.

Currently, the Church is in the betrothal stage, where we have pledged ourselves to Christ. The Bridegroom is preparing our future home, and we await His return to take us to Himself. When Jesus returns for His Bride at the Rapture, it is the fulfillment of His promise to bring us into that union. After the wedding ceremony in Heaven, He will return with His Bride to establish His Millennial Kingdom on earth (Revelation 19:7-9).

As we've discussed in this book, this imagery invites us to live with an "even more so" mentality, fully engaged in devotion, love, and preparation for the moment our Bridegroom returns.

BOOK OF LIFE

The Book of Life is mentioned throughout Scripture as a record of those who belong to God and have eternal life. Revelation 20:15 (KJV) states, *"And whosoever was not found written in the book of life was cast into the lake of fire."* For believers, being written in the Book of Life guarantees eternal salvation. During the Tribulation, those who worship the beast and take the mark will have their names blotted out of this book, sealing their eternal fate.

The Book of Life also carries a solemn warning: the possibility of names being blotted out. In Revelation 3:5 (KJV), Jesus declares, *"He that overcometh, the same shall be clothed in white raiment; and I will not blot out his name out of the book of life...."*

Some scholars suggest that the Book of Life is different from the Book of the Living mentioned in the Old Testament. For example, Psalm 69:28 refers to the *"book of the living,"* which some interpret as a record of those who are physically alive rather than a book of eternal life. The Book of Life, by contrast, pertains to eternal salvation and those who are destined to be with God forever. Moreover, this should not be confused with the *"book of remembrance"* referenced in Malachi 3:16, which is said to contain the names of those who fear the Lord and honor His name, recording their faithfulness and devotion. Each of these "books" serves a different purpose within God's divine plan, representing different aspects of His relationship with humanity.

BOWLS OF WRATH

The Bowls of Wrath, also known as the Bowl Judgments, are a series of seven judgments described in the book of Revelation that signify the final outpouring of God's wrath upon a rebellious world during The Great Tribulation. These judgments are described in Revelation 16, where each bowl represents a specific, devastating plague that God will pour out, ranging from grievous sores to rivers turning into blood, to global darkness and intense heat.

The pouring out of each bowl shows the culmination of God's patience and the consequence of humanity's refusal to repent despite previous warnings (Revelation 16:9-11). These bowls of wrath are an integral part of the eschatological timeline and are distinct from the seals and the trumpets.

C

CAUGHT UP

The phrase "caught up" refers to the Rapture of the Church, which is described in 1 Thessalonians 4:16-17 (KJV): "*For the Lord himself shall descend from heaven with a shout, with the voice of the archangel, and with the trump of God: and the dead in Christ shall rise first: Then we which are alive and remain shall be* **caught up** *together with them in the clouds, to meet the Lord in the air: and so shall we ever be with the Lord.*" This event marks the moment when believers, both living and dead, will be physically removed from the earth to meet Christ in the air. The term *caught up* comes from the Greek word *harpadzo*, meaning "to snatch or seize suddenly, just in the nick of time."

When the Bible was translated into Latin (the Vulgate), the Greek word *harpadzo* was translated into the Latin word *rapiemur*, which comes from the root *raptus* (meaning to seize or to carry off).

From the Latin *rapiemur* (or *raptus),* the English word *rapture* was derived. The term *rapture* entered the English language as a term for being "caught up" or "seized," and it eventually became the popular term used to describe the event of believers being taken to meet Christ in the air.

Greek *harpadzo* → Latin *rapiemur* → English "rapture."

Though the word *rapture* itself doesn't appear in most English translations of the Bible, it is found in the Latin Bible.

CHILIASM

Chiliasm, also known as Millenarianism, is the belief that Jesus Christ will establish a literal thousand-year reign on earth after His Second Coming, based on Revelation 20:1-6. The term *chiliasm* comes from the Greek *chilia*, meaning "thousand," and underscores the belief in a future, tangible Kingdom where Christ reigns physically, fulfilling God's promises to Israel and all nations.

Revelation 20 explicitly mentions "a thousand years" six times, making the duration significant. Old Testament prophecies, including Isaiah 2:2-4 and Isaiah 11:6-9, speak of a future time of peace and harmony, aligning with this millennial expectation. Early church fathers such as Justin Martyr and Irenaeus also taught a literal millennium, suggesting they inherited this understanding directly from the apostles. The early Christians saw this as the time when Jesus would physically reign.

In the fourth century, Augustine introduced amillennialism, which viewed the thousand-year reign as a symbolic period representing the Church Age, and this view became dominant. However, premillennialism resurfaced during the Reformation and gained further traction with the development of Dispensationalism in the 19th century, emphasizing a literal interpretation of Scripture.

The central argument for chiliasm is a consistent, literal interpretation of prophetic texts and a belief that God will fulfill His promises to Israel in a tangible way. Revelation 20 and the teachings of the early church suggest that Christ's reign is not merely symbolic but will be a real and glorious fulfillment of God's Kingdom on earth.

CHURCH AGE

See Age / Age of Grace

D

DANIEL'S SEVENTIETH WEEK

This phrase refers to the final seven-year period described in Daniel 9:24-27, commonly understood as the seven-year Tribulation.

Daniel's prophecy outlines 70 "weeks" or *heptads* (seven-year periods) that are determined upon Israel and Jerusalem to accomplish God's purposes. Sixty-nine of these weeks have already been fulfilled, with the seventieth week set to begin with a peace treaty signed between the antichrist and Israel. The Church will be raptured before Daniel's 70th week begins, as this period is primarily concerned with the purification of Israel and the judgment of the nations. This topic is discussed in more detail in the chapter on the Tribulation.

DAY OF THE LORD

The Day of the Lord is a recurring biblical theme referring to a future time when God will intervene directly in human history to bring judgment and establish His Kingdom. This period begins with the Tribulation and culminates with the Second Coming of Christ and the establishment of His Millennial Kingdom. Several Old Testament prophets, as well as the New Testament, mention the Day of the Lord, emphasizing both its severity and its significance in God's redemptive plan (Joel 2:31, Zephaniah 1:14-18, 2 Peter 3:10).

The Day of the Lord includes the entire Tribulation and the outpouring of God's wrath on a sinful world. The Rapture occurs before the Day of the Lord, as God's Church is promised deliverance from this wrath (1 Thessalonians 5:9).

DISPENSATIONALISM

Dispensationalism is a theological system that interprets the Bible through the lens of distinct periods or "dispensations" in which God interacts with humanity in different ways.

Dispensationalism emphasizes a literal interpretation of biblical prophecy, particularly in relation to Israel and the end times. It views the Church and Israel as distinct entities with separate roles in God's plan, with the Church being raptured before the Tribulation so that God can once again focus on fulfilling His promises to Israel.

DOCTRINE OF IMMINENCY

The Doctrine of Imminency teaches that Christ's return for His Church (the Rapture) could happen at any moment, with no specific event needing to precede it. This belief encourages Christians to live in a constant state of readiness. Verses including 1 Thessalonians 4:16-17 and Titus 2:13 highlight the expectation of Christ's sudden return. The Rapture will occur before the Tribulation, and believers should remain alert and prepared for the Lord's return at any moment.

DRAGON

The dragon in Revelation 12 is a symbolic representation of satan. Described as a great red dragon with seven heads and ten horns, satan is portrayed as the one who deceives the whole world and seeks to destroy God's people. He is cast out of Heaven along with his angels and wages war against the "woman" (Israel) and her off-spring (the saints). The dragon empowers the antichrist and the false prophet, leading a global rebellion against God during the Tribulation. Although satan will intensify his efforts during the Tribulation, his defeat is certain, culminating in his binding at the start of the Millennium (Revelation 20:1-3).

DUAL FULFILLMENT

Dual fulfillment refers to a prophetic concept where a single prophecy has both an immediate or partial fulfillment in history and a more complete, ultimate fulfillment at a later time. This idea allows a single event to foreshadow a greater, future event, demonstrating

God's ability to weave multiple layers of meaning into His Word. Many biblical prophecies have this dual characteristic, fulfilling a purpose in their original context while pointing to a greater, end-times fulfillment.

For example, the abomination of desolation is a prime instance of dual fulfillment. The desecration of the temple by Antiochus Epiphanes in 168 BC served as an initial fulfillment, while Jesus's words in Matthew 24:15 point to a future, ultimate fulfillment involving the antichrist in the last days.

This concept underscores the richness of Scripture, where past events serve as types or shadows of what is yet to come, making prophecy applicable to both its immediate audience and future believers. It also demonstrates God's sovereign control over history, showing that He works through different ages to bring His ultimate purposes to pass.

E

EAGLE'S WINGS

In Revelation 12:14 (KJV), the woman (Israel) is given the *"wings of a great eagle"* so that she can fly into the wilderness and be protected during The Great Tribulation. The imagery of eagle's wings is often seen as symbolic of God's supernatural protection and deliverance. Some suggest that this could be a reference to the United States of America but many nations, including Rome, used eagles and their wings as symbols. Ultimately we know that God will lead His remnant to a place of refuge (some believe this could be Petra). The eagle's wings symbolize God's ability to swiftly and safely remove His people from imminent danger, a reminder of His care for Israel even during the darkest times.

ELDERS (24 ELDERS)

The 24 elders are seen around the throne of God in Revelation 4–5. These elders, dressed in white robes and wearing crowns, represent the redeemed people of God. The number 24 may symbolize the 12 tribes of Israel and the 12 apostles, bringing together both Old and New Testament believers. All 24 could represent the Church as well. The presence of these 24 elders in Heaven at the beginning of the Tribulation is evidence that the Church has already been raptured. Their dress and their song indicates that the Church is represented here. The elders are seen worshipping the Lamb, Jesus Christ, and casting their crowns before Him, reflecting the rewards and authority given to the faithful at the Bema Seat Judgment.

ESCHATOLOGY

Eschatology is the study of end-time events as revealed in the Bible. This includes the Rapture, the Tribulation, the Second Coming of Christ, the Millennial Kingdom, and the final judgment. There are several differing views on eschatology, including Pre-Tribulation, Post-Tribulation, and amillennial perspectives. The study of eschatology is vital for understanding God's prophetic plan for humanity and His ultimate victory over evil.

EVERLASTING GOSPEL

The *"everlasting [eternal] gospel"* is mentioned in Revelation 14:6-7 (NIV), where an angel proclaims it to *"every nation, tribe, language, and people."* This Gospel calls people to fear God and give Him glory because the hour of His judgment has come. This moment occurs during the Tribulation, when God extends a final call for repentance to the inhabitants of the earth before the final judgments are poured out. This proclamation appears to be distinct from the Church's mission and is a call to acknowledge God's sovereignty and worship Him before it's too late.

EUPHRATES RIVER

The Euphrates River plays a significant role in the end-time events described in Revelation 16:12, where it is dried up to prepare the way for the kings of the east. This event occurs during the sixth Bowl Judgment, allowing armies from the east to gather for the final battle at Armageddon. The drying up of the Euphrates is symbolic of God's preparation for the end-time showdown between good and evil. Demonic locusts of some kind will fly out of this river and kill one third of mankind. This is one of the few judgments where God's chosen people are marked and protected during the tribulation. In recent years we have been seeing this river drying up at historic rates.

F

FALSE PROPHET

The false prophet is the second beast described in Revelation 13:11-18. He will rise to power during the Tribulation and will act as a religious leader who promotes the worship of the antichrist, performing signs and wonders to deceive the inhabitants of the earth. The false prophet will mandate the infamous "mark of the beast" as a sign of allegiance to the antichrist, and without it, people will not be able to buy or sell. The false prophet is part of the satanic trinity (satan, the antichrist, and the false prophet), and his role is to lead people away from God during the Tribulation.

FALLING AWAY

See Apostasy

FEASTS OF GOD/ISRAEL

The Feasts of God are seven annual biblical festivals given by God to the Israelites in the Old Testament, found primarily in Leviticus 23. Each feast holds prophetic significance related to God's redemptive plan. These feasts not only commemorate historical events but also foreshadow future prophetic fulfillments in Jesus Christ and the end times. The major feasts are:

- *Passover* – Represents Jesus's sacrificial death as the Lamb of God.

- *Unleavened Bread* – Symbolizes the removal of sin, foreshadowing Christ's sinless life and death.

- *Firstfruits* – Represents Christ's resurrection as the "firstfruits" of those who will be raised from the dead.

- *Pentecost* – Represents the birth of the Church through the outpouring of the Holy Spirit.

- *Feast of Trumpets* – Many see this as a foreshadowing of the Rapture, where a trumpet will sound and the Church will be caught up to meet Christ.

- *Day of Atonement* – Points to Israel's future national repentance and reconciliation with God.

- *Feast of Tabernacles* – Represents the Millennial Kingdom when God will dwell with His people.

The first four feasts have already been fulfilled through Christ's first coming, while the final three will be fulfilled during the Rapture, Tribulation, and Millennial Kingdom.

FIG TREE

In Matthew 24:32-35, Jesus uses the fig tree as a symbol to describe the signs of the end times. He says that when its branch becomes tender and puts forth leaves, you know that summer is near. In the same way, when believers see the signs He described unfolding (such as wars, famines, and false prophets), they can know that His return is near.

In another place Jesus refers to *"all the trees."* In both instances where Jesus references the fig tree (Matthew 24:32-33, Luke 21:29-31), He stresses its significance while also mentioning all the other trees. Some interpret this to suggest that Jesus isn't specifically highlighting Israel, but it's important to note that Jesus specifically mentions it in both places. Even when other trees are mentioned, the emphasis remains on the fig tree, which has long been recognized as a representation of Israel.

Several Scriptures confirm that the fig tree is a symbol for Israel. Hosea 9:10 (NKJV) says, *"I found Israel like grapes in the wilderness; I saw your fathers as the firstfruits on the fig tree in its first season...."* Likewise, Jeremiah 24 speaks of *"good figs"* and *"bad figs,"* clearly representing different conditions of the people of Israel. Another reference can be found in Joel 1:7, where the destruction of a fig tree symbolizes Israel's suffering. These passages help us understand that when Jesus refers to the fig tree blossoming, He is pointing to the national rebirth of Israel, making it a key sign of the approaching end times.

The rebirth of Israel in 1948 is a key prophetic event as well as the 6 Day War in 1967. These events are seen as a fulfillment of prophecy and a sign that the world is entering the final stages before the Tribulation and the Second Coming of Christ.

FIRST RESURRECTION

The First Resurrection refers to the resurrection of believers who have died, which occurs at different points in the end times, beginning with the Rapture of the Church (1 Thessalonians 4:16-17). The First Resurrection includes all who are raised to eternal life, including Old Testament saints, Church Age believers, and Tribulation martyrs. This is in contrast to the Second Resurrection, which will occur after the Millennial Kingdom and will include the resurrection of the wicked for judgment at the Great White Throne Judgment (Revelation 20:5-6). We discuss the harvest cycles in Israel and how it relates in a previous chapter.

FOUR HORSEMEN

The Four Horsemen of the Apocalypse appear in Revelation 6:1-8 as part of the Seal Judgments that are unleashed during the Tribulation. These horsemen represent different aspects of judgment that will come upon the earth:

- *The White Horse* – Symbolizes the rise of the antichrist, who comes with a bow and a crown, conquering and seeking global domination.
- *The Red Horse* – Represents war and bloodshed, as peace is taken from the earth.
- *The Black Horse* – Symbolizes famine and economic collapse, with scarcity and inflated prices for basic goods.
- *The Pale Horse* – Represents death, followed by Hades, as widespread death from famine, disease, and violence ravages the earth.

FULLNESS OF THE GENTILES

The fullness of the Gentiles refers to the completion of God's plan to bring salvation to the Gentiles (non-Jewish people). This phrase is linked to Romans 11:25 (NIV), where Paul writes, *"I do not want you to be ignorant of this mystery, brothers and sisters, so that you may not be conceited: Israel has experienced a hardening in part until the full number of the Gentiles has come in."* Once this appointed number of Gentiles enters the faith, God's focus will shift back to Israel, and *"all Israel shall be saved"* (Romans 11:26 NIV), ushering in a time of restoration for the Jewish people and fulfillment of His covenant promises.

This concept highlights God's overarching plan of redemption that involves both Gentiles and Jews, pointing toward a future time when Israel's spiritual blindness will be lifted and they will recognize their Messiah. This "fullness" is a key event that leads into the culmination of the end times, emphasizing God's desire to reach all peoples before the final fulfillment of His promises to Israel.

G

GOG AND MAGOG

Gog and Magog are prophetic names mentioned in Ezekiel 38–39 and Revelation 20:8. In Ezekiel's prophecy, Gog is the leader of a coalition of nations that some suggest will invade Israel in the last days, and Magog is often associated with a region or nation north of Israel. This invasion is seen as a major end-time event where God will intervene supernaturally to protect Israel, resulting in the total destruction of Gog's armies. Some scholars believe this event occurs before or at the beginning of the Tribulation, while others place it during the Tribulation itself.

Others connect Gog and Magog with a future coalition that includes nations like Russia, Iran, and Turkey. In Revelation 20:8, Gog and Magog reappear at the end of the Millennial Kingdom as symbolic representations of a final rebellion against God. This shows that even after 1,000 years of Christ's righteous reign, satan will still find followers to oppose God.

GRAPES OF WRATH

The Grapes of Wrath is a biblical metaphor used to describe the outpouring of God's judgment during the end times. In Revelation 14:19-20 (NKJV), it is written that the earth's wickedness is harvested and thrown into *"the great winepress of the wrath of God,"* resulting in widespread destruction. This vivid imagery signifies the crushing judgment that will come upon the unrepentant nations during the final days of the Tribulation, culminating in the Battle of Armageddon. The phrase is often associated with God's retributive justice, demonstrating His righteous anger toward sin and rebellion.

> *I have trodden the winepress alone; and of the people there was none with me: for I will tread them in mine anger, and trample them in my fury; and their blood shall be sprinkled upon my garments, and I will stain all my raiment*
>
> (Isaiah 63:3 KJV).

GREAT MULTITUDE

In Revelation 7:9-14, a great multitude is seen before the throne of God, worshipping Him. This multitude consists of believers from every nation, tribe, people, and language who have come out of The Great Tribulation. They are described as having *"washed their robes and made them white in the blood of the Lamb."* This great multitude is often understood to be Tribulation saints or those who come to faith in Christ during the Tribulation and are martyred for their testimony.

GREAT TRIBULATION

The Great Tribulation refers to the second half of the seven-year Tribulation period, which begins at the midpoint when the antichrist commits the abomination of desolation in the temple. Jesus speaks of this time in Matthew 24:21 (KJV), saying, *"For then shall be great tribulation, such as was not since the beginning of the world to this time, no, nor ever shall be."* During this period, God's wrath will intensify with the Trumpet and Bowl Judgments, and unprecedented suffering will come upon the earth. The Pre-Tribulation view teaches that the Church will not experience The Great Tribulation, as believers will have been raptured beforehand. The Great Tribulation is primarily focused on Israel and the nations, as God brings judgment and purifies His people. Learn more in the chapter on the Tribulation.

GREAT WHITE THRONE JUDGMENT

The Great White Throne Judgment is the final judgment described in Revelation 20:11-15, where all the dead who have not been part of the First Resurrection will stand before God. This judgment takes place after the Millennial Kingdom and the final defeat of satan. All those who are judged at the Great White Throne are unbelievers, and their names are not found in the Book of Life. They will be judged based on their works and will be cast into the lake of fire, which is the second death. Believers will not face this judgment, as they will have already been rewarded at the Bema Seat Judgment after the Rapture.

H

HARLOT OF BABYLON

The harlot of Babylon is a symbolic figure described in Revelation 17 as a great prostitute who sits on many waters, representing a corrupt religious system that aligns itself with political powers during the Tribulation. She is associated with luxury, immorality, and persecution of the saints, symbolizing the world's false religious systems and their opposition to God. The harlot is said to be *"drunk with the blood of the saints"* because of her persecution of believers. Eventually, the political leaders she is allied with will turn on her and destroy her. Some associate this with the Catholic church but we do know that this will be a future world religion that will dominate the first half of the Tribulation but will be destroyed when the antichrist assumes full control. Babylon itself represents a global system of corruption and rebellion against God.

HEAVEN

Heaven is the dwelling place of God, His angels, and the redeemed. It is described in Revelation 21–22 as the eternal home of believers, where there will be no more death, sorrow, or pain. After the Rapture, believers will be taken to Heaven to be with Christ, and they will return with Him at the Second Coming to reign during the Millennial Kingdom. Ultimately, believers will dwell in the New Jerusalem, a heavenly city, for eternity.

HELL

Hell is the final destination for the unrighteous after the Great White Throne Judgment. Described as a place of eternal punishment, Revelation 20:14 refers to it as the *"lake of fire,"* which is the second death. All those whose names are not found in the Book of Life will be cast into the lake of fire, including satan, the antichrist, and the false prophet. Hell is the final abode of all who reject God's offer of salvation through Jesus Christ.

HORNS

Horns often symbolize strength, power, or authority, particularly of kings and kingdoms. In Daniel 7 and Revelation 13, horns are used to describe world rulers or empires. For example, the antichrist is symbolized as having ten horns, representing ten kings or kingdoms that will submit to his authority during the Tribulation. The ultimate defeat of these powers is predicted, leading to Christ's victorious return and the establishment of His Kingdom.

HOUR OF TEMPTATION

The hour of temptation is mentioned in Revelation 3:10, where Jesus promises the church of Philadelphia that He will keep them from *"the hour of temptation, which shall come upon all the world, to try them that dwell upon the earth."* This phrase is understood to refer to the time of the Tribulation, specifically the global testing and judgment that will take place. The promise to be kept from this hour is seen as evidence of a Pre-Tribulation Rapture, when the Church will be removed from the earth before the Tribulation begins. The *"temptation"* here refers to a time of intense trial, testing, and divine judgment, not merely moral temptation. We discuss this in more detail in this book.

I

IMAGE OF THE BEAST

The image of the beast is mentioned in Revelation 13:14-15, where the false prophet creates an image of the antichrist (the beast) and commands everyone to worship it. This image is given the ability to speak and even to kill those who refuse to worship it. The antichrist will demand global worship through this idolatrous image. Some speculate that this could involve advanced technology, such as artificial intelligence.

I write about this in my book, *Summoning the Demon: AI, Aliens and the Antichrist.*

INCENSE

In Scripture, incense is often symbolic of the prayers of God's people. In Revelation 8:3-4, an angel offers incense with the prayers of the saints before God's throne. This image of incense rising before God is a reminder that the prayers of believers are heard and treasured by Him. Even during the chaotic events of the Tribulation, the prayers of the saints, including those martyred for their faith, will play a significant role in God's unfolding plan. The use of incense in the tabernacle and temple also points to the intercessory role of Christ as our High Priest, who continually presents our prayers before the Father.

ISRAEL (ROLE IN THE END TIMES)

Israel plays a central role in end-time prophecy. The Tribulation, or Daniel's seventieth week, is primarily focused on Israel and the fulfillment of God's covenant promises to them. While the Church is raptured, God will turn His attention back to Israel, bringing them through a time of intense trial and purification, as described in Zechariah 13:8-9. The 144,000 Jewish evangelists in Revelation 7 will be sealed and protected by God to proclaim the Gospel during the Tribulation. The Millennial Kingdom will also see Israel restored as the center of Christ's reign on earth, as prophesied throughout the Old Testament.

J

JACOB'S TROUBLE

Jacob's trouble refers to a time of unparalleled distress for Israel, prophesied in Jeremiah 30:7 (KJV), which says, *"Alas! For that day is great, so that none is like it: it is even the time of Jacob's trouble; but he shall be saved out of it."* This period is widely understood to be the Tribulation when Israel will face unprecedented persecution and trials under the rule of the antichrist. God promises that even though this period will be one of intense suffering, He will save a remnant of Israel through it. The deliverance of Israel at the end of the Tribulation aligns with prophecies such as Zechariah 12:10, where they will recognize Jesus as their Messiah.

JEHOSHAPHAT (VALLEY OF)

The Valley of Jehoshaphat is mentioned in Joel 3:2 as the place where God will gather the nations for judgment. It is traditionally associated with the Kidron Valley, which runs between Jerusalem and the Mount of Olives. This valley is believed to be the site of the final judgment of the nations, also known as the Judgment of the Nations or the Sheep and Goats Judgment. This judgment is separate from the Great White Throne Judgment and takes place after Christ's Second Coming, before the start of the Millennial Kingdom.

JERUSALEM

Jerusalem is central to biblical prophecy, particularly in the end times. It is the city where Jesus will return to set up His Millennial Kingdom, as prophesied in Zechariah 14:4, where His feet will stand on the Mount of Olives. Throughout the Tribulation, Jerusalem plays a key role as the epicenter of spiritual and political activity. The antichrist will desecrate the temple in Jerusalem during the abomination of desolation (Matthew 24:15), and the two witnesses will prophesy in the city before being killed (Revelation 11:8). Despite its temporary occupation by the antichrist, Jerusalem will ultimately be restored as the capital of Christ's Kingdom during the Millennium. In the eternal state, the New Jerusalem will descend from Heaven, representing the eternal dwelling place of God with His people (Revelation 21:2).

JUDGMENT SEAT OF CHRIST (BEMA SEAT)

The Judgment Seat of Christ, also known as the Bema Seat, is where believers will stand to be judged for their works and service to the Lord. This judgment does not determine salvation, as that is already secured by faith in Christ; rather, it determines the rewards believers will receive for their faithfulness. Second Corinthians 5:10 (KJV) says, *"For we must all appear before the judgment seat of Christ, that every one may receive the things done in his body, according to that he hath done, whether it be good or bad."* The term *bema* refers to a platform where judges would award prizes in athletic competitions, but it also refers to the place where a city's judge sat to render decisions.

The Judgment Seat of Christ occurs after the Rapture, and believers will be rewarded for their service, obedience, and stewardship. The rewards mentioned in Revelation 2–3 (like crowns and authority) may be dispensed at this time as well. The Rapture of the Church and this Judgment are connected and happen in succession.

K

KEY OF DAVID

The key of David is mentioned in Revelation 3:7, where Jesus is described as the one who holds the key of David. This phrase refers to Jesus's authority and His power to open and close doors that no one else can. The key gives Him the authority to grant or deny access to the Kingdom and His will. This is also a fulfillment of Isaiah 22:22, where Eliakim is given the key to the house of David, symbolizing authority over the king's household. The church of Philadelphia is promised that the door of opportunity will remain open to them, as Christ holds this key. It could also be a reference to the same door John saw in Revelation 4:1 which some believe to be representative of the Rapture.

KING OF KINGS

The title King of kings is used to describe Jesus Christ in Revelation 19:16, where He returns as the conquering King at His Second Coming. It signifies His ultimate authority over all earthly rulers and kingdoms. Unlike His first coming, where He came as the suffering servant, His Second Coming will reveal Him as the victorious King who will judge the nations and establish His Kingdom.

KINGDOM OF THE BEAST

The kingdom of the beast refers to the global empire that the antichrist will establish during the Tribulation. This kingdom is described in Revelation 13 and Revelation 17, where the antichrist, empowered by satan, will have authority over all the nations of the earth. The kingdom will be characterized by tyranny, persecution of believers, and the enforcement of the mark of the beast. The antichrist's kingdom is referred to as a beast because of its ferocious nature and its opposition to God's people. However, this kingdom will be short-lived, as it will be destroyed when Christ returns at the Second Coming. The kingdom of the beast is contrasted with the Kingdom of God, which will be established after the defeat of the antichrist.

KNOWLEDGE SHALL INCREASE

The phrase *"knowledge shall increase"* is found in Daniel 12:4 (KJV), where Daniel is told to *"shut up the words, and seal the book, even to the time of the end: many shall run to and fro, and knowledge shall be increased."* This is often interpreted to mean that as the end times approach, there will be a rapid increase in both technological advancements and spiritual understanding, particularly in relation to prophetic insights. Many believe this passage indicates that as we draw closer to the Tribulation and the return of Christ, people will gain more understanding of Bible prophecy.

L

LAKE OF FIRE

The lake of fire is the final place of punishment for satan, the antichrist, the false prophet, and all those who reject Christ, as described in Revelation 20:14-15. It is referred to as the *"second death,"* where both death and Hades are cast, and it is a place of eternal torment. Unlike Hades, which is a temporary place of the dead, the lake of fire is the permanent place of judgment. The lake of fire is reserved for those who are not part of God's redeemed, marking their final and eternal separation from God.

LAMB OF GOD

The Lamb of God is a title given to Jesus Christ that signifies His role as the sacrificial Lamb who takes away the sins of the world. This phrase comes from John 1:29 (KJV), where John the Baptist, upon seeing Jesus, declares, *"Behold the Lamb of God, which taketh away the sin of the world."* In the Old Testament, lambs were sacrificed as an offering for sin, foreshadowing the ultimate sacrifice of Jesus. The imagery of a lamb represents innocence, submission, and the willingness to be sacrificed.

In Isaiah 53:7, the Messiah is described as being led *"as a lamb to the slaughter,"* further pointing to Jesus's sacrificial death. The Lamb of God concept finds its fulfillment in Jesus's death on the Cross, where He became the perfect and final sacrifice for humanity's sins, fulfilling the requirements of the law and reconciling humanity to God. The book of Revelation also emphasizes this imagery, depicting Jesus as the victorious *"Lamb slain from the foundation of the world"* (Revelation 13:8), highlighting both His sacrifice and His triumph over sin and death.

In Revelation 5:5-6 (KJV), John recounts, *"And one of the elders saith unto me, Weep not: behold, the Lion of the tribe of Judah, the Root of David, hath prevailed to open the book, and to loose the seven seals thereof. And I beheld, and, lo, in the midst of the throne and of the four beasts, and in the midst of the elders, stood a Lamb as it had been slain, having seven horns and seven eyes, which are the seven Spirits of God sent forth into all the earth."*

The modern imagery often portrays this as a small, gentle lamb, but the true picture John saw was far more intimidating. This was not a helpless, fluffy lamb but an adolescent ram, one that still bears the wounds of sacrifice. The sight was meant to be awe-inspiring and even terrifying, showing a blood-soaked ram with seven horns and seven eyes. As the antichrist rises with his seven heads and ten horns, Jesus stands as the true, ultimate power, His seven horns proclaiming His superiority, with a horn for each of the usurper's attempts to dominate. It is a declaration that He holds full authority and that no false power can prevail against Him.

LAMB'S BOOK OF LIFE

The Lamb's Book of Life is mentioned several times in Revelation, most notably in Revelation 20:12 and Revelation 21:27. It contains the names of all those who have accepted Christ as their Savior, ensuring their eternal life. Those whose names are written in the Book of Life will not face eternal judgment and will enter the New Jerusalem. The absence of a name in this book results in being cast into the lake of fire. (See Book of Life.)

LAODICEA

Laodicea was one of the seven churches mentioned in the book of Revelation (Revelation 3:14-22). Jesus addressed the church in Laodicea with some of the most direct and sobering rebukes in all of Scripture. The church is described as "lukewarm," neither hot nor cold and because of this, Jesus declared that He would *"spew thee out of my mouth"* (Revelation 3:16). The lukewarm nature of Laodicea symbolizes a form of Christianity that is complacent, self-satisfied, and indifferent, lacking the fervor and passion that true faith should produce.

Jesus told them that while they claimed to be rich, they were in fact *"wretched, miserable, poor, blind, and naked"* (Revelation 3:17 KJV). The city was famous for its banking, textile industry, and a medical school that produced an eye salve. Jesus used these familiar symbols to call them to repentance, urging them to *"buy of me gold tried in the fire,"* *"white raiment,"* and *"anoint thine eyes with eyesalve, that thou mayest see"* (Revelation 3:18 KJV).

Laodicea serves as a warning to modern believers about the dangers of spiritual complacency and self-reliance. Jesus stands at the door and knocks (Revelation 3:20), offering fellowship to those who open the door.

LAST DAYS

The last days refer to the period between Christ's first coming and His Second Coming, a time of increasing wickedness, spiritual deception, and the spread of the Gospel. The term is used frequently in the New

Testament, including in 2 Timothy 3:1, where Paul warns of perilous times in the last days, and Acts 2:17, where Peter quotes Joel's prophecy that God will pour out His Spirit in the last days.

LAST TRUMP

See "What about the Last Trump?" in Chapter 9.

LITTLE HORN

The little horn is a symbol found in Daniel 7:8 (KJV), where the prophet describes seeing a small horn emerging among ten horns, uprooting three of them. This little horn represents a powerful, emerging ruler who grows in dominance and whose influence surpasses the others, *"speaking great things"* or boasting arrogantly.

Most scholars interpret this little horn as a reference to the antichrist, a future leader who will rise from the nations and establish a significant authority during the end times. The description given, speaking pompous words, making war against the saints, and prevailing over them, aligns with the depiction of the antichrist in Revelation 13. He will seek to defy God, deceive many, and wage war against God's people.

LOCUSTS (DEMONIC PLAGUE)

The locusts described in Revelation 9:1-11 during the fifth Trumpet Judgment are not ordinary locusts but represent a demonic army unleashed from the abyss. These creatures are given the power to torment those who do not have the seal of God on their foreheads for five months. Their appearance is described as terrifying, with faces like humans, crowns of gold, and tails like scorpions. The protection given to the 144,000 Jewish evangelists also highlights that some will be supernaturally shielded from this particular horror, but not others.

LUCIFER

Lucifer, meaning "light-bearer," is the name traditionally associated with satan before his fall from Heaven. The name comes from Isaiah 14:12 (KJV) where it says, *"How art thou fallen from heaven, O Lucifer, son of the morning!"* Satan, once an angel of high rank, was cast out of Heaven due to his rebellion against God. In the end times, satan will empower the antichrist and lead the final rebellion against God. However, his ultimate defeat is assured, as he will be cast into the lake of fire for eternity (Revelation 20:10).

M

MAN OF SIN

The man of sin, also known as the man of lawlessness, is a title given to the antichrist in 2 Thessalonians 2:3-4. He will rise to power during the Tribulation, declaring himself to be God and demanding worship from all people. The man of sin will deceive the world through signs and wonders, leading a rebellion against God. The man of sin will dominate the world politically and spiritually during the Tribulation, but will ultimately be defeated by Christ at His Second Coming. (See antichrist.)

MARANATHA

The term *Maranatha* is an Aramaic phrase meaning "Our Lord, come" or "The Lord is coming." It was used as a greeting and an expression of hope among early Christians, reminding each other of the imminent return of Jesus Christ. The apostle Paul used Maranatha in 1 Corinthians 16:22 (KJV), emphasizing the believer's longing for Christ's return. This expectation of Jesus's return serves as both encouragement and motivation, urging believers to live holy and faithful lives while anticipating the blessed hope of His appearing

(Titus 2:13). In the midst of trials and uncertainties, Maranatha stands as a powerful declaration of hope, reminding us that Jesus is coming soon to set all things right.

MARK OF THE BEAST

The mark of the beast is mentioned in Revelation 13:16-18, where it is described as a mark that will be required for all people to buy or sell during the Tribulation. The mark is associated with the antichrist (the beast) and represents allegiance to his regime. The number of the beast, 666, is linked to this mark, and those who receive it are aligning themselves with satan's kingdom. This mark will be a literal, visible mark, possibly linked to modern technology like biometric systems or implants, but no one can know for sure. Those who refuse the mark will be persecuted, but they will be spared from God's eternal judgment.

The concept of the mark of the beast has stirred up a great deal of alarm, and rightly so, especially as our generation is witnessing the rapid development of technology that could make such a mark feasible. Despite the fear and hysteria, no one should be concerned about accidentally receiving the mark of the beast. This isn't something that can happen without full awareness. Scripture makes it clear that receiving the mark involves a deliberate act of allegiance to the antichrist and a conscious rejection of God. There will be no confusion, no gray area. It will be a clear decision to worship the beast and reject God, leaving no room for ambiguity.

MARRIAGE SUPPER OF THE LAMB

The marriage supper of the Lamb is a celebratory event described in Revelation 19:7-9 (KJV), rejoicing over Christ (the Lamb) being united with His Bride (the Church). The imagery of a wedding banquet highlights the joy and intimacy of the relationship between Christ and His Church.

Some suggest that following the marriage of the Lamb, Jesus returns to the earth accompanied by His Bride, the Church (Revelation 19:14). At this time, tribulation saints are resurrected to join in the celebration as guests, along with the Old Testament saints (Daniel 12:1-2). This grand feast will mark the beginning of Christ's Millennial Reign and could take place during the 75-day interval mentioned in Daniel 12:11-12, between Christ's return and the establishment of His earthly Kingdom. It's a celebration that will unite all of God's redeemed across history, highlighting His triumph and their faithfulness.

MILLENNIAL KINGDOM

The Millennial Kingdom is the 1,000-year reign of Christ on earth, described in Revelation 20:1-6. After His Second Coming, Jesus will establish His Kingdom on earth, ruling from Jerusalem, and fulfilling the promises made to Israel. During this time, satan will be bound in the abyss, and peace and righteousness will prevail around the world. This period will be characterized by the fulfillment of Old Testament prophecies about Israel's restoration and global peace. It is distinct from the eternal state, which comes after the Millennium and the final judgment.

MILLENNIUM

The Millennium refers to the thousand-year reign of Jesus Christ on earth, described in Revelation 20:1-6. During this period, satan is bound and unable to deceive the nations, and Christ reigns with justice and righteousness, fulfilling God's promises of peace and restoration. The Millennium is characterized by unparalleled prosperity, harmony, and the direct rule of Jesus as King of kings, allowing humanity to experience the fullness of His righteous governance.

The Millennium is mentioned six times in Revelation 20, each time specifying a duration of one thousand years, emphasizing that this is a literal time period, not a figurative one. This is further evidenced by the fact that it is a specific sentencing period for satan, who is bound for one thousand years and then loosed briefly for one last attempt to deceive the nations (Revelation 20:7-8). Such a specific duration and sequence of events, including satan's binding and release, support the understanding of a literal thousand-year reign of Christ.

This time period is also when resurrected believers reign alongside Christ (Revelation 20:4-6). Those who survived the Tribulation and gave their lives to Christ will enter into the Millennium in natural bodies, repopulating the earth. The Millennium fulfills the promises made to Israel in the Old Testament, with Jesus ruling from Jerusalem, and shows God's perfect justice and the fulfillment of His covenant promises. At the end of the thousand years, satan will be released briefly to deceive the nations one last time, leading to his ultimate defeat and the establishment of the eternal state. This period is merely preparation for God the Father to come and dwell among His people in the eternal state.

MYSTERY BABYLON

Mystery Babylon is described in Revelation 17 as the symbolic representation of a corrupt global religious, financial, and political system that opposes God and persecutes His people. The term *mystery* suggests that Babylon's true nature is hidden until it is revealed in the end times. Babylon's fall, described in Revelation 18, marks the collapse of this system and the beginning of God's final judgment on the world. The destruction of Babylon is significant because it signals the end of human rebellion and the imminent return of Christ to establish His Kingdom.

MYSTERY OF LAWLESSNESS

The *"mystery of lawlessness"* is mentioned in 2 Thessalonians 2:7 (NKJV), referring to the hidden but active force of rebellion against God that will culminate in the rise of the antichrist. This mystery is already at work in the world, though it is currently restrained by the Holy Spirit within the Church. At the Rapture, the restraining influence of the Holy Spirit through the Church will be removed, allowing lawlessness to reach its full expression under the antichrist's reign. This term highlights the spiritual forces that oppose God and seek to deceive humanity, which will become fully visible during the Tribulation.

N

NEW HEAVEN AND NEW EARTH

The new heaven and new earth is the ultimate restoration of creation described in Revelation 21:1, where John sees a new heaven and new earth, for the first heaven and the first earth have passed away. This marks the final and eternal state where God's people will live in His presence forever. After the Millennial Kingdom and the final judgment, God will make all things new, removing the curse of sin and death. This is the culmination of God's redemptive plan, where He dwells with His people in perfect peace and righteousness for eternity.

NEW JERUSALEM

The *"New Jerusalem"* is described in Revelation 21:2 (NKJV) as a glorious city that descends from Heaven, prepared as a bride adorned for her husband. This is the eternal home for believers. The city is filled with the glory of God and is described in great detail, with streets of gold, gates made of pearl, and walls adorned with precious stones. It represents the culmination of God's promise to dwell with His people forever.

NUMBER OF THE BEAST

The number of the beast, 666, is mentioned in Revelation 13:18 as the number of the antichrist, and it is tied to the mark of the beast. This number has been the subject of much speculation, as John says it is the number of a man, and calculating it reveals the identity of the beast. Those who take the mark of the beast and associate themselves with this number will face eternal judgment.

O

OCCUPY

The command to *"Occupy till I come"* comes from Jesus's parable in Luke 19:13 (KJV), where a nobleman tells his servants to engage in business with his resources until he returns. The word *occupy* in this context is translated from the Greek word *pragmaeuomai*, meaning to do business, trade, or actively engage in productive work. For believers, this command is a reminder to stay actively engaged in God's work until Christ's return. It encourages us to spread the Gospel, serve others, and live faithfully, making the most of the opportunities we have while awaiting Jesus's return.

Healthy Rapture teaching encourages and motivates us to occupy, being salt and light in a world that desperately needs the hope we carry.

OLIVET DISCOURSE

The Olivet Discourse, recorded in Matthew 24-25, Mark 13, and Luke 21, is Jesus's in-depth teaching about the events of the last days. Delivered from the Mount of Olives, this discourse encompasses prophetic insights into the signs of His Second Coming, The Great Tribulation, the abomination of desolation, and the urgent call for believers to remain watchful.

It is crucial to note that much of Jesus's teaching here is directed specifically toward Israel. For instance, His instruction to *"flee to the mountains"* when they see the abomination of desolation clearly refers to those in Judea, which indicates an audience that is predominantly Jewish and relevant to the circumstances during the future Tribulation.

A key aspect of understanding the Olivet Discourse is recognizing the differences between the accounts in Matthew 24 and Luke 21. Matthew 24 focuses heavily on end-time events and is addressed primarily to a Jewish audience, with the abomination of desolation serving as a key sign for those in Judea during the Tribulation. Luke 21, however, includes references to earlier historical events, such as the destruction of Jerusalem in AD 70, in addition to the broader warnings about the last days. Luke's perspective is more tailored to a mixed audience, reflecting both immediate and future fulfillments of Jesus's prophetic words. Thus, Matthew emphasizes the future tribulation period, while Luke contains a combination of near-term and end-time events, giving a more detailed historical and prophetic context.

ONE WORLD GOVERNMENT

The concept of a one world government is closely tied to the rise of the antichrist during the Tribulation. In Revelation 13:7, the beast (antichrist) is described as having authority over every tribe, people, language, and nation, indicating global political and economic control. This one-world system will involve a centralized government that forces people to submit to the rule of the antichrist. This government will be marked by tyranny, the enforcement of the mark of the beast, and persecution of believers who resist the antichrist's authority.

ONE WORLD RELIGION

The one world religion refers to the false religious system that will emerge during the Tribulation and unite people in worship of the antichrist. In Revelation 17, this system is symbolized by the harlot who sits on many waters, representing the global influence and power of this false religious entity. The false prophet will play a key role in promoting the worship of the antichrist and deceiving the world with miraculous signs (Revelation 13:13-14). This system will be short-lived, as it will be destroyed by the antichrist himself during the second half of the Tribulation.

OUTPOURING OF THE HOLY SPIRIT

The outpouring of the Holy Spirit is prophesied in Joel 2:28-29 and quoted by Peter in Acts 2:17 as the beginning of the fulfillment of this prophecy. In the end times, there will be a renewed outpouring of the Holy Spirit, empowering believers to preach the Gospel with boldness, accompanied by signs and wonders. According to 2 Chronicles 7:14, revival is promised to all those who seek it, even the final generation. No matter how dark it gets, revival is available to every hungry heart.

OVERCOMERS

Overcomers are mentioned in the letters to the seven churches in Revelation 2–3. They are believers who remain faithful to Christ despite persecution, temptation, and the trials of life. Each church is given promises to those who *"overcome,"* including rewards such as the right to eat from the tree of life (Revelation 2:7), receive a new name (Revelation 2:17), and rule with Christ (Revelation 3:21). These promises apply to believers who live victoriously through the power of Christ. Overcomers are those who trust in Jesus (1 John 5:4).

P

PAROUSIA

Parousia is a Greek term meaning "presence" or "coming," and in biblical eschatology it refers specifically to the Second Coming of Jesus Christ. Some use the term to encompass both the Rapture and the Second Coming. The *Parousia* refers primarily to Christ's visible return to earth at the end of the Tribulation to defeat the antichrist, judge the nations, and establish His Millennial Kingdom (Revelation 19:11-16).

PARTIAL RAPTURE THEORY

The partial Rapture theory suggests that only faithful, spiritually mature believers will be taken in the Rapture, while carnal or luke-warm Christians will be left behind to face the Tribulation. This viewpoint emphasizes the need for believers to be "watchful" and "ready," implying that only those who are living obediently and faithfully will qualify for the Rapture when it occurs.

While I don't subscribe to the idea that only the so-called "super saints" will be raptured, we must acknowledge the consistent and urgent warnings Jesus gave to watch, be ready, and live faithfully (Luke 21:36, Mark 13:33-37). These warnings would seem unnecessary if every believer were guaranteed to be taken, regardless of their spiritual state. The admonition to *"watch and pray always"* implies a readiness that every believer should strive for, and while all who are truly in Christ will be saved, there is still a call to live prepared for His sudden return, ready to meet Him when He comes.

Maybe this should shift our focus away from the idea of a "partial Rapture" involving different classes of believers and instead challenge us to consider what it truly means to be a believer. Perhaps the question is not whether only part of the Church will be taken, but rather whether those left behind were ever genuinely saved to begin with.

If we redefine what it means to be a true believer, one whose life reflects faithfulness, readiness, and an ongoing relationship with Jesus, then maybe the Rapture isn't a selective event for "super saints," but rather the fulfillment of His promise to all who are genuinely His. It's possible that everyone who is truly saved will be caught up, while those left behind were simply those who had deceived themselves, thinking they were ready, yet lacking the genuine saving faith required to be part of Christ's Bride. As Jesus warned in Matthew 7:21 (NIV), *"Not everyone who says to me, 'Lord, Lord,' will enter the kingdom of heaven, but only the one who does the will of my Father who is in heaven."* This verse serves as a reminder that the true believers are those who are actively living out their faith while trusting in His grace alone.

PRETERISM

Preterism is the view that most or all of the prophecies concerning the end times were fulfilled in the first century, particularly with the destruction of Jerusalem and the temple in AD 70. Preterists believe that the events described in Matthew 24 and much of Revelation are not future occurrences but historical ones.

PROPHECY (BIBLICAL PROPHECY)

Biblical prophecy refers to the divine foretelling of future events as revealed in Scripture. Approximately one-third of the Bible is prophetic, much of it concerning the end times.

R

RAPTURE

The Rapture refers to the event when Jesus Christ will return to take believers (the Church) from the earth to meet Him in the air, as described in 1 Thessalonians 4:16-17 and 1 Corinthians 15:51-52. This event is imminent, meaning it could happen at any moment, and it will involve both the resurrection of dead believers and the transformation of living believers into glorified bodies. The Rapture is not only a deliverance from wrath but also a moment of joyous reunion with Christ, as believers are caught up to be with Him forever.

REBUILDING OF THE TEMPLE

The rebuilding of the temple refers to the future construction of the Jewish temple in Jerusalem, which will occur during or just before the Tribulation. Second Thessalonians 2:4 and Revelation 11:1-2 indicate that the antichrist will desecrate this temple by proclaiming himself to be God and setting up the abomination of desolation within it. The rebuilding of the temple is a key prophetic sign, signaling the nearing of the Tribulation period and the fulfillment of end-time prophecy.

The Temple Institute in Jerusalem nearly has everything in place to begin this process. We are in the last days.

RESTRAINER

The Restrainer is mentioned in 2 Thessalonians 2:6-7 (NKJV), where Paul speaks of a force that is currently holding back the man of lawlessness (the antichrist) from being revealed. The Restrainer is the Holy Spirit working through the Church. Once the Church is raptured, the Holy Spirit's restraining influence will be removed, allowing the antichrist to rise to power and the full force of lawlessness to be unleashed during the Tribulation. This concept underscores the belief that the Church plays a vital role in holding back the darkness and chaos that will dominate the earth during the Tribulation.

We're not afraid of the antichrist. The antichrist is afraid of us.

REVELATION

The book of Revelation, also known as the Apocalypse, is the final book of the Bible, written by the apostle John, that reveals the events of the last days, the Second Coming of Christ, and the final judgment. The book provides symbolic and literal visions of the Tribulation, the rise of the antichrist, the judgments of God, and the establishment of the new heaven and new earth. Revelation serves as a road map for understanding God's ultimate plan for humanity and the defeat of evil, but more than that, it's a revelation of Jesus Christ.

S

SAINTS

In the context of end-time prophecy, *saints* can refer to different groups of believers depending on the timeline both in the Old and New Testaments. While the antichrist will be given power to persecute saints during the Tribulation, Jesus promised in Matthew 16:18 that the gates of hell would not prevail against the Church, which is one reason why Pre-Tribulation scholars believe the Church is not present during this period of intense persecution.

SATAN

Satan, also known as the devil, is the ultimate accuser of God and humanity. He plays a significant role in the events of the end, particularly during the Tribulation, when he empowers the antichrist and wages war against the saints. Revelation 12 describes satan being cast down from Heaven, filled with fury because he knows his time is short. Satan's final defeat will come at the end of the Tribulation when Christ returns, and satan is bound for 1,000 years in the abyss during the Millennial Kingdom (Revelation 20:1-3). After a brief release, he will be cast into the lake of fire for eternity (Revelation 20:10).

SCOFFERS

The Bible predicts that in the last days, scoffers will come, mocking the promise of Jesus's return and ridiculing the hope of believers (2 Peter 3:3-4). These scoffers question the certainty of Christ's coming, using the apparent delay as a reason to doubt its reality. Peter writes:

> *Knowing this first, that there shall come in the last days scoffers, walking after their own lusts, And saying, Where is the promise of his coming? for since the fathers fell asleep, all things continue as they were from the beginning of the creation*
> (2 Peter 3:3-4 KJV).

These scoffers are often those who should know better but choose to ignore God's promises due to their sinful desires. Their mockery is rooted in spiritual blindness, and their skepticism ignores the fact that God's timeline is not bound by human understanding. The warnings about scoffers emphasize the importance of believers holding fast to their hope, understanding that God's delay is an act of mercy, allowing time for more people to repent (2 Peter 3:9).

Often people will say, "Every generation has thought they were the last..." and they are absolutely correct. Nearly every generation, except this one, has lived with that urgency. Interestingly, the lack of urgency we see today is, in itself, a fulfillment of prophecy. The presence of scoffers is a specific indicator that the return of Jesus is drawing nearer. So, ironically, those who ridicule our hope are themselves proof that we are on the verge of His return.

SEAL JUDGMENTS

The Seal Judgments are the first series of judgments that unfold in the book of Revelation, beginning in Revelation 6 when Jesus, the Lamb of God, opens the seals of a scroll. Each seal unleashes a specific judgment upon the earth, including war, famine, death, and widespread devastation. These judgments mark the beginning of the Tribulation and are followed by the Trumpet and Bowl Judgments, which intensify in severity. These judgments are part of God's wrath being poured out on a rebellious world, and the Church is not present during this time, having been raptured before these events occur.

SECOND COMING (SECOND ADVENT)

The Second Coming of Jesus Christ refers to His physical return to earth at the end of the seven-year Tribulation, as described in Revelation 19:11-16. Unlike the Rapture, where Christ comes to take believers up into the air, the Second Coming involves Christ returning with His saints to defeat the antichrist, judge the nations, and establish His Millennial Kingdom. The Second Coming is distinct from the Rapture, which happens before the Tribulation, while the Second Coming occurs after it. At the Second Coming, Christ will fulfill His role as King of kings and Lord of lords, bringing an end to the reign of evil and establishing peace on earth.

SECOND DEATH

The Second Death is mentioned in Revelation 20:14 and refers to eternal separation from God in the lake of fire. After the Great

White Throne Judgment, those who have rejected Christ will face this second death, which is far more severe than physical death, as it involves the soul's eternal punishment. Believers, having part in the first resurrection (at the Rapture), are not subject to the second death. Instead, they are granted eternal life with Christ, while those who face the second death are those who rejected God's offer of salvation.

SECRET RAPTURE

The term *secret rapture* is a derogatory phrase coined by critics of the Pre-Tribulation Rapture doctrine, suggesting that believers will be quietly and secretly taken away without anyone knowing. However, this concept is a distortion of what Pre-Tribulation believers actually teach. No prominent advocate of the Pre-Tribulation Rapture holds that the event will be secret. This resurrection/rapture of believers will be no more secret than the resurrection of our Messiah.

While the Rapture will be sudden and without warning (*"as a thief in the night,"* 1 Thessalonians 5:2 KJV), the aftermath will be anything but secret. The world will be left shocked, confused, and in disarray as millions of believers are taken from earth in an instant. It is precisely because of the Rapture's dramatic impact that many will turn to God, realizing that the event they were warned about has come to pass. The disappearance of believers, the sudden emptiness of workplaces, schools, homes, and the inexplicable absence of countless individuals will be an undeniable testament to the truth of the Bible. Though world government will attempt to explain this away as some kind of plague, enemy attack, or even UFOs, it will prompt many to seek answers; and as a result, numerous people will come to faith during the beginning of the Tribulation.

SEED OF THE WOMAN

The seed of the woman is a reference to the prophetic promise found in Genesis 3:15, often called the *protoevangelium,* or "first gospel." In this verse, God speaks to the serpent, saying:

> *And I will put enmity between thee and the woman, and between thy seed and her seed; it shall bruise thy head, and thou shalt bruise his heel*
>
> (Genesis 3:15 KJV).

This verse is the first prophetic hint of the coming Messiah. The seed of the woman refers to a descendant of Eve who would ultimately defeat satan. Unlike the natural course of human reproduction, which typically refers to the seed of a man, this prophecy uniquely points to a supernatural birth, a virgin birth, which finds its fulfillment in the birth of Jesus (Matthew 1:23). The reference to the woman's seed foreshadows that Jesus, as the Savior, would crush the head of the serpent, symbolizing His ultimate victory over satan and sin through His death and resurrection.

Furthermore, the phrase *"thy seed"* (referring to the serpent) could allude to the existence of the Nephilim. Genesis 6 describes how fallen angels (the *"sons of God"*) mated with human women, giving rise to the Nephilim, a hybrid offspring that served as an attempt by satan to corrupt the human lineage. This rebellion and contamination of human genetics was a direct assault on the *"seed of the woman"* promised in Genesis 3:15, aimed at thwarting the coming of the Messiah.

Daniel 2:43 (KJV) further hints at these hybrid entities in the end times:

> *And whereas thou sawest iron mixed with miry clay, they shall mingle themselves with the seed of men: but they shall not cleave one to another, even as iron is not mixed with clay.*

This cryptic verse is understood by many to reference an unnatural mingling of beings, possibly akin to the days of Noah when the Nephilim existed. The persistence of these entities or their influence ties back to the age-old conflict between the serpent's seed and the seed of the woman, a conflict that culminates in the rise of the antichrist and in Christ's ultimate victory.

SEVENTY WEEKS OF DANIEL

The seventy weeks of Daniel is a prophecy found in Daniel 9:24-27, which outlines God's plan for Israel and the world. The seventy "weeks" refer to seventy sets of seven years, totaling 490 years. This prophecy covers the period from the decree to rebuild Jerusalem until the end of the age. The first 69 of these weeks (483 years) have already been fulfilled, culminating in the death of the Messiah. The final week (the 70th week) represents the seven-year Tribulation, during which the antichrist will rise to power, make a covenant with Israel, and break it halfway through, triggering The Great Tribulation. This is one of the most stunning prophecies in the Bible.

SHEEP AND GOATS JUDGMENT

The Sheep and Goats Judgment is described in Matthew 25:31-46, where Jesus separates the nations into two groups: the "sheep," who are blessed and inherit the kingdom, and the "goats," who are cursed and cast into eternal punishment. This judgment occurs at the end of the Tribulation, following Christ's Second Coming, and involves the people who survived the Tribulation.

While some suggest that the Sheep and Goats Judgment, mentioned in Matthew 25:31-46, is based on how the nations treated Israel, this interpretation does not align with the broader biblical message regarding salvation and entry into Christ's Kingdom. First, the

Bible makes it clear that during the Tribulation period, all nations will turn against God and Israel (Revelation 16:14, Zechariah 14:2). Therefore, treating this judgment purely as a matter of how they supported Israel is inconsistent with the overall prophetic narrative.

Second, Scripture is unequivocal about the requirement for salvation, faith in Jesus Christ. There is no alternate path. People will not qualify to enter Christ's Millennial Kingdom solely based on their actions toward Israel; rather, they will be judged according to their response to Jesus as He revealed Himself to them and His prophets. The righteous among them will be those who responded to the call of faith, allowing God to work in their hearts to produce fruit that aligns with His righteousness. This aligns with the consistent biblical teaching that entry into God's Kingdom is predicated on faith and transformation through Christ, not merely humanitarian efforts or national alignment.

SON OF PERDITION

The term *son of perdition* is a title given to the antichrist, as seen in 2 Thessalonians 2:3 (KJV):

> *Let no man deceive you by any means: for that day shall not come, except there come a falling away first, and that man of sin be revealed, the son of perdition.*

The phrase *son of perdition* means "the one doomed to destruction." The term emphasizes the fate of the antichrist as someone destined for damnation.

This same term was also used to describe Judas Iscariot in John 17:12 (NKJV): *"While I was with them in the world, I kept them in Your name. Those whom You gave Me I have kept; and none of them is lost except the son of perdition, that the Scripture might be fulfilled."* Judas and the antichrist share this title because they are both betrayers. Judas betraying Jesus personally, and the antichrist betraying humanity and leading the ultimate rebellion against God.

The *"son of perdition"* will be revealed in the end times, exalting himself above all gods, demanding worship, and persecuting the saints who live through the Tribulation (Daniel 7:25). The title highlights both the pride and the doomed fate of the antichrist. Despite the power and terror that he wields during his brief reign, his end is certain. When Jesus returns at the Second Coming, the antichrist will be defeated and cast into the lake of fire (Revelation 19:20), fulfilling his title as the son of perdition.

T

TEN NATIONS

Ten nations refers to a coalition of ten kingdoms or leaders that will arise in the last days, forming a power bloc under the authority of the antichrist. This concept is rooted in passages including Daniel 7 and Revelation 17, where the emergence of ten "horns" or ten "kings" is described.

In Daniel 7:24, the ten horns represent ten kings who will come from a revived form of the Roman Empire. Likewise, Revelation 17:12-13 (NKJV) states:

> *The ten horns which you saw are ten kings who have received no kingdom as yet, but they receive authority for one hour as kings with the beast. These are of one mind, and they will give their power and authority to the beast.*

These ten nations or leaders will be instrumental in the establishment of the antichrist's rule, handing over their power to him in unity. The exact identity of these ten nations is not definitively given in Scripture, and there have been numerous speculations about their modern equivalents, ranging from the European Union to other emerging geopolitical alliances.

TIME, TIMES, AND HALF A TIME

"Time, times, and half a time" is a prophetic phrase found in Daniel 7:25, Daniel 12:7, and Revelation 12:14 that represents a specific period of time lasting three and a half years. This term is often used to refer to the latter half of the Tribulation, also known as The Great Tribulation.

- "Time" refers to one year.
- "Times" refers to two years.
- "Half a Time" refers to half a year.

In total, this phrase denotes three and a half years, which aligns with other scriptural references to the same period, often expressed as 42 months (Revelation 11:2, Revelation 13:5) or 1,260 days (Revelation 11:3, Revelation 12:6). This precise measurement of time underscores the literal interpretation of these prophecies.

Daniel 7:25 (KJV) describes how the antichrist will oppress the saints for this exact period of time:

> *And he shall speak great words against the most High, and shall wear out the saints of the most High, and think to change times and laws: and they shall be given into his hand until a time and times and the dividing of time.*

Revelation 12:14 speaks of the woman (representing Israel) being protected in the wilderness for "a time, times, and half a time" from the serpent (the devil), highlighting God's supernatural protection during the latter half of the Tribulation.

This consistent usage of three and a half years signifies a literal second half of the Tribulation, emphasizing the intense persecution and divine judgment that will take place before Christ's return. Some argue that this prophecy was fulfilled in the past (a preterist view), but these references to precise time periods, coupled with a global scope, align more with the future events during The Great Tribulation as described in Revelation.

TREE OF LIFE

The tree of life is a profound symbol found throughout the Bible, representing eternal life, divine sustenance, and God's ultimate plan for humanity's redemption. It first appears in the Garden of Eden in Genesis 2:9, where it stands at the center of the garden alongside the tree of the knowledge of good and evil:

> And out of the ground made the Lord God to grow every tree that is pleasant to the sight, and good for food; the tree of life also in the midst of the garden, and the tree of knowledge of good and evil
>
> (Genesis 2:9 KJV).

In Eden, the tree of life was accessible to Adam and Eve, granting them ongoing physical and spiritual life. After the Fall, however, humanity was banished from the Garden to prevent access to the tree of life and the possibility of living eternally in a sinful state:

> Then the Lord God said, "Behold, the man has become like one of Us, to know good and evil. And now, lest he put out his hand and take also of the tree of life, and eat, and live forever"—therefore the Lord God sent him out of the garden of Eden
>
> (Genesis 3:22-23 NKJV).

The tree of life reappears in the closing chapters of the Bible in Revelation 22, representing healing in the New Jerusalem:

> *In the midst of the street of it, and on either side of the river, was there the tree of life, which bare twelve manner of fruits, and yielded her fruit every month: and the leaves of the tree were for the healing of the nations*
>
> (Revelation 22:2 KJV).

The tree of life is also referenced in Proverbs, where it symbolizes wisdom, righteousness, and fulfilled desires:

> *She is a tree of life to them that lay hold upon her: and happy is every one that retaineth her*
>
> (Proverbs 3:18 KJV).

> *The fruit of the righteous is a tree of life; and he that winneth souls is wise*
>
> (Proverbs 11:30 KJV).

> *Hope deferred maketh the heart sick: but when the desire cometh, it is a tree of life*
>
> (Proverbs 13:12 KJV).

In Revelation, access to the tree of life is granted to those who overcome and obey God's commands:

> *Blessed are they that do his commandments, that they may have right to the tree of life, and may enter in through the gates into the city*
>
> (Revelation 22:14 KJV).

This imagery highlights the restoration and redemption that is central to God's plan for humanity.

TRIBULATION / THE GREAT TRIBULATION

See chapter on Tribulation in this book.

TRUMP OF GOD

See "What about the Last Trump?" in Chapter 9.

TWINKLING OF AN EYE

The twinkling of an eye refers to the speed at which the transformation of believers will occur at the Rapture. In 1 Corinthians 15:52 (KJV), Paul writes: *"In a moment, in the twinkling of an eye, at the last trump: for the trumpet shall sound, and the dead shall be raised incorruptible, and we shall be changed."* This phrase underscores the instantaneous nature of the Rapture, where believers will be given glorified bodies in an instant, faster than the blink of an eye.

In terms of speed, it's much faster than a blink, which takes roughly 300 to 400 milliseconds. The *"twinkling"* refers to a moment of light catching the eye, a fleeting instance that occurs almost instantaneously. Regardless of exact timing, the key point is that it will happen faster than anyone can react. When Jesus calls His Church, believers will be instantly transformed and caught up.

TWO WITNESSES

The two witnesses are end-time prophets described in Revelation 11:3-12 who will testify in Jerusalem. These individuals will perform miracles, including calling down fire from Heaven, turning water into blood, and striking the earth with plagues. Their ministry will last for 1,260 days (3½ years), after which they will be killed by the antichrist. However, after three days, they will be resurrected and taken up to Heaven in full view of the world.

These two figures could possibly be Moses, Elijah, Enoch, or even two entirely new individuals we haven't yet encountered in history. There's much debate over their identities, but each of these candidates carries compelling reasons to be among the two witnesses described in Revelation 11.

Moses and Elijah: Many believe Moses and Elijah could be the two witnesses because of the miracles they perform, which echo the powers these prophets displayed during their lifetimes, Moses turning water to blood and calling plagues (Exodus 7:17-20) and Elijah calling fire from Heaven (1 Kings 18:36-38).

Elijah and Enoch: Another theory suggests Elijah and Enoch since these are the only two individuals in Scripture recorded as never experiencing physical death. Elijah was taken up to Heaven in a whirlwind (2 Kings 2:11), and Enoch was taken by God in a rapture (Genesis 5:24). Hebrews 9:27 states that it is appointed for men to die once, making some believe these two are preserved for this particular end-time mission.

Unknown individuals: It's also entirely possible that these two witnesses are people we've never heard of before, prophets raised specifically for this unique role during the Tribulation. The Bible doesn't give their names, which opens the door for the possibility of fresh servants chosen for the prophetic times ahead.

The important takeaway is not necessarily their identities but their purpose and the authority they are given. These two witnesses will testify for 1,260 days (Revelation 11:3), prophesying during a time of severe judgment. Their ministry will stand as a bold declaration of God's truth in a world dominated by deception, and their eventual resurrection and ascension will serve as a powerful sign to the world of God's power and sovereignty.

U
UNIVERSALISM

Universalism is the belief that all people, regardless of faith or behavior, will eventually be saved and reconciled to God. This idea runs counter to traditional Christian teaching, which says that salvation is only through faith in Jesus Christ. The Bible clearly distinguishes between those who are saved and those who are not, especially in the context of end-time judgment, where unbelievers face the Great White Throne Judgment and the second death (Revelation 20:11-15).

V
VIALS (BOWL JUDGMENTS)

See Bowls

W
WATCHFULNESS

Watchfulness is a key attitude that believers are instructed to maintain as they await the return of Christ. Jesus repeatedly urges His followers to "watch" and be ready for His return, as seen in Matthew 24:42 (KJV): *"Watch therefore, for ye know not what hour your Lord doth come."*

If there is one word that could summarize all New Testament eschatology, it would be the word, "WATCH."

WHITE THRONE JUDGMENT

The Great White Throne Judgment is the final judgment described in Revelation 20:11-15, where all the dead who were not part of the first resurrection will stand before God to be judged according to their works. Those whose names are not found in the Book of Life will be cast into the lake of fire, representing eternal separation from God. Pre-Tribulation theology teaches that this judgment occurs after the Millennial Kingdom and is distinct from the Judgment Seat of Christ, which is reserved for believers and concerns their rewards, not their eternal destiny. The White Throne Judgment is the final event in God's plan before the creation of the new heaven and new earth.

WORMWOOD

Wormwood is a term mentioned in Revelation 8:10-11 during the blowing of the third trumpet, one of the judgments that occur during the Tribulation. In this passage, a great star named Wormwood falls from Heaven, turning a third of the rivers and springs bitter, causing many people to die from drinking the poisoned waters:

> *And the third angel sounded, and there fell a great star from heaven, burning as it were a lamp, and it fell upon the third part of the rivers, and upon the fountains of waters; and the name of the star is called Wormwood: and the third part of the waters became wormwood; and many men died of the waters, because they were made bitter*
> (Revelation 8:10-11 KJV).

Wormwood refers to both the name of the star and a bitter, toxic substance. The name Wormwood comes from a bitter herb used in ancient times, often associated with sorrow and judgment in the Bible (Jeremiah 9:15, Lamentations 3:19).

The identity of Wormwood, whether a literal star, asteroid, or something else, remains debated, but its impact is clear: it brings physical and spiritual bitterness and judgment upon the earth during the Tribulation.

WRATH OF GOD

The Wrath of God refers to the righteous judgment and punishment that God pours out on the unbelieving world during the Tribulation. Described vividly throughout the book of Revelation, especially in the Seal, Trumpet, and Bowl Judgments, the Wrath of God is not merely human or demonic affliction but divine retribution for rebellion against Him. First Thessalonians 5:9 assures believers that they are *"not appointed to wrath."* This period will be characterized by God's direct intervention, punishing sin, bringing justice, and preparing for the return of Christ.

Y

YESHUA

Yeshua is the Hebrew name for Jesus, meaning "salvation" or "the Lord saves."

Z

ZION

Zion is a term with rich biblical significance, referring both to the city of Jerusalem and, symbolically, to the dwelling place of God and His people. In the context of end-time prophecy, Zion often represents the future restoration of Israel and the reign of the Messiah from Jerusalem during the Millennial Kingdom. Isaiah 2:2-3 and

Micah 4:2 prophesy that in the last days, the law will go out from Zion, and the nations will come to Jerusalem to worship the Lord. Zion is where Jesus will return to rule the earth after the Tribulation and establish His throne in Jerusalem.

> *But ye are come unto mount Sion, and unto the city of the living God, the heavenly Jerusalem, and to an innumerable company of angels, to the general assembly and church of the firstborn, which are written in heaven, and to God the Judge of all, and to the spirits of just men made perfect, and to Jesus the mediator of the new covenant, and to the blood of sprinkling, that speaketh better things than that of Abel.*
>
> *See that ye refuse not him that speaketh. For if they escaped not who refused him that spake on earth, much more shall not we escape, if we turn away from him that speaketh from heaven: Whose voice then shook the earth: but now he hath promised, saying, Yet once more I shake not the earth only, but also heaven. And this word, Yet once more, signifieth the removing of those things that are shaken, as of things that are made, that those things which cannot be shaken may remain.*
>
> *Wherefore we receiving a kingdom which cannot be moved, let us have grace, whereby we may serve God acceptably with reverence and godly fear: For our God is a consuming fire*
>
> (Hebrews 12:22-29 KJV).

NOTES

INTRODUCTION

1. "Eschatology," Merriam-Webster.com Dictionary, Merriam-Webster, https://www.merriam-webster.com/dictionary/eschatology; accessed November 9, 2024.

CHAPTER 1

1. Mark Ross, "In Essentials Unity, In Non-Essentials Liberty, In All Things Charity," Ligonier Ministries, September 1, 2009; https://www.ligonier.org/learn/articles/essentials-unity-non-essentials-liberty-all-things#:~:text=Philip%20Schaff%2C%20the%20distinguished%20nineteenth,the%20early%20seventeenth%20century%2C%20Rupertus; accessed November 9, 2024.

2. "Where did the term 'rapture' come from?" Bible.org; https://bible.org/question/where-did-term-8216rapture%E2%80%99-come; accessed November 9, 2024.

CHAPTER 2

1. Jeff Diamant, "About four-in-ten U.S. adults believe humanity is 'living in the end times,'" Pew Research Center, December 8, 2022; https://www.pewresearch.org/ short-reads/2022/12/08/about-four-in-ten-u-s-adults-believe-humanity-is-living-in-the-end-times/; accessed November 9, 2024.

2. "Vigilant," Merriam-Webster.com Dictionary, Merriam-Webster, https://www.merriam-webster.com/dictionary/vigilant; accessed November 9, 2024.

3. A.W. Tozer, *Preparing for Jesus' Return: Daily Live the Blessed Hope* (Ada, MI: Baker Publishing Group, 2012), 23-24.

CHAPTER 3

1. "Eternity Stamped on our Eyeballs," The Daily Grace Co., January 28, 2019; https://thedailygraceco.com/blogs/the-daily-grace-blog/eternity-stamped-on-our-eyeballs?srsltid=AfmBOopgKMG D9ZJ5LfOwxH_byWa17Hsn1tfXHx5tMew67uf0inwmF8l9; accessed November 9, 2024.

2. A.W. Tozer, *Preparing for Jesus' Return: Daily Live the Blessed Hope* (Ada, MI: Baker Publishing Group, 2012), 33.

3. Grant R. Jeffrey, *Triumphant Return: The Coming Kingdom of God* (Toronto: Frontier Research Publications, 2001), 61.

4. "Pragmatism," Merriam-Webster.com Dictionary, Merriam-Webster, https://www.merriam-webster.com/dictionary/pragmatism.

5. "Practical," Merriam-Webster.com Dictionary, Merriam-Webster, https://www.merriam-webster.com/dictionary/practical.

6. "Escapism," Merriam-Webster.com Dictionary, Merriam-Webster, https://www.merriam-webster.com/dictionary/escapism.

CHAPTER 4

1. Chuck Missler, *Cosmic Codes: Hidden Messages From the Edge of Eternity* (Cocoa, FL: Koinonia House, 1999).

2. A.W. Pink, *Gleanings from Genesis* (Chicago, IL: Moody Bible Institute of Chicago, 1922), 78.

CHAPTER 6

1. "Snatched Out of the Very Jaws of the Devil!" Grace Gems, https://gracegems.org/05/07/Whitefield.html; accessed November 10, 2024.

2. "Top 250 Ravenhill Quotes," QuoteFancy, 2024, https://quotefancy.com/leonard-ravenhill-quotes; accessed November 10, 2024.

CHAPTER 7

1. "Philadelphia Experiment," Naval History and Heritage Command, November 20, 2017, https://www.history.navy.mil/research/library/online-reading-room/title-list-alphabetically/p/philadelphia-experiment.html; accessed November 11, 2024.

CHAPTER 9

1. Paul J. Alexander, *The Byzantine Apocalyptic Tradition* (Berkeley, CA: University of California Press, 1985), 210.

2. "Irenaeus—Ground Zero for the Rapture Controversy in the Early Church," Soothkeep, https://soothkeep.info/irenaeus-ground-zero-for-the-rapture-controversy-in-the-early-church/; accessed November 11, 2024.

3. C. Taylor, *The Shepherd of Hermas* (London: Society for Promoting Christian Knowledge, 1906), Vision 4.

4. H. Orton Wiley, *Christian Theology,* chapter 34: The Second Advent (Kansas City, MO: Nazarene Publishing House, 1940).

5. Victorinus, *Commentary on the Apocalypse of the Blessed John* (Whitefish, MT: Kessinger Publishing, 2010), *6.14.*

6. Dr. David R. Reagan, "The Origin of the Concept of a Pre-Tribulation Rapture" Lamb & Lion Ministries; https://

christinprophecy.org/articles/the-origin-of-the-concept-of-a-pre-tribulation-rapture/; accessed November 13, 2024.

7. William Watson, *Dispensationalism Before Darby* (Silverton, OR: Lampion Press, 2015), 232.

8. Ephraim the Syrian, *Sermon on Repentance and Judgement and the Separation of the Soul from the Body.*

9. Ken Johnson, *The Rapture* (CreateSpace, 2009).

10. Nesrine Malik, "Why the World Can Get Worse by Constantly Saying It's Getting Better," The Correspondent, September 30, 2020; https://thecorrespondent.com/720/why-the-world-can-get-worse-by-constantly-saying-its-getting-better; accessed November 13, 2024.

ABOUT ALAN DIDIO

After experiencing a radical spiritual encounter at the age of seventeen, Alan DiDio was born again; instantly transforming him from a dogmatic atheist to a passionate follower of Jesus. Taught in a Word-based church, he learned early on how to stand in faith. Not long after giving his life to Christ, Bishop Alan went to Bible College and continued serving with an international ministry, working on staff for nearly seven years. In that time, he gained experience in every possible area of ministry from running an international prayer center to traveling across the country spreading the Gospel.

Since then, Alan DiDio founded Encounter Ministries and launched The Encounter Charlotte in his home state, North Carolina. Through Encounter Ministries he has taken the Gospel to nations including Pakistan, China, Israel, Haiti, and Guatemala. Bishop Alan is the best-selling author of multiple books and host of the Encounter Today on YouTube. His media ministry alone reaches millions of people around the world with the Gospel of Jesus Christ.

In 2022, Bishop Alan was ordained a bishop and overseer in City Harvest Network. He and his wife, Tera, have two children and consider family to be the most important ministry any believer is called to.

YOUR
Prophetic
COMMUNITY

Sign up for a **FREE** subscription to the Destiny Image digital magazine and get awesome content delivered directly to your inbox!

destinyimage.com/signup

Sign up for Cutting-Edge Messages that Supernaturally Empower You

- Gain valuable insights and guidance based on biblical principles
- Deepen your faith and understanding of God's plan for your life
- Receive regular updates and prophetic messages
- Connect with a community of believers who share your values and beliefs

Experience Fresh Video Content that Reveals Your Prophetic Inheritance

- Receive prophetic messages and insights
- Connect with a powerful tool for spiritual growth and development
- Stay connected and inspired on your faith journey

Listen to Powerful Podcasts that Propel You into God's Presence Every Day

- Deepen your understanding of God's prophetic assignment
- Experience God's revival power throughout your day
- Learn how to grow spiritually in your walk with God

In the Right Hands, This Book Will Change Lives!

Most of the people who need this message will not be looking for this book. To change their lives, you need to **put a copy of this book in their hands.**

Our ministry is constantly seeking methods to find the people who need this anointed message to change their lives. **Will you help us reach these people?**

Extend this ministry by sowing 3 books, 5 books, 10 books, or more today, and become a life changer! Your generosity will be part of catalyzing the Great Awakening that many have been prophesying and praying for.